SEXUALITY

Fourth edition

Jeffrey Weeks

Routledge
Taylor & Francis Group

LONDON AND NEW YORK

First published 2017
by Routledge
2 Park Square, Milton Park, Abingdon, Oxon OX14 4RN

and by Routledge
711 Third Avenue, New York, NY 10017

Routledge is an imprint of the Taylor & Francis Group, an informa business

British Library Cataloguing in Publication Data
A catalogue record for this book is available from the British Library

Library of Congress Cataloging-in-Publication Data
Names: Weeks, Jeffrey, 1945– author.
Title: Sexuality / by Jeffrey Weeks.
Description: 4 Edition. | New York : Routledge, 2016. | Revised edition of the
    author's Sexuality, 2009. | Includes bibliographical references.
Identifiers: LCCN 2016014251 | ISBN 9781138022881 (hardback) |
    ISBN 9781138022898 (pbk.) | ISBN 9781315776811 (ebook)
Subjects: LCSH: Sex. | Sex customs.
Classification: LCC HQ21 .W379 2016 | DDC 306.7—dc23
LC record available at https://lccn.loc.gov/2016014251

ISBN: 978-1-138-02288-1 (hbk)
ISBN: 978-1-138-02289-8 (pbk)
ISBN: 978-1-315-77681-1 (ebk)

Typeset in Minion Pro
by Apex CoVantage, LLC
Printed and bound by CPI Group (UK) Ltd, Croydon, CR0 4YY

SEXUALITY

The new edition of *Sexuality* displays the qualities which have made this book a key text for understanding human sexuality. Jeffrey Weeks blends deep empirical knowledge with theoretical sophistication and a sensitivity to the politics of sexuality. Framing and shaping the analysis is an acute understanding of the world-wide changes that are remaking sexuality and gender, dramatized by the globalization of sex and the rise of cybersex. These changes have opened unprecedented opportunities for sexual interaction and sexual choice, but also posed new sexual dangers and anxiety. Debates about the regulation and control of sexuality, and the intersection of various dimensions of power and domination are contextualised by a sustained argument about the importance of agency in remaking sexual and intimate life, above all for women and for LGBTQ people. Particular attention is given to the question of same-sex marriage which came to symbolize the transformations that have taken place. These controversies in turn feed into debates about intimate citizenship and human sexual rights in a rapidly changing world.

Jeffrey Weeks is Emeritus Professor of Sociology at London South B<

KEY IDEAS

Series Editor: PETER HAMILTON

Designed to complement the successful *Key Sociologists*, this series covers the main concepts, issues, debates, and controversies in sociology and the social sciences. The series aims to provide authoritative essays on central topics of social science, such as community, power, work, sexuality, inequality, benefits and ideology, class, family, etc. Books adopt a strong 'individual' line, as critical essays rather than literature surveys, offering lively and original treatments of their subject matter. The books will be useful to students and teachers of sociology, political science, economics, psychology, philosophy, and geography.

Contents

Editor's foreword to the first edition

We are, as Jeffrey Weeks points out in this book, almost programmed into thinking of our sexuality as a wholly natural feature of life. It is of course a truism that sexual relations are but one form of social relations, but we are nonetheless accustomed to think also of social relations as 'natural', at least in the commonsense world. Yet it is the task of sociology and the other social sciences to 'deconstruct' naturalism, and to determine how actions are given their meaning and significance via social interaction. Why in principle should not sexuality be treated as socially conditioned a phenomenon as, say, chess-playing or cuisine? The liberationist philosophies of the post-war generation have accustomed us to a search for a 'natural' and unrepressed sexuality, as if there were at bottom some essential form of sexual relations whose expression lies in an extra-moral domain. Yet simultaneously the same generation has also been the site of a resurgence of homosexuality, of transvestism, of pederasty, and of fierce and critical debate about the negotiation of gender identity. As the philosopher–historian Michel Foucault pointed out, sexuality is no more (or no less) than a historical construct. Its meaning and expression is no wider or extensive than its specific social or historical manifestations, and explaining its forms and variations cannot be accomplished without examining and explaining the context in which they are located.

Jeffrey Weeks has written extensively on what we might call the new sociology of sexuality, and is representative of the way in which what was a slightly 'marginal' academic interest has come to full respectability. It is slightly ironic that sexuality should appear to have increased its hold over aspects of popular culture (cf. the mass of sexual media currently available in Western societies and the ubiquity of sexual imagery in advertising) at the same time as the new perspectives on sexuality attempt to deconstruct it as a cultural expression. However, our preoccupation with sexuality does mean that it is more necessary than ever to interpret and elucidate this all-pervasive ideology.

One important feature of the present interest in sexuality is its linkage with a parallel concern with questions of family, kinship and household organization. The massive expansion of 'family history' as a site of academic research, has itself more empiric parallels in the growth of social policy initiatives, social intervention in the lives of families, indeed the emergence of a field of bio-politics in which the state can be seen as attempting to regulate and control. Both psychological and social therapies devote great attention to the sexual dimension of their clients' lives. This is not perhaps an entirely new feature of social control, for the Church and the village community were at least as concerned about regulating and organizing sexual behaviour in Western societies of the pre-industrial era, as is the modern state. But what is different and qualitatively new is the attention paid to the rationalization of sexuality, and its subjection to scientific study, in modern Western society.

In the detailed and carefully argued discussion of the sociology of sexuality which Jeffrey Weeks has written, the connection of sexuality to its socio-historical context is explored in ways which reveal just how completely sex is socially constructed. This naturally raises problems about sexual morality which are likely to cause a certain amount of unease. For if sexuality is at base a social convention of almost infinite variety, then nothing is either 'right' or 'wrong'. Clearly – as Weeks is concerned to stress – the issue cannot be left there. We are rational and intelligent beings who have the capacity to choose the moral codes under which we live – or at least to negotiate modifications and adaptations to them.

Peter Hamilton

Author's preface to the
SECOND EDITION

This short book has in a sense been my intellectual manifesto. It summarizes a debate, and my position in that. But nothing stops still. It is now some 18 years since I completed the first edition of this book, and a great deal has happened to me, and the world of sexuality.

The book has been happily in print throughout that period. It has been translated into Spanish and Japanese as a whole, and sections have appeared in a variety of other languages. My views have not changed fundamentally since the book was first published. But the scholarship of sexuality has experienced a transformation. What seemed an esoteric subject for a historian and sociologist in the 1980s, has now become a mainstream topic, taught in all universities across the Western world and beyond. There has been a mountain of new research, and a continent of publications. It seemed time, therefore, to look again at *Sexuality* to see whether it was fit for purpose for new readers in the twenty-first century.

When my editor approached me to do a new edition, I confess I hesitated. On the one hand, the essay on sexuality that I wrote in the mid-1980s had a certain integrity, reflecting the passions, preoccupations and priorities of the time in which it was written. As such, I am told, it had achieved a sort of classic status, and I am deeply grateful for all those readers who have contributed to that. I was reluctant to change a dot or comma. On the other hand, there is no point in keeping what was intended as an active intervention in contemporary debates in a deep freeze while the world moves on. Many of the issues that engaged me in the 1980s are still live; new issues have emerged, on which I have strong opinions. I believe the approaches I put forward in the 1980s still have relevance to an understanding of the present. But they needed refreshing by taking account of the new scholarship. So I allowed myself to be persuaded that a new edition was indeed needed. This is the result.

The structure of this new edition remains broadly the same as in the first edition. But within that structure I have taken the opportunity to rewrite and update every chapter, both to amplify my arguments as necessary, and to take into account the changes both in the world, and in the literature which tries to understand it. The book is therefore about a third longer again than the first edition. But it remains, I hope, true to my original intentions, and a concise guide to the debates about the history and social organization of sexuality. The interested reader can follow through my own views in the other books I have written on sexuality and intimacy, which are listed in the suggestions for further reading. I have also tried in that section to reflect a broad selection of other work. One of the arguments of the book is that sexuality is in part being shaped and reshaped by the ways in which we think and write about it. This book represents part of my own contribution to that necessary process.

Jeffrey Weeks

London, 2003

Author's preface to the
third edition

The last edition, published in 2003, offered a thorough re-write of the original text, introducing a wide a range of debates and issues that had scarcely surfaced in the mid 1980s. For example, the second edition was able to introduce readers to debates on evolutionary psychology which had largely replaced the socio-biology discussed in the first edition. Globalization, and the notion of 'global sex', was introduced as a key concept, while the comparatively new debates about 'intimacy' and 'sexual citizenship' reshaped much of the last half of the book.

In this form, *Sexuality* continued to appeal to a wide range of readers, and has been a key text for a variety of university courses. I have been told on numerous occasions by various people I meet at conferences and seminars at home and abroad how important the book has been for their thinking about sexuality, and how useful it is for students. It is, however, now some five years since the second edition was published. There has been a spectacular expansion of works on sexuality during this period, and sexuality, intimacy and gender have become normal parts of the curriculum as well as part of the general conversation in our culture. The time now seems ripe for a new edition which takes on board the debates in the twenty-first century.

My aim has been to offer a refreshing and updating of the book, to ensure that it remains at the cutting edge of the subject. The structure remains broadly the same, but each chapter has been carefully revised in the light of current scholarship, and some 10,000 extra words have been added to the previous length. My purpose throughout has been to maintain the intellectual unity and integrity of the book, while ensuring that it remains in the forefront of debates about the sexual. So this new edition further advances the debate on globalization: in relation to our understanding of global interactions and patterns of difference, and to closely linked concepts, such as cosmopolitanism and neo-liberalism.

Post-Foucauldian analyses have tended to emphasize not only power but also governance, seeing the sexual matrix almost exclusively in terms of regulation and control. In this new edition I introduce a renewed emphasis on agency in relation to erotic and intimate life – not only the agency of social movements, but the impact of the millions of individual decisions about love, sex and relations that shape the contours of contemporary life, on a global scale. These decisions are shaped by a vast diversity of experiences. These are not random differences, but structured by intersecting power relations and subjectivities. An analysis of these, especially the relations of class, gender and race/ethnicity, was developed in the first two editions, but is further developed in this edition. I have also taken the opportunity, in the light of post-9/11 developments, to look again at the power of religion in many parts of the world, including the USA, in shaping moral policy.

In relation to dissident sexualities, the conceptual unity suggested by the relatively new LGBTQ (Lesbian, Gay,

Bisexual, Transgender, Queer) label signifies real shifts in the world of non-heterosexuality, and I have explored these in the new edition. Two issues particularly stand out. The first is the increasing salience of the transgender debate over the past decade, which is radically challenging gender essentialism. The second is the high impact of same-sex marriage, divisive both within the LGBTQ world, and in the wider culture, and yet a key mobilizing issue for activists across the west, and beyond. These feed into debates about what is 'transgressive', 'normal', 'ordinary'; into the nature of heteronormativity; and into the meanings of diversity and choice.

I also return to the debates over moralities and ethics which I first explored in the original edition. To what extent, for example, can one claim gains in the privileged West when human sexual rights are residual in much of the Global South? To what extent are sexual rights and intimate citizenship really secure in the West itself? Such questions in turn resonate with other debates about recognition, social justice, suffering and global citizenship, and these issues are explored in Chapters 5 and 6.

Finally, the Suggestions for Further Reading and the Bibliography have been thoroughly updated, and offer, I hope, a useful starting point for further study.

It has been an enjoyable challenge once again to digest the crucial issues raised by thinking about sexuality into the confines of a short book. I hope that the reader will in turn enjoy exploring the result, and will find it a stimulation to further reading and research. That, in the end, is the justification for this book.

Jeffrey Weeks
London, March 2009

AUTHOR'S PREFACE TO
FOURTH EDITION

I am privileged and grateful for the opportunity once again to introduce a new edition of this book. The extraordinary thing about writing on sexuality is how rapidly the subject changes. In large part this of course reflects the real world, where we appear to be going through a period of unprecedented transition in behaviour and attitudes, with global resonance. In part it reflects changing empirical research and theoretical speculation, with the emergence of new objects of interest or concern. In part, it is a result of a rapidly changing politics of sexuality, with the emergence of new sexual subjectivities and forms of agency.

A short book like this can barely do justice to the rapid evolution of the topic. What I offer is not a detailed account of all the shifts in the sexual landscape but a framework for understanding them. This remains a work that is rooted in the belief that we can best understand sexuality and gender in terms of the historical, social and cultural contexts in which they are made, contested, lived and remade. Sexuality as an idea, a concept, a historical apparatus, a mass of embodied practices and experiences is fundamentally a human construct, and as such is inevitably in constant flux. Which does not mean that nothing stays the same. There are long continuities in sexual attitudes and practices, so that even as we feel we have shaken off traditional values, the repressed can readily return to bite us. Yet no observer of sexual mores and values over the years since this book was first published can doubt that the world can readily be turned up-side down. In the mid-1980s, same-sex marriage was a twinkle in the eyes of a few activists. Now it is on the way to becoming an ordinary everyday experience in many parts of the world. Transgender issues were grossly ignored. Now even conservative politicians speak knowingly of gender fluidity, while hyper-masculine sports stars come out as trans. Child sex abuse was covered up and denied. Now revelations about it can destroy public figures and the power of churches and other public institutions.

These are just three examples where attitudes, policies and practices have rapidly evolved. It would be easy but facile to assume from this that we are on some automatic trajectory to a better, more humane, more tolerant and accepting world. Alongside the many progressive changes that have taken place are continuing violence and abuse, cruelty and ignorance, hate and phobic reactions. Sexuality has become a focus of hope for a better world through the claims for human sexual rights. It has also become a political tool to mobilize extreme nationalist, racist or religious movements.

In this new edition, as in the previous ones, I attempt to capture the complexity of the world of sexuality. Each chapter has been carefully revised to embrace new knowledge. New ideas and arguments have been introduced as appropriate. The Further Reading and Bibliography has been thoroughly updated. I have sought to keep the book at the cutting edge of the subject.

Sexuality offers an introduction to a vital subject and theme, and a contribution to critical sexualities studies. But I hope the reader will find here more than that: a book that also offers a way of understanding the sexual world, providing a guide to the perplexed, a map for the explorer and an inspiration for further reading and research.

Jeffrey Weeks
London, March 2016

Acknowledgements to the First Edition

It is now over ten years since I first began writing on the history and sociology of sex. During that time I have incurred many intellectual and emotional debts. There is no space here to record the names of all the people who have helped me. I refer readers to the acknowledgements in my previous books, full details of which are given in the Suggestions for Further Reading at the end of this book. All I can do here is to thank them all once again, and to free them from any obligation to agree with everything (or anything) I say here.

Some debts are immediate, however. I must thank Peter Hamilton for asking me to write this book, Caradoc King for encouraging me to do so, Barbara Giddins for patiently transferring my early drafts into legible type which allowed me to rethink, rejig and rewrite, and Janet Hussein for (as ever) typing an impeccable final draft. My gratitude, as always, goes to Chetan Bhatt, Micky Burbidge and Angus Suttie for sustaining me during its writing. But my greatest debt is to my students, whose questions, doubts, anxieties and stimulation have forced me to think through many of the issues I tackle here. I therefore dedicate this book to my students – past, present and (government policy permitting) future. I hope they get as much from this essay as I got from them.

Acknowledgements to the second edition

My debts to other writers and to many more generations of students continue to grow. I hope I have done them justice in this new edition. I want particularly to thank my colleagues at London South Bank University for their support as I have tried to combine writing about sexuality with increasing managerial responsibilities. I owe a special debt to the following: Ros Edwards, Clare Farquhar, Philip Gatter, Brian Heaphy, Janet Holland, Rachel Thomson, Matthew Waites.

Sadly, a number of friends and colleagues who supported me in various ways as I wrote the first edition have since died. I still miss and mourn them, especially Angus Suttie. My greatest debt is to Mark McNestry. I can simply thank him for everything.

ACKNOWLEDGEMENTS TO THE
THIRD EDITION

As I began work on this new edition, a conference, 'Making History Personal', was held at Manchester University to mark my retirement (at last) from managerial responsibilities. It gave me renewed energy to continue writing on sexuality and intimate life. I therefore want to particularly thank the following for their kind and generous comments, and for the intellectual stimulation they always give me: Matt Cook, Brian Heaphy, Ken Plummer, Sheila Rowbotham, Carol Smart, Matthew Waites, and everyone who attended and participated in the day – the memory of which I will always cherish. I also want to thank Peter Aggleton and Henrietta Moore for the many dinners we have had together, ostensibly to discuss the future of sexuality research, but also to talk about everything else. One of the results of our discussions has been the establishment of the London Sexuality Forum, and I thank the participants for the challenging debates we have enjoyed together.

My debts to Mark McNestry, my life partner, grow ever greater as the years pass. Once again, all I can do is to thank him for everything.

ACKNOWLEDGEMENTS TO THE
FOURTH EDITION

It is easy to lament the loneliness of the long-distance writer. Writing is a solitary business, but in a subject like sexuality it is alleviated by the support and generosity of many others. I thank once again the numerous people mentioned in my acknowledgements to previous editions. My debt to others increases as the years go by and, whether knowingly or not, they made this book possible. I won't repeat their names, but I express once again my warmest gratitude.

In the past few years I have had the pleasure and privilege of extensive foreign travel where I have been able to observe at first hand the changes that are reshaping the sexual world, and given the opportunity to float the ideas developed in this book. I warmly thank all who invited me to address conferences, give lectures and meet students and other colleagues, and who provided generous hospitality and friendship. I especially want to thank Mariela Castro Espin, Paula Sequiera, Luis Perelman, Antonio Garcia Pasarán, Esther Corona, Constantine Phellas, Delphine Hautois, Françoise Orazi, Anne Verjus, Marion Maudet, Cécile Thomé, Frédéric Simon and Rommel Mendès-Leite. Sadly, Rommel died as I was revising this book. He was the inspiration and general editor for the

French publication of the 3rd edition of this book. I honour and cherish his memory.

In so many ways, my partner Mark McNestry made this book possible. I can only offer again my gratitude and thanks.

1

INTRODUCTION
Languages of sex

THE SIGNIFICANCE OF SEXUALITY

Sexuality today is spoken about, written about, debated and preached about as never before. Traditionally, *who* could legitimately speak of sexuality and the body was tightly regulated by Churches and states, priests and politicians, the medical profession and various types of experts, with others – whether poets or novelists, polemicists or preachers, reformers or activists – seeking spaces where they could. The many regimes of silence did not stop the masses thinking about it, or living and doing it, but their voices were rarely heard or when heard not listened to. Now increasingly we have a mass democracy speaking of sexuality: through the globalized media, on television, in chat shows, confessional programmes, soap operas, reality shows, documentaries and advertisements; in cyberspace via social networks, dating and pick up sites and apps, blogs, microblogs and vlogs, chat rooms, through to the mysterious files of the 'dark web'; and in the myriad forums and intimacies of everyday life. We can all claim to be experts today, true to ourselves in our own fashion.

Yet the more expert we become in talking about sexuality, the greater the difficulties we often seem to encounter in trying to understand it. Despite sustained attempts over many years to 'demystify' sex, and despite several decades of much proclaimed – or condemned – 'liberation', 'liberalism' and 'permissiveness' – especially in the West – the erotic still arouses acute moral anxiety and confusion among many people, not least the self-declared guardians of our morals. The focus might change, but the obsession remains, even grows.

That is because sexuality is a focus for powerful feelings, and this gives it a seismic sensitivity, making it a transmission belt for a wide variety of needs and desires: for love and anger, tenderness and aggression, intimacy and adventure, romance and predatoriness, altruism and exploitation, pleasure and pain, empathy and power. We experience the erotic very subjectively, and in a host of often contradictory ways.

At the same time, the very mobility of sexuality, its chameleon-like ability to take many guises and forms, so that what for one might be a source of warmth and attraction, for another might be a cauldron of fear and hate, insult and humiliation, makes it a peculiarly sensitive conductor of cultural influences, and hence of social, cultural and political divisions. Not surprisingly, therefore, especially since the nineteenth century, with growing force through the twentieth century into the twenty-first, sexuality has become the focus of fierce ethical and moral debate: between traditional moralists (of various religious hues, or of none) and progressive reformers; between the high priests of sexual restraint and the advocates of sexual freedom; between the defenders of male privilege and those who challenged it; and between the forces of moral regulation – the upholders of 'traditional values' – and a host of radical sexual oppositions, some of whom attack each other as much as they challenge sexual orthodoxy and injustice. And in a world of what Plummer (2015) calls 'cosmopolitan sexualities', it has become a challenging field of transnational interactions and potential conflicts, embracing both the claims for universal sexual rights and social justice and the perpetuation of divisions and social and sexual ills and injustices.

In the past, such controversies might have been regarded as marginal to the mainstream of political life, whatever their importance for those closely involved. Increasingly over the past decades, however, sexual issues have moved ever closer to the centre of political concerns. In North America and Europe from the 1980s, new conservative forces, variously called the New Right, the Moral Majority, the Christian Right and so on, mobilized considerable political energies through their emphasis on the so-called 'social issues': an affirmation of the sanctity of family life, hostility to homosexuality and sexual diversity, fear of gender ambiguity and a fierce reassertion of traditional demarcations between the sexes. Institutionalized forms of homophobia, transphobia and biphobia have proved powerful weapons for building political constituencies for conservative politics and new forms of nationalism, from the USA to post-Soviet Russia and post-colonial states in Africa and Asia. So-called 'fundamentalists', whether Christian, Islamic, Jewish or Hindu, or of no settled religion, have placed the body and its bitterly contested pleasures at the centre of their efforts to draw the curtain on the apparent failures of the present, and to go back to the future by reconstructing neo-traditional societies, marked by rigid distinctions between men and women, the harsh punishment of sexual transgressors, and a bitter rejection of Western secularism. If fundamentalism is a response to uncertainty and ambiguity, a search for meaning and clarity in a conflicted world (Ruthven 2004), then its continued potency tells us something profound about our continuing fears and confusions.

At the same time, such extreme reactions can be read as a back-handed compliment to the millions of individuals across the globe who in their own ways, and under the force of dramatic social and cultural change, have engaged in 'everyday experiments' in living (Giddens 1992), and helped to transform the ways in which sexuality is lived. It is also a testimony to the success of feminism and the lesbian, gay, bisexual, transgender and queer (LGBTQ) movements and international campaigns for sexual and reproductive rights in challenging many of the 'traditional values' and received norms of sexual behaviour, identities and relationships on a global scale, in a world of intense and unprecedented globalization. New discourses of human sexual rights seek to explore the complex relationship between the particular experiences of the erotic and universal values that can respect what we do differently and affirm what we have in common. The ground rules of the debates over sexuality and gender have irreversibly

shifted, so that they no longer appear the peculiar obsession of the West, but of real concern in the Global South
where they are similarly enmeshed in relations of power,
domination and resistance in this era of what Altman
(2001) has called 'global sex'.

WORDS AND MEANINGS

Yet amidst all this intensity and fury, alongside the energy
and contestation, a fundamental question recurs: what is
this phenomenon we call sexuality? The core argument
of this book is that not only does sexuality have a variety
of histories and social meanings, but that the concept of
sexuality, and its various related terms, also have a history
and a clear social and cultural context. Perhaps, I shall
suggest, the truth of sexuality is that it has no inner truth,
but speaks for a vast range of possible truths.

That, of course, is not how it has been seen. In the West,
at least, the erotic has had a special relationship with the
nature of virtue and Truth (with a capital T) since before
the triumph of Christianity. Through (what we now
call) their sexualities, individuals have been expected to
find themselves and their place in the world. What was
mooted in the debates of late antiquity, codified by the
early Christian disquisitions on the flesh and personalized
in the procedures of the Catholic confessional and Prot-
estant witness before God, reached an apotheosis in the
nineteenth century as medicine and psychology, sexology
and pedagogy, took on a role, alongside the Churches, of
establishing moral and social standards. By the end of the
nineteenth century, as critics observed at the time, doctors

had adopted some of the attributes of a new priesthood, and many of its members seemed as certain of their views as the old. But the increasing politicization of the sexual in the past hundred years or so offers new possibilities and consequent challenges: not just of moral control and its inevitable converse, sexual transgression and dissidence, but of political analysis, opposition and change. This makes it all the more necessary that we know what we are talking about when we speak of sexuality, that we clarify the meaning (or, more accurately, meanings) of this complex phenomenon.

This is an easy aim to proclaim. It is a notoriously more hazardous task to carry out. All of us have so much invested in our own concept of what is the 'true sex' that we find it difficult enough to understand dispassionately the sexual needs and behaviour of our closest contemporaries, let alone the infinitely more ambiguous desires of our predecessors or contemporaries in other cultures. The mists of time and the various disguises of prejudice conveniently obscure other ways of living a sexual life and the merits of diverse sexual cultures. This resilient will not to know is backed up by an assumption which is deeply embedded in perhaps all cultures, but strongly in the West: that our sexuality is the most spontaneously natural thing about us. It is the basis for some of our most passionate feelings and commitments. Through it, we experience ourselves as real people; it gives us our identities, our sense of self, as men and women, as heterosexual and homosexual, 'normal' or 'abnormal', 'natural' or 'unnatural'. Sex has become, as the French philosopher Michel Foucault famously put it, 'the truth of our being' (Foucault 1979). But what is this 'truth'? And on what basis can we call something 'natural' or 'unnatural'? Who has the right to lay down the laws of sexuality? The magic quality of words gives us some clues to a convoluted history.

Let us start with the term 'sex' and its common uses. Its very ambiguity signals difficulty. We learn very early on from many sources that 'natural' sex is what takes place with members of the 'opposite sex'. 'Sex' between people of the 'same sex' is therefore, by definition, 'unnatural'. So much has usually been taken for granted. But the multiple meanings of the word 'sex' in these last few sentences should alert us to the real complexity of the question. The term refers both to an act and to a category of person, to a practice and to a gender. Modern culture has assumed an intimate connection between the fact of being biologically male or female (that is, having 'appropriate' sex organs and reproductive potentialities) and the correct form of erotic behaviour (usually genital intercourse between men and women). The earliest usage of the term 'sex' in English, in the sixteenth century, referred precisely to the division of humanity into the male section and the female section (that is, to differences of what later was to be called gender). This eventually gave rise to the idea that 'sex' is the basic biological datum on which the cultural and social divides of gender are built. The other dominant meaning today, and one current since the early nineteenth century, refers to physical relations between these polarized sexes, 'to have sex'. The word 'sexuality' (the abstract noun referring to the quality of being 'sexual') developed its modern meanings in the second half of the nineteenth century. It named the personalized sexual feelings that distinguished one person from another (*my* sexuality), while hinting at that mysterious essence that attracts us to each other. It also came to mean the whole apparatus and institutional forms that we now take for granted: sexuality as a continent of knowledge, culture, beliefs, practices, identities and social and political concern (Weeks 2011: 198–200).

The social processes through which these mutations of meaning have taken place are complex. But the implications are clear, for they are ones we still live with, even as they are questioned, demystified or deconstructed. In the first place, there is a continuing assumption of a sharp distinction and polarization between 'the sexes', a dichotomy of interests, even an antagonism ('the battle of the sexes') which can only be precariously bridged. Men are men and women are women; women are, in the vastly popular but highly misleading cliché, from Venus and men are from Mars – and this is Truth embodied in the dominant structures of heterosexuality, from which everything else remains a falling away. One reason both homosexuality and transgender were long tabooed is that they both depend on this dichotomy even as they seek to transgress and transcend it. Second, there is a belief that 'sex' is an overpowering natural force, a 'biological imperative', mysteriously located in the genitals (especially the wayward male organs) that sweeps all before it (at least if you are male) like hamlets before an avalanche, and that somehow bridges this divide, like a rainbow over a chasm. Third, this gives rise to a pyramid-like model of sex, to a sexual hierarchy stretching downwards from the apparently Nature-endowed correctness of heterosexual genital intercourse to the bizarre manifestations of 'the perverse', hopefully safely buried at the base but unfortunately always erupting in dubious places.

Much has changed during the past few generations. We are much more tolerant of difference and diversity. There has been a re-evaluation of the relationships between men and women, men and men and women and women, and a growing recognition of gender ambiguity, ambivalence and fluidity. Transgender, long feared or despised, is as I write being touted as the new civil rights issue of our time. But traditional views of the world of sex and gender remain deeply embedded in our cultures, part of the air we breathe. They provide an ideological justification for apparently uncontrollable male lust, and therefore for the fact of rape and violence, for the downgrading of female sexual autonomy, and for the way we treat those sexual minorities who are different from ourselves, as well as for the more acceptable verities of love, relationships and security. Since the late nineteenth century, moreover, this approach has had the ostensibly scientific endorsement of the broad tradition known as sexology, the 'science of desire'. Sexologists such as Richard von Krafft-Ebing, Havelock Ellis, Auguste Forel, Magnus Hirschfeld, Sigmund Freud and many others, sought to discover the true meaning of sex by exploring its various guises: the experience of infantile sexuality, relations between the sexes, the influence of the 'germ plasm', the hormones and chromosomes and the gene, the nature of the 'sexual instinct', and the nature and causes of sexual perversions. They often disagreed with one another; they frequently contradicted themselves. In the end, even the most dedicated had to admit to a certain defeat. Freud confessed to the difficulty of agreeing 'any generally recognized criterion of the sexual nature of a process' (Freud 1916–17: 323), and although today we may claim to be a little more confident in knowing what is 'sexual' or not, we are still in as much of a fog as those pioneers in interpreting its implications. The revolution in genetics we are now living through, in its mapping of DNA, its search for the genes for this attribute or another (the 'gay gene' being perhaps the most notorious), has not fundamentally challenged, in fact has often confirmed, the difficulties and perils of this endless quest to understand the mysteries of sex.

The science of sex has had important positive effects in extending our knowledge of sexual behaviours, and I have no desire to denigrate its real achievements. Without it we would be enslaved to an even greater extent than we are to myths and nostrums. On the other hand, in its search for the 'true' meaning of sex, in its intense interrogation of sexual difference, its obsessive categorization of sexual perversities, and precise specifications of sexual 'disorders', it has contributed to the codification of a 'sexual tradition', a more or less coherent body of assumptions, beliefs, prejudices, rules, methods of investigation and forms of moral regulation, which still shape the way we live our sexualities. Is sex threatening and dangerous? If we want to believe that, we can find justification not only in a particular Christian tradition but in the writings also of the founding fathers of sexology, and in many of their scientific successors. Is sex, on the other hand, a source of potential freedom, whose liberatory power is only blocked by the regressive force of a corrupt civilization ('beneath the cobblestones, the beach' as the student revolutionaries in Paris, 1968, headily proclaimed)? If so, then justification can again be found in works of polemicists and 'scientists' from the nineteenth century to the present, embracing not only socialist pioneers such as Charles Fourier and Edward Carpenter, Freudo-Marxists like Wilhelm Reich and Herbert Marcuse, but also more ostensibly sober-suited 'social book-keepers' like Alfred Kinsey.

Whatever our moral and political values, it has been difficult to escape the naturalistic fallacy that the key to our sex lies somewhere in the recesses of 'Nature', and that sexual science provides the best means of access to it, tidying up the world by sweeping messy things into neat pigeonholes (Davis 1983: 272, note 1). Unfortunately, the 'mess' keeps returning with the wind, endlessly confusing our gaze.

SEXUALITIES IN HISTORY AND SOCIETY

Against the certainties of this tradition, I intend, in this short book, to offer an alternative way of understanding sexualities. This involves seeing the sexual not as a primordially 'natural' phenomenon but rather as a product of social and historical forces. 'Sexuality', I shall argue, is a 'fictional unity', that once did not exist, and at some time in the future may not exist again. It is an invention of the human mind. As Carole S. Vance once suggested, the most important organ in humans is located between the ears (Vance 1984). This does not mean we can simply ignore the massive edifice of sexuality which envelops us. In the heyday of theoretical deconstruction, it was argued that 'sexuality is without the importance ascribed to it in our contemporary society . . . it does not exist as such, because there is no such thing as sexuality' (Heath 1982: 3). Here we see a reduction to absurdity of a valuable insight. Of course, sexuality exists as a palpable social presence, shaping our personal and public lives. But I am suggesting that what we define as 'sexuality' is a historical construction, which brings together a host of different biological and mental possibilities, and cultural forms – gender and sexual identities, bodily differences, reproductive capacities, needs, desires, fantasies, erotic practices, institutions and values – which need not be linked together, and in other cultures have not been.

All the constituent elements of sexuality have their source either in the body or the mind, and I am not attempting to deny the limits posed by biology or emotions and mental processes. But the capacities of the body and the psyche are given meaning only in social relations. The next chapter, on 'The invention of sexuality', will attempt to justify this argument, while Chapters 3 and 4 will look at the implications of this approach for thinking about gender and sexual identities, and the fact of sexual diversity.

These chapters amount to a critique of what in the 1980s and 1990s came to be known as an 'essentialist' or 'naturalist' approach to sexuality and gender: that is a method which attempts to explain the properties of a complex whole by reference to a supposed inner truth or essence, the assumption 'that in all sexological matters there must be a single, basic, uniform pattern ordained by nature itself' (Singer 1973: 15). This is a *reductionist* method in that it reduces the complexity of the world to the imagined simplicities of its constituent units; and it is

deterministic in that it seeks to explain individuals as automatic products of inner propulsions, whether of the genes,
the instinct, the hormones or the mysterious workings of
the dynamic unconscious.

Against such an approach, I shall argue that the meanings we give to 'sexuality' are socially organized, sustained
by a variety of languages, which seek to tell us what sexuality is, what it ought to be – and what it could be. Existing
languages of sexuality, embedded in moral treatises, laws,
educational practices, psychological theories, medical definitions, social rituals, pornographic or romantic fictions,
popular music, as well as in commonsense assumptions
(most of which disagree) set the horizon of the possible.
They all present themselves as true representations of our
intimate needs and desires. The difficulty lies in their contradictory appeals, in the babel of voices they bring forth.
In order to make sense of them, and perhaps to go beyond
the current limits on the possible, we need to learn to trans-
late these languages – and to develop new ones. This has
been one of the tasks of those who have sought, in recent
years, to problematize the apparent unity of this world of
sexuality, and to develop a *critical*, non-essentialist, historically rooted study of the sexual. From social anthropology, sociology and post-Kinsey sex research, there
has come a growing awareness of the vast range of sexual
practices that exist in other cultures and within our own
culture. Other cultures, Ruth Benedict noted a long time
ago, act as laboratories 'in which we may study the diversity of human institutions' (Benedict 1980: 12). An awareness that the way we do things is not the only way of living
can provide a salutary jolt to our ethnocentricity. It can

also force us to ask questions about why things are as they are today. Other cultures, and subcultures, are a mirror to our own transitoriness. The names of anthropologists, sex researchers like Alfred Kinsey and social psychologists and sociologists such as John Gagnon, Wiliam Simon and Ken Plummer recur in these pages because they tell us that variety, not uniformity, is the norm. At the same time, the new theorists of globalization have made us aware that the new energies unleashed on the world are producing unpredictable patterns as the global and the local, the 'glocal' intermesh, clash and engender new social possibilities for the organization of human sexualities.

The social, however, does not imprint itself on blank sheets of paper. If sexuality is largely social it is also embodied. Material bodies provide the potentialities on which sexuality draws, and are the focus of the powerful feelings, emotions and psychic process which structure individual subjectivities. Psychology was a constitutive aspect of the new sexology at the end of the nineteenth century (Davidson 2001), but it has also offered ways of challenging its naturalism and essentialism. The legacy of Freud and his theory of the dynamic unconscious, though fiercely contested, has been a major source of the new sexual theory: what goes on in the unconscious mind often contradicts the apparent certainties of conscious life. The life of the mind – of fantasies above all – reveals a diversity of desires to which the human being is heir. It unsettles the apparent solidities of gender, of sexual need, of identity and subjectivity. As Rosalind Coward graphically said, 'In the private life of the mind, nothing is certain, nothing is fixed' (Coward 1984: 204).

Alongside these developments, the emergence of new forms of social and cultural history from the 1970s and 1980s, with their emphasis on the history of populations, 'mentalities' and cultural formations and representations, and the experiences and beliefs of the downtrodden and oppressed, those 'hidden from history', as much as stories of the powerful, has posed new questions about the past as well as the historic present. *The History of Sexuality* by Michel Foucault (1979) has had a spectacular influence on modern thinking about the sexual because it grew out of, as well as contributed to, this fertile development of our historical understanding. Foucault, like Freud two generations earlier, stands at a crossroads of sexual thought, important as much for the questions he raises as for the answers he provides.

Finally, and perhaps most powerfully of all, the emergence of new forms of sexual agency, both individual and through social movements concerned with sexuality – second-wave feminism, the 'lesbian, gay, bisexual, transgender, queer, querying' and other radical sexual movements. These have fundamentally challenged many of the certainties of the sexual tradition, and as a result have produced new insights into the intricate forms of power and domination that shape our sexual lives. The politics of homosexuality and bisexuality have placed on the agenda questions about sexual preference, identity and choice, the arbitrariness of sexual categorizations, the significance of entrenched homophobia and biphobia, and the nature of 'compulsory heterosexuality' and heteronormativity. Transgender activists have challenged the fixity and arbitrariness of gender and explored the fluidity and malleability of the body and identity. The women's movement has forced a recognition of the multiple forms of female sexual subordination, from endemic male violence and misogyny to sexual harassment and a pervasive language of sexual denigration and abuse. It has asked challenging questions about sexual autonomy, consent and reproductive rights, desires and pleasure.

These movements often pose as many questions as answers. Differences have emerged between men and women, men and men, women and women, homosexuals and heterosexuals, black and white. But through the clash of very real differences we are being forced to rethink what we understand by 'sexuality' because of a growing awareness of the tangled web of intersecting influences and forces – politics, economics, class, race, ethnicity, geography and space, gender, age, ability and disability, faith, morals and values – that shape our emotions, needs, desires and relationships.

So what does a non-essentialist theory of sexuality mean for the politics of sexuality and for sexual ethics in a feverishly globalizing and digitalizing world? These are the topics I examine in Chapters 5 and 6. They pose perhaps the most difficult challenges of all. The sexual tradition assumed that your sex was your fate or destiny: what you desired was what you were. Sexuality pinned you down like a butterfly to the table. If you break with this tradition, if you reject the idea that sexuality embodies its own values and goals, then you are faced with complex problems of alignment and choice. How do we respond to questions which have come to dominate sexual debates in recent years – about the queer assault on the normal, the significance of same-sex marriage, sexual fluidity and gender non-conformity? Confronted by such uncertainties, it is all too easy to retreat into moral or political absolutes, to reassert again, against all the odds, against all the evidence, that there is a true sexuality that we must find at all costs.

The aim of this book is to challenge such absolutes without falling into the trap of saying no values are possible, 'anything goes'. 'Sexuality' is a deeply problematic concept, and there are no easy answers to the challenges it poses. But if we begin to ask the correct questions, then we might find the way through the maze. We shall not find at the end of the journey a prescription for correct behaviour or ultimate Truth. But we might find a framework which allows us to come to terms with diversity – and to re-find, in sexuality, new opportunities for creative relationships, agency, choice and common values which bridge the gap between the individual and the social, the particular and the universal.

2

THE INVENTION OF SEXUALITY

A BRIEF HISTORY OF THE HISTORY OF SEXUALITY

We cannot escape history, even as we try to divine its inner meanings. We live history, even as we seek to dwell in the moment. History shapes our possibilities at the same time as we attempt to reshape and remake it. Our sense of agency, of being able to mould our possibilities, is a defining characteristic of being human, but that agency is always fashioned by what is historically possible and feasible. This is true of all cultural phenomena. It is especially true of sexual cultures.

But until relatively recently, few writers seriously concerned themselves with sexual history. The distinguished American historian, Vern Bullough (1976) famously declared that sex in history was a 'virgin field'. This may have been a dubious pun but it was useful in underlining an important, if often overlooked, reality. 'Sexuality' was much talked about and written about, but our historical knowledge about it remained pretty negligible. Those would-be colonizers who ventured into the field tended either to offer transcultural generalizations or to subsume the subject under more neutral and acceptable labels ('marriage', 'the family' and 'morals', especially). Sexuality seemed marginal to the broad acres of orthodox history.

Over the past few decades, however, much has changed, sometimes dramatically. There has been a major explosion of historical writings about sexuality (Weeks 2016). We now know a great deal about such topics as marriage and the family; prostitution; homosexuality, the forms of legal and medical regulation; pre-Christian, Christian and non-Christian (including Islamic, Jewish and Hindu) moral codes; masculinities; women's bodies and health; illegitimacy and birth control; rape and sexual violence; the evolution of gay, lesbian, bisexual or transgender identities; the structures of heteronormativity; and the importance of diverse sexual cultures, social networks and oppositional sexualities. In recent years sexual history has gone global, with a growing interest in transnational history, and the impact of colonial and post-colonial regimes of power, domination and resistance. Historians have deployed sophisticated methods of family reconstitution and demographic history, intensively searched for new – or interrogated old – documentary sources, and made full use of oral and life history interviews to reconstruct the subjective or the tabooed experience. Encouraged by a vigorous grass-roots history, fed by the impact of modern feminism and LGBTQ politics, and made urgent by the impact of the HIV/AIDS crisis which required better knowledge of human sexual behaviours, there is now an impressive library of articles, pamphlets, books and archives, and a mass of cyber-dialogue about all aspects of sexual history.

Sex research, the sociologist Ken Plummer once noted, makes you 'morally suspect' (Plummer 1975: 4). But the history of sexuality is now in danger of becoming a respectable field of study, with a high degree of professional recognition, its own specialist journals and an interested, even passionate, audience. Writing about sexuality, and especially the history of sexuality, no longer seems quite such a bizarre and marginal activity as it once did. There is even a blooming recognition that the history of sexuality tells us more than the wheres, hows and whys of the erotic in the past: it throws a dazzling, searching light on our confusing and confused present, in all its complexities.

But having said this, we are still left with a dilemma – as to what exactly our object of study is. I can list, as I did above, a number of activities that we conventionally designate as being concerned with the sexual; but what is it that connects them? What is the magic element that defines some things as sexual and others not? There are no straightforward answers to these questions. At the heart of our concern, clearly, is an interest in the relations between men and women, men and men, women and women. One particular form of human interaction is the process of biological and social reproduction. No historian of sexuality would dare to ignore that. But a history of reproduction is not a history of sex. As Alfred Kinsey bitingly observed:

> Biologists and psychologists who have accepted the doctrine that the only natural function of sex is reproduction

have simply ignored the existence of sexual activity which is not reproductive. They have assumed that heterosexual responses are a part of an animal's innate, 'instinctive' equipment, and that all other types of sexual activity represent 'perversions' of the 'normal instincts'. Such interpretations are, however, mystical.

(Kinsey et al. 1953: 448)

Most erotic interactions, even between those we easily call 'heterosexual', do not lead to procreation. And there are many forms of non-heterosexual sex, among women, and among men. Some of these patterns involve intercourse of one sort or another. Others do not. Most have at least the potentiality of leading to orgasm. Yet some activities which are clearly sex-related (for example, transgender practices) are not directly or necessarily linked with sexual activities. In recent years a new category of 'asexuality' has emerged not simply as a clinical definition but as a badge of pride and social identity. Not even intimacy seems a clear enough criterion for judging what is sexual. Some activities we quite properly describe as sexual (masturbation is a good example) are solo practices, even if mediated by fantasy or stimulated by pornography and sexually explicit material on- or offline. Some aspects of intimacy have nothing to do with sex; and some sex is not intimate. In the age of cybersex, mediated anonymously through millions of network connections, bodily intimacy is in danger of being displaced altogether, and the distinctions between men and women, heterosexual and homosexual, adults and children, the beautiful, the ugly and the damned, may dissolve easily in the millions of possible interactions in cyberspace.

Modern sexual scientists who wish to explain every manifestation of social life by reference to the 'timeless energy of the selfish genes', the dance of DNA or the mating games of our remote ancestors on the African savannah half a million years ago, may see some biological logic in all of these activities. The rest of us, wisely in my opinion, are probably a little more sceptical. We are rather more than the 'survival machines – robots blindly programmed to preserve the molecule' – that the populist biologist Richard Dawkins (1978) once described so vividly and misleadingly.

A SUBJECT IN CONSTANT FLUX

So what is a history of sexuality a history of? My rather disappointing answer would be that it is a history without a proper subject; or rather as Robert Padgug (1979) has suggested, a history of a subject in constant flux. It is often as much a history of *our* changing preoccupations about how we should live, how we should enjoy or deny our bodies, as about the past. The way we write about our sexuality tells us as much about the present and its concerns as about this past.

We are not, of course, the first generation to speculate about the past of sexuality, nor the first to be so revealing about our preoccupations in doing so. Some sense of the past has always been an important element for those that have been thinking about the meaning and implications of erotic life. In her book *Patriarchal Precedents*, Rosalind Coward (1983) described the complex and heated debates in the last half of the nineteenth century about the

nature of contemporary family and sexual forms. Pioneering social scientists saw in sexuality a privileged site for
speculations on the very origins of human society. From
this flowed conflicting theories about the evolution and
development of the various patterns of sexual life. Had the
modern family evolved from the primitive clan, or was it
already there, 'naturally', at the birth of history? Did our
ancestors live in a state of primitive promiscuity, or was
monogamy a biological necessity and fact? Was there once
an Eden of sexual egalitarianism before what Friedrich
Engels (1972: 120) called the 'world historical defeat of the
female sex', or was patriarchal domination present from
the dawn of culture? On the resolution of such debates
depended attitudes not only to existing social forms (marriage, sexual inequality, the double standard of morality)
but also to other, 'primitive' cultures that existed contem-
poraneously with the Western in other (often colonized)
parts of the world. Could we find clues to our own evolutionary history in the rites and behaviours of aboriginal
peoples, apparently stunted on the ladder of progress? Or
did these people tell us something else about the variability of cultures?

We have still not fully escaped the effects of these evolu-
tionist controversies. For much of the twentieth century,
ethnocentric racist theories and practices were legit-
imized by reference to the primitive condition of other
races – a position hallowed, no doubt unintentionally,
by the founding father of evolutionary biology himself.
In the last paragraphs of his *The Descent of Man* (1871),
Charles Darwin commented on the blood of more primitive creatures flowing through the native peoples he had

met on his early investigatory voyages. Even those who extolled the virtues of the sexual freedom of non-industrial societies fell back on a belief that their peoples were somehow 'closer to nature', more 'spontaneous' and free of the stifling conventions of complex modern society. Similarly, many of the feminist debates of the 1970s and 1980s about the permanence of patriarchal male domination re-cultivated the ground so feverishly worked over a century previously. Yet from the 1920s, the older questions about the evolution of human culture were being displaced by a new anthropological approach, which asked different questions about sexuality.

This was associated in the first place with writers such as Bronislaw Malinowski and Margaret Mead. They recognized the danger of trying to understand our own prehistory by looking at existing societies. As a result, there was a new effort to try to understand each particular society in its own terms. This gave rise to a kind of cultural relativism in looking at other sexual mores, and a recognition of the validity of different sexual systems, however exotic they may have looked by the standards of twentieth-century industrial societies. This new approach was highly influential in helping to put Western culture, with all its discontents, into some sort of context. Moreover, by recognizing the diversity of sexual patterns all over the world, it contributed to a more sympathetic understanding of the diversity of sexual patterns and cultures within Western societies, made up as they were and are of intersecting but differentiated sexual cultures. Social anthropology helped to provide a critical standard by which we could begin to judge the historical nature of our own norms and values.

For long the most famous example of this genre, Margaret Mead's romantic (and now much criticized) picture of 'coming of age' in Samoa, was enormously influential in the 1930s in large part because it seemed to demonstrate that the (repressive) American way of dealing with the problem of adolescence was neither desirable, inevitable, nor necessary (Mead 1977; compare Freeman 1983).

There were, however, difficulties. On the one hand, there was the danger of attempting to understand all sexual acts by their function, as finely tuned responses to the claims of society. For Malinowski, a grasp of the laws of society needed to be matched by a scientific understanding of the laws of nature, and he paid homage to the sexological work of Havelock Ellis, and gave critical respect to Freud for helping him to grasp 'the universally human and fundamental' (Malinowski 1963: 167). Malinowski saw cultures as delicate mechanisms designed to satisfy a basic human nature; in the process, the status of 'the natural' was not so much questioned as reaffirmed, although now it was less a product of evolution and more of basic instinctual needs. On the other hand, the endorsement of an 'infinite plasticity' of human needs by Ruth Benedict, Margaret Mead and their followers led not to a more historical account of sexual patterns but to a descriptive anthropology in which readers were offered wonderful, shimmering evocations of the sexual lives of other peoples, but little sense of why these patterns were as they were. In the absence of any theory of determinative structures or of historical processes, again essentialist assumptions surreptitiously reasserted themselves.

The originality of attempts since the 1970s to develop a more social and historical approach to sexuality lies in their willingness to question the naturalness and inevitability of the sexual categories and assumptions we have inherited. The sociologists/social psychologists John Gagnon and William Simon have talked of the need which may have existed at some unspecified time in the past to *invent* an importance for sexuality – perhaps because of under-population and threats of cultural submergence (Gagnon and Simon 1973). The French philosopher Michel Foucault went further by attempting to query the very category of 'sexuality' itself. In a now famous passage he wrote:

> Sexuality must not be thought of as a kind of natural given which power tries to hold in check, or as an obscure domain which knowledge tries gradually to uncover. It is the name that can be given to a historical construct.
>
> (Foucault 1979: 105)

Except, of course, he did not use that last word in the original French – he spoke rather of a *dispositif*, a deployment or apparatus of sexuality. Nevertheless, Foucault's work has made a vital contribution to recent discussions on the historical invention of sexuality precisely because it burst onto and grew out of work that was already creatively developing in sociology, anthropology and in radical social history in challenging naturalistic assumptions about the sexual. It helped to give a focus for questions already being formed. To questions about what shaped sexual beliefs and behaviours, a new one was added, concerning the history of the idea of sexuality itself. For Foucault, sexuality was a relationship of elements and discourses, a series of meaning-giving practices and activities, a social apparatus which had a history – with complex roots in the pre-Christian and Christian past, but achieving a modern conceptual unity, with diverse effects, only within the modern world.

The most important result of this historical approach to sexuality is that it opens the whole field to critical analysis and assessment. It becomes possible to relate sexuality to other social phenomena. Three types of question then become critically important. First: how is sexuality shaped, how is it articulated with economic, social and political structures; in a phrase, how is it socially and historically constructed? Second: how and why has the domain of sexuality achieved such a critical organizing and symbolic significance in Western culture; why do we think it is so important? Third: what is the relationship between sex and power; what role should we assign class divisions, patterns of male domination and racism? Coursing through each of these questions is a recurrent preoccupation: if sexuality is constructed by human agency, to what extent can it be changed? This is the question I shall attempt to deal with in succeeding chapters. The first three I shall examine in turn in the rest of this chapter.

THE 'SOCIAL CONSTRUCTION' OF SEXUALITY

At the heart of 'the social construction of sexuality' is a quite straightforward concern, with 'the intricate and multiple ways in which our emotions, desires and relationships are shaped by the society we live in' (Cartledge and Ryan 1983: 1). It is basically concerned with the ways in which sexualities have been shaped in a complex history, and in tracing how sexual patterns have changed over time. It is preoccupied with the historical and social organization of the erotic (Stein 1992; Seidman 2014).

In practice, most writers on our sexual past have assumed that sex is an irresistible natural energy barely held in check by a thin crust of civilization. For Malinowski:

> Sex is a most powerful instinct . . . there is no doubt that masculine jealousy, sexual modesty, female coyness, the mechanism of sexual attraction and of courtship – all these forces and conditions made it necessary that even in the most primitive human aggregates there should exist powerful means of regulating, suppressing and directing this instinct.
>
> (Malinowski 1963: 120)

'Sex', as he put it in another paper, 'really is dangerous', the source of most human trouble from Adam and Eve onwards (Malinowski 1963: 127).

In these words we can still hear echoes of the pioneering sexologist Richard von Krafft-Ebing's view at the end of the nineteenth century of sex as an all-powerful instinct which demands fulfilment against the claims of morals, belief and social restrictions (Krafft-Ebing 1931). But even more orthodox academic historians spoke in rather similar language. Lawrence Stone, for instance, in *The Family, Sex and Marriage* sensibly rejects the idea that 'the id' (the energy of the Freudian unconscious) is the most powerful and unchanging of all drives. He suggests that changes in protein, in diet, in physical exertion and in psychic stress all have an effect on the organization of sex. Yet he still speaks of 'the super ego' (our internalized system of values) at times repressing and at other times releasing the sexual drive, which eloquently reproduces the ancient traditional picture of sexuality as a pool of energy that has to be contained or let go (Stone 1977: 15).

These approaches assume that sex offers a basic 'biological mandate' which presses against and must be restrained by the cultural matrix. This is what I mean by an essentialist approach to sexuality. It takes many forms. Liberatory theorists such as Wilhelm Reich and Herbert Marcuse tended to see sex as a beneficent force which was repressed by a corrupt civilization (Weeks 1985). Sociobiologists or evolutionary psychologists on the other hand see all social forms as in some unspecified way, emanations of basic genetic material. Yet they all argue for a world of nature which provides the raw material we must use for the understanding of the social. Against all these arguments I want to stress that sexuality is shaped by social forces. Far from being the most natural element in social life, the most resistant to cultural moulding, it is perhaps one of the most susceptible to social organization, and becomes meaningful only through its social forms and social organization. Moreover, the forces that shape and mould the erotic possibilities of the body vary from society to society. 'Sexual socialization', Ellen Ross and Rayner Rapp wrote in the early stages of this historicizing of sexuality, 'is no less specific to each culture than is socialization to ritual, dress or cuisine' (Ross and Rapp 1984: 109). This puts the emphasis firmly where it should belong – on society and social relations rather than on nature.

I do not wish to deny the importance of biology. The physiology and morphology of the body provides the pre-conditions for human sexuality. Biology conditions and limits what is possible. Embodiment matters. But the patterns of sexual life are not dictated by biology. We cannot reduce human behaviour to the mysterious workings of the DNA, the eternal gene or 'the dance of the chromosomes' (Cherfas and Gribbin 1984). I prefer to see in biology a set of potentialities, which are transformed and given meaning only in social relationships. Human consciousness and human history are very complex phenomena, not simply reflections of Nature.

This theoretical stance has many roots: in the sociology and anthropology of sex, in the revolution in psychoanalysis and in the new social and cultural history. But despite these disparate starting points, it coheres around a number of common assumptions. First, there is a general rejection of sex as an autonomous realm, a natural domain with specific effects, a rebellious energy that the social controls. We can no longer set 'sex' against 'society' as if they were separate domains. Second, there is a widespread recognition of the social variability of sexual forms, beliefs, ideologies, identities and behaviour, and of the existence of different sexual cultures. Sexuality has a history, or more realistically, many histories, each of which needs to be understood both in its uniqueness and as part of an intricate pattern. There are indeed sexualities rather than a single sexuality. Third, we must abandon the idea that we can fruitfully understand sexual history in terms of a dichotomy of pressure and release, repression and liberation. The sexual is not a head of steam that must be capped lest it destroy us; nor is it a life force we must release to save our civilization. Instead we must learn to see that sexualities are produced in society in complex ways. They are a result of diverse social practices that give meaning to human activities, of social definitions and self-definitions, of struggles between those who have power to define and regulate, and those who resist. 'Sexuality' is not a given, it is a product of negotiation, struggle and human agency.

Nothing is sexual, Plummer suggested in one of the founding statements of the new sociology of sexuality, but the naming makes it so (Plummer 1975). If this is the case, it follows that we need to move gingerly in applying the dominant Western definitions to non-Western cultures. Both the significance attributed to sexuality and attitudes to the various manifestations of erotic life vary enormously. Some societies display so little interest in erotic activity that they have been labelled more or less 'asexual'. Others use the erotic to open up sharp dichotomies, between those who can be included in the community of believers, and those who must be forcibly excluded; between those open to salvation, and the sinners who are not. Islamic cultures have, it is claimed by one of its leading historians, developed a lyrical view of sex with sustained attempts at integrating the religious and the sexual. Bouhdiba writes of 'the radical legitimacy of the practice of sexuality' in the Islamic world – as long, that is, as it was not homosexual, which was 'violently condemned' by Islam, or involved extra-marital activity by women, who might be condemned to death under Sharia law (Bouhdiba 1985: 159, 200). The practice, needless to say, has been more varied (compare Massad 2007). The Christian West, notoriously, has seen in sex a terrain of moral anguish and conflict, setting up an enduring dualism between the spirit and the flesh, the mind and the body. It has had the inevitable result of creating a cultural configuration which simultaneously disavows the body while being obsessively preoccupied with it.

Within the wide parameters of general cultural attitudes, each culture names different practices as appropriate or inappropriate, moral or immoral, healthy or perverted. Western culture, at least as codified by the Roman Catholic and evangelical traditions, continues formally at least to define appropriate behaviour in terms of a limited range of acceptable activities. Monogamous marriage between partners of roughly equal age but different genders remains the most widely accepted norm (though not, of course, necessarily or even today generally the reality) and, despite many changes, a readily accepted gateway to adulthood and sexual activity. Homosexuality, on the other hand, despite remarkable shifts in attitudes over recent generations, still carries in many quarters a heavy legacy of taboo. The HIV/AIDS crisis in the 1980s and 1990s revealed the contradictory attitudes of most Western countries and has fed into forms of political homophobia in the Global South.

Other cultures, on the other hand, have not found it necessary to issue the same injunctions or develop the same dichotomies. The anthropologists Ford and Beach (1965) famously found that only 15 per cent of 185 different societies surveyed restricted sexual liaisons to single mateships. Kinsey's figures suggested that beneath a surface conformity, Western practices are as varied: in his 1940s sample, 50 per cent of males and 26 per cent of females had extra-marital sex by the age of 40 (Kinsey et al. 1953). Even more unsettling was the evidence that the heterosexual/homosexual binary divide, which has done so much to define Western attitudes since the nineteenth century, was something less than universal.

Marriage has not been inevitably heterosexual, even before contemporary claims for the recognition of same-sex marriage. Among the Nuer, older women 'marry' younger women; and there is a great deal of emerging evidence that even in early Christian Europe male partnerships were sanctified by the Church almost as if they were marriages (Edholm 1982; Boswell 1994). Homosexuality has not been universally tabooed. There have been various forms of institutionalized homosexuality, from puberty rites in various tribal societies, to pedagogic relations between older men and youths (as in Ancient Greece), to the integrated transgender partnerships (the berdache) among native Americans, and transgendered identities among other peoples, from Brazil to the Philippines (Parker 1991, 1999; Herdt 1994; Johnson 1997; Parker et al. 2000).

Many in the West, not least those adhering to the formal positions of the Roman Catholic Church, still tend to define the norms of sex in relationship to one of the possible results – reproduction. For long centuries of Christian dominance it was *the only* justification of sexual relations. Other cultures, however, have sometimes failed even to make the connection between copulation and procreation. Some societies only recognize the role of the father, others the mother. The Trobriand Islanders according to Malinowski saw no connection between intercourse and reproduction. It was only *after* the spirit child entered the womb that intercourse assumed any significance for them, in moulding the character of the future child (Malinowski 1929).

Sexual cultures are precisely that: culturally specific, shaped by a wide range of social and historical factors. National cultures are frequently made up of a variety of competing local sexual traditions, cultures and conventions, some dominant, some subordinate, others uneasily co-existing (see discussion in Weeks 2007). Each culture makes what Plummer calls 'who restrictions' and 'how restrictions'. 'Who restrictions' are concerned with the gender of the partners, the species, age, kin, race, caste or class which limit whom we may take as partners. 'How restrictions' have to do with the organs that we use, the orifices we may enter, the manner of sexual involvement and sexual intercourse: what we may touch, when we may touch, with what frequency, and so on (Plummer 1984). These regulations take many forms: formal and informal, legal and extra-legal. They tend not to apply in an undifferentiated way for the whole of society. For instance, there are usually different rules for men and women, shaped in ways which subordinate women's sexuality to men's. Erotic minorities tend to develop their own norms and values. There are different rules for adults and children. These rules are often more acceptable as abstract norms than as practical guidelines. But they provide the permissions, prohibitions, limits and possibilities through which erotic life is constructed.

THE ORGANIZATION OF SEXUALITY

Five broad areas stand out as being particularly crucial in the social organization of sexuality: kinship and family systems, economic and social organization, social regulation, politics, and the development of 'cultures of resistance'.

Kinship and family systems

Kinship and family systems *appear* as the most basic and unchanging forms of all – pre-eminently the 'natural' focus of sexual socialization and experience. The taboo on incest, that is the prohibition of sexual involvement within certain degrees of relationship, seems to be a universal law, marking the passage, it has been often argued, from a state of nature to human society: it has been seen as constitutive of culture. (It is also the basis for one of the most enduring collective myths – that of Oedipus, who unknowingly killed his father and married his mother, and then had to pay the painful price of this infringement of the Law.) Yet the forms of the taboo vary enormously. In the Christian traditions of the Middle Ages, marriage to the seventh degree of relationship was prohibited. Today, marriage to first cousins is generally allowed. In the Egypt of the pharaohs, sibling marriages were permitted, and in some cases, so were father–daughter marriages, in the interests of preserving the purity of the royal line (Renvoize 1982; Jones 2009). Today, father–daughter incest is among the most tabooed of activities. The existence of the incest taboo illustrates the need of all societies to regulate sex – but not how it is done. Even 'blood relationships' have to be interpreted through the grid of culture.

Every society, the American social anthropologist and sexual theorist Gayle Rubin influentially argued, had a 'sex-gender system' by which the biological raw materials of sex and reproduction were shaped by human, social and historical interventions, and developed into conventional patterns of social life, into which varieties of sexual life had to fit, or transgress and resist (Rubin 1974: 165). The truth is that kin ties are not *natural* links of blood but are social relations between groups, often based on residential affinities and hostile to genetic affinities. As Marshall Sahlins argued:

> human conceptions of kinship may be so far from biology as to exclude all but a small fraction of a person's genealogical connections from the category of 'close kin', while at the same time, including in that category, as sharing common blood, very distantly related people or even complete strangers. Among these strangers (genetically) may be one's own children (culturally).
>
> (Sahlins 1976: 75)

Who we decide are kin and what we describe as 'the family' are clearly dependent on a range of historical factors, shaped by class, geography and different religious, cultural, racial and ethnic differences. On a global scale, the Swedish sociologist Göran Therborn has suggested that there are five basic types of family forms within broad religious frameworks, which provide the framing contexts for sexuality and gender patterns: sub-Saharan African (shaped by Animist beliefs); European and North American (shaped by Christian systems); South Asian (Hindu); East Asian (Confucian and Buddhist); and West Asian / North African (Islam) (Therborn 2004). Clearly, as Therborn acknowledges, the reality on the ground is much more complex, with a number of sub-forms, and considerable change over time. In his discussion of Therborn's book, Plummer (2015: 147) suggests the existence of what he calls 'global tectonic plates' moving slowly and organizing forms of life at a deep level. These include world religions which, far from declining as secularists hoped, are burgeoning in many parts of the world; civilizational regions, as discussed by Therborn; dramatic migratory shifts of population leading to diasporas, colonizations and hybrid populations; and social divisions, especially those based on economics, class and disparities of wealth and poverty, gender, race and ethnicity, and age as well as the cultural and political conflicts which reflect and magnify such divisions. It is not surprising that the future of the family has become a central focus of controversy in many parts of the world. The pluralization of family patterns – including 'families of choice', based on friendships networks and chosen kin (Weeks et al. 2001) – can be seen as either a signal mark of growing toleration or a perilous sign of social decline.

Family patterns are shaped and re-shaped by economic and social factors, by faiths, by rules of inheritance and by state interventions to regulate marriage and divorce or to support the family by social welfare or taxation policies. All these affect the likely patterns of sexual life: by encouraging or discouraging the rate of marriage, age of marriage, incidence of reproduction, attitudes to non-procreative or non-heterosexual sex, acceptance of cohabitation, or single parenthood, the relative power of men over women, and now, with the growing recognition of same-sex marriage and the rise of 'queer domesticities' (Cook 2014), even the relevance, or not, of the heterosexual/homosexual binary divide. All these factors are important in themselves. They are doubly important because the family is the arena in which most people, certainly in Western cultures, gain some sense of their individual sexual needs, subjectivities and identities, and if we follow psychoanalysis, it is the arena where our desires are organized from a very early stage indeed. As kin and family patterns change, so will attitudes and beliefs concerning sexuality.

Economic and social organization

Attempts to directly relate sexual systems to wider economic and social formations in terms of causation, function, determination or need have not on the whole been successful, despite valiant efforts from functionalist sociologists, feminist theorists of patriarchy, Marxists or critics of contemporary neo-liberalism. Sexuality is too diverse, historically variable and recalcitrant, and as sexual history shows, too subject to the contingencies of social practices to have any confidence in broad generalizations. But social and economic forces do inevitably provide the context, open the opportunities and set the limits within which sexual and intimate life is shaped. Domestic patterns can be changed by economic forces, by the class divisions to which economic change gives rise, by the degree of urbanization and of rapid industrial and social change, by migrations and other transnational flows of people, even by sex tourism and by trafficking of peoples. Labour migrations have, for example, variously affected patterns of courtship, mateship arrangements, ethnic and racial intermingling, the incidence of illegitimacy rates, or the spread of sexual diseases. The proletarianization of the rural population in early nineteenth-century England helped to contribute to the massive rise of illegitimacy during this period, as old courtship patterns were broken by economic and industrial dislocation – a case of 'marriage frustrated' rather than a conscious sexual revolution. Work conditions can dramatically shape sexual lives. A good example of this is provided by the evidence from the 1920s and 1930s in Britain that women who worked in factories tended to be much more familiar with methods of artificial birth control, and thus could limit their family size to a greater degree, than women who worked solely in the home or in domestic service (Gittins 1982).

The relations between men and women are constantly affected by changes in economic and social conditions. The growing involvement of married women in the paid workforce from the 1950s and 1960s in most Western countries inevitably affected the patterns of domestic life, even if it took much longer to transform beyond recognition the traditional division of labour in the household. Increasing economic opportunities for women and the emergence of a consumer society have been important elements in the 'rise of women' since the 1960s, perhaps the most important social transformation of the twentieth century. It has gone hand in hand with greater recognition of the sexual autonomy of women, and of more individualized attitudes towards sexuality generally. Between the 1960s and the first decade of the twenty-first century there was a great transition in sexual values, based on the weakening of traditional institutions such as the family and authoritarian religion, giving rise to new patterns of intimate life based more than ever before on sexual agency and choice (Giddens 1992; Weeks 2007).

Such changes are no longer confined to the highly industrialized heartlands of the North of the globe. The processes of globalization are sweeping away old economic, social and cultural boundaries. Many of its manifestations are not new. Mass movements of peoples, within countries, and across states and continents, have been among the dominant forces of the past few hundred years – through imperialism and colonization, the slave trade, the disruptive effects of war, voluntary migration and enforced resettlements. All these have disrupted traditional patterns of life, and settled sexual values and behaviours, as men and women, adults and children have been brought together and violently parted, with unpredictable results on sexual mores – from enforced segregation of the sexes to an international sex-trade, from the disruption of traditional patterns of courtship and marriage to the epidemic spread of HIV/AIDS. All the evidence suggests that contemporary global trends are speeding up these processes, creating dramatic new patterns of 'global sex'. Sexuality may not be *determined* by the developing modes of production, but the rhythms of economic and social life provide the basic preconditions and ultimate limits for the organization and 'political economy' of sexual life (Altman 2001).

Social regulation

If economic life establishes some of the fundamental rhythms, the actual forms of regulation of sexuality have a considerable autonomy. Formal methods of regulating sexual life vary from time to time depending on the significance of religion, the changing role of the state, the existence or not of a moral consensus which regulates marriage patterns, divorce rates and incidence of sexual unorthodoxy, and even the location of cultures and states within the international order. Colonialism and imperial expansion by European powers in the nineteenth century profoundly reshaped the sexual systems and gender orders of the subordinated peoples of the world as well as those of the metropolitan countries, and continue to shape post-colonial attitudes towards what are regarded as Western sexual patterns (notably homosexuality).

One of the critical shifts of the last hundred years in most highly industrialized countries has been the move away from moral regulation by the churches to a more secular mode of organization through medicine, education, psychology, social work and welfare practices. That does not necessarily mean the diminution of religion. In some ways, the apparent secularization of late industrial societies has heightened the importance of faith-based interventions as they react to what they see as the undermining of traditional values. While European countries have become increasingly indifferent to religious practices, other parts of the world have witnessed waves of religious enthusiasm and revivalism. As Micklethwaite and Wooldridge (2009) affirmed, 'God is back', spurred in many ways by the

Americanization of religion. Evangelical Christianity in the USA itself owed much of its initial energy in the early twentieth century to profound rejection of the apparent triumph of Darwinian ideas of evolution, with science ostensibly rejecting the religious view of life. The USA, as the most religious of contemporary late industrial societies, has seen since the 1970s a powerful resurgence of the power of religion in politics, with abortion, (secular) sex education, homosexuality and especially same-sex marriage becoming touchstone issues for moral conservatives. Anti-Darwinism has produced its own reaffirmation of a religious viewpoint in contemporary Creationism, which a high proportion of American citizens apparently support. The wider rise of fundamentalist movements globally has a similar anti-secular and anti-scientific drive, even as they are sustained and promoted, like American evangelicalism and social conservatism, by all the sophisticated technologies that modern science has wrought (Bhatt 1997; Ruthven 2004). Yet even as we must acknowledge the power of contemporary religious revivalism, we should also recognize that these movements are in large part reactions to the rise of sexual modernism. Traditional religious organizations closely linked to earlier imperial expansionism, like the Episcopal/Anglican churches and even the Roman Catholic Church, are now riven by debates over the role of women and lesbians and gays in the priesthood, not to mention same-sex marriage. There are LGBTQ groups for Muslims as well as Christians in Western societies. Such manifestations are, however, anathema to more conservative cultures – and especially their leaders – in the Global South.

Whatever the intentions of moral leaders, politicians and law-makers, medics and psychologists, it is important to recognize that the success of their interventions are not necessarily pre-ordained. As often as not, sexual life is altered by the unintended consequences of social action as much as through the intention of the protagonists. Laws banning obscene publications, more often than not, give rise to court cases that publicize them. Banning sexually explicit films gives them a notoriety they might not otherwise deserve. Laws and prohibitions designed to control the behaviour of erotic minorities can actually give rise to an enhanced sense of identity and cohesion amongst them. This certainly seems to be the case with the refinement of the laws relating to male homosexuality since the late nineteenth century in Europe and North America, which coincide with the strengthening of same-sex ways of being (Weeks 2016/1977). The waves of homophobia in parts of Africa, western Asia and eastern Europe in recent years, with often devastating effects on individual lives, have similarly often worked to consolidate LGBTQ identities (see contributions to Aggleton et al. 2012). In the same way, injunctions against artificial birth control methods can make people aware of their existence. It is surely no accident that Italy, the home of the Papacy, which strictly forbids abortion and birth control, has one of the lowest birth rates in Europe, while still remaining formally Catholic. Catholics in their millions use modern means to control fertility despite the firm and fierce injunctions against them. Although religion can still be decisive, especially in those countries dominated by religious ideologues, people are increasingly willing to decide for themselves how they want to behave. Morality is being privatized, even in deeply religious cultures.

It is not only formal methods which shape sexuality; there are many informal and customary patterns which are equally important. The traditional forms of regulation of adolescent courtship can be critical means of social control. It is very difficult to break with the consensus of one's village or one's peer group in school, and this is as much true today as it was in the pre-industrial societies. A language of sexual abuse ('slags', 'sluts', 'whores' in familiar Anglo-Saxon usage) works to keep girls in line, and to enforce conventional distinctions between girls who do and girls who don't. In Britain, despite increasing acceptance of same-sex love at all levels of society, 'gay' has become a familiar term of abuse in school playgrounds and in youth-oriented media. Such informal methods enforced by strictly adhered to unspoken rules often produce, by contemporary standards, various bizarre manifestations of sexual behaviour. One such example is provided by the traditional form of courtship in parts of England and Wales up to the nineteenth century known as 'bundling', which involved intimate but fully clothed rituals of sex play in bed. Closer to the present, we can find the equally exotic phenomenon of 'petting', which much preoccupied moralists and parents until the 1960s. Petting is dependent on the belief that while intercourse in public is tabooed, other forms of play, because they are not defined as *the* sex act, may be intimately engaged in. Kinsey noted in the early 1950s that:

> Foreign travellers [to America] are sometimes amazed at the open display of such obviously erotic activity . . . There

is an increasing amount of petting which is carried on in such public conveyances as buses, trams, and airplanes. The other passengers have learned to ignore such activities if they are pursued with some discretion. Orgasm is some- times achieved in the petting which goes on in such public places.

(Kinsey et al. 1953: 259)

Petting itself becomes insignificant when the taboos against sexual intercourse before marriage are relaxed, as they have been in most Western societies since the 1960s. Implicit in such phenomena are intricate though only semi-conscious rules which limit what can and cannot be done. Informal methods of regulation can have important social effects – in limiting, for example, illegitimate con- ceptions. They have often been enforced in the past by cus- tomary patterns of public shaming, rituals of humiliation and public mocking – examples include the 'charivari' and 'rough music' in Britain, which have widespread echoes across the globe – which serve to reinforce the norms of the community.

Politics

These formal and informal methods of control exist within an ever-changing political framework. The balance of political forces at any particular time can determine the degree of legislative control or moral intervention in sex- ual life. The general social climate provides the context in which some issues take on a greater significance than oth- ers. The existence of skilled 'moral entrepreneurs' able to articulate and call up inchoate currents of opinion can be decisive in enforcing existing legislation or in conjuring up new. The success of the New Right in America during the 1970s and 1980s in establishing an agenda for sexual conservatism by campaigning against sexual liberals and/ or sexual deviants underlined the possibilities of political mobilization around sex. In particular, the anti-abortion position of many moral conservatives opened up a fundamental divide in American politics that became a central feature of the so-called 'culture wars' for the next 40 years.

But examples abound across the world of the exploitation of sexual issues to advance or consolidate a political agenda – whether President Mugabe mixing anti-colonial and anti-gay messages to shore up his crumbling support in Zimbabwe, or President Putin endorsing anti-gay legislation in Russia to strengthen his nationalist base, or fundamentalist regimes such as Iran or Saudi Arabia asserting their purity by stoning adulterers and executing homosexuals. At the same time, we can see the emergence of new claims for sexual and intimate citizenship from those previously disenfranchised by traditional sexual regimes, and of new discourses of human sexual rights on a global scale to combat continuing prejudices, discriminations and oppressions (Correa et al. 2008; Plummer 2015).

Cultures of resistance

The history of sexuality is not a simple history of control; it is also a history of opposition and resistance to moral codes. Forms of moral regulation give rise to transgressions, subversions and cultures of resistance, great and

small, local and transnational. Female networks of knowledge about sexuality, especially birth control and abortion, can be seen across history and cultures. As Angus
McLaren put it, 'In studying abortion beliefs it is possible
to glimpse aspects of a separate female sexual culture that
supports the independence and autonomy of women from
medical men, moralists and spouses' (McLaren 1984: 147).
There is a long history of such alternative knowledges.
A classic local example is provided by the widespread use
of the lead compound diachylon as an abortifacient in the
late nineteenth century and early twentieth century in the
Midlands of England. Widely used as an antiseptic, it was
accidentally discovered that this could be used to induce
abortions, and there is evidence of its subsequent spread
as a prophylactic among working-class women up to the
outbreak of the First World War (McLaren 1978: 390).

Other examples of cultural resistance come from the
emergence of the subcultures and networks established
by the sexually marginalized. There is a long history of
subcultures of male same-sex networks throughout the
history of the West, manifest for instance in Italian towns
of the late Middle Ages and in England from the late seventeenth century. These have been critical for the emergence of modern same-sex and gender non-conforming
identities, which have been largely formed in these wider
social networks. More recently, over the past 100 years or
so, there have been series of explicit oppositional political movements organized around sexuality and sexual
issues. The classic example is the rise of 'first wave' feminism in the second half of the nineteenth century, and
'second-wave' feminism from the 1960s. A rich and ever

growing historical excavation has demonstrated the long-standing existence of sex reform movements often closely linked to campaigns for homosexual rights: the modern gay and lesbian movements have antecedents going back to the nineteenth century in countries like Germany and Britain (Weeks 2016/1977; Cook 2003).

These local cultures of resistance are important in themselves. They have been given a new resonance, however, through the development since the 1970s of national and international social movements, of women, of lesbian, gay, bisexual, transgender and queer peoples, and of human rights campaigns which have politicized and internationalized cultures of opposition, and given them a new resonance in global discourse (for example, see Adam et al. 1999; Bamforth 2005; Paternotte and Tremblay 2015).

WHY SEXUALITY IS IMPORTANT

Moral concern

All societies have to make arrangements for the organization of erotic life. Not all, however, do it with the same obsessive concern as the West. Throughout the history of the West, since the time of the Ancient Greeks, what we call sexuality has been an object of moral concern, but the concept of sexual life has not been the same. For the Ancient Greeks, concern with the pleasures of the body – *aphrodisia* – was only one, and not necessarily the most important, of the preoccupations of life, to be set alongside dietary regulations and the organization of household relations. And the object of debate was quite different too.

Freud, with his usual perceptiveness, was able to sum up one aspect of this difference:

> The most striking distinction between the erotic life of antiquity and our own no doubt lies in the fact that the ancients laid the stress upon the instinct itself, whereas we emphasize its object.
>
> (Freud 1905: 149)

The West has been largely preoccupied *with whom* people have sex, the ancients with the question of excess or over-indulgence, activity and passivity. Plato would have banned pederasty from his city not because it was against nature, but because it was in excess of what nature demands. Sodomy was excessively licentious, and the moral question was not whether two men had had sex, but whether they were active or passive. Passive homosexual activities and the people who practised them were rejected, not because they were homosexual but because they involved a man acting like a woman or child. This is a distinction we can see across many cultures, where homosexual activity among men was tolerated as long as it did not 'feminize' the man (Veyne 1985: 27; Halperin 1990, 2002). Northern European and American societies, on the other hand, have since the nineteenth century at least been obsessively concerned with whether a person is normal or abnormal, increasingly defined in terms of whether they are heterosexual or homosexual. These societies seek the truth of subjectivity in the organization of sexual desires. The differences between the two patterns represent a major shift in the organizing significance given to sexuality.

Key moments

The development of the dominant Western model is the product of a long and complicated history. But there seem to be several key moments in its evolution. One came with innovations of the first century AD in the classical world, before the generalized advent of a Christianized West. It was represented by a new austerity and by a growing disapproval of *mollities*, that is, sex indulged in purely for pleasure. The Church accepted and refined the view that husbands should not behave incontinently with wives in marriage. The purpose of sex was reproduction, so sex outside marriage was obviously for pleasure and hence a sin. As Flandrin wrote, 'marriage was a kind of preventive medicine given by God to save man from immorality' (Flandrin 1985: 115). The sins of the flesh were a constant temptation from the divine path.

The second crucial moment came in the twelfth and thirteenth centuries, after a series of intense critical and religious struggles, with the triumph of the Christian tradition of sex and marriage. This did not necessarily affect everyone's behaviour in society. What it did do was to establish a new norm which was enforced by both the religious and the secular arm. Marriage was a matter of family arrangement for the good of families. So for two people thrown together often as strangers, a tight set of rules had to be elaborated. As a result, 'the couple were not alone in their marriage bed: the shadow of the confessor loomed over their frolics' (Flandrin 1985: 115). Theologians and canonists discussed the sex lives of married couples to the last detail, not simply as an intellectual game but to provide detailed answers to practical moral questions.

The third crucial and decisive moment occurred in the eighteenth and nineteenth centuries with the increasing definition of sexual normality in terms of relations with the opposite sex, and the consequent categorization of other forms as aberrant (Laqueur 1990). This last change is the one of which we are immediate heirs. It was represented by a shift from the religious organization of moral life to increasingly secular regulation embodied in the emergence of new medical, psychological and educational norms. There was a move from the ancient idea that men and women constituted but one sex, with women's bodies but an inverted form of the male, towards recognizably modern notions of two, oppositional or complementary genders. Alongside this, new typologies of degeneracy and perversion emerged and there was a decisive growth of new sexual categorizations and identities, less concerned with age distinctions than with new binaries between heterosexuality and homosexuality (Trumbach 1998). Homosexuality moved from being a category of sin to become a psychosocial disposition. Sexology, the new would-be science of desire, began to speculate about the laws of sex and 'sexuality' finally emerged as a separate continent of knowledge with its own distinct effects.

The homosexual category and new binaries

The emergence of the category of homosexuality and 'the homosexual' illustrates what was taking place. Same-sex activities are of course widespread in all cultures and there is a sustained history of homoeroticism both in the West and across all other cultures. But the idea that there is such a thing as *the* homosexual person is a relatively new one. All the evidence suggests that before the eighteenth century, homosexuality, interpreted in its broadest sense as involving erotic activities between people of the same gender, certainly existed, but 'homosexuals' in any meaningful modern sense, did not. Certain acts such as sodomy were severely condemned: in Britain they carried the death penalty, formally at least, until 1861, and subsequently by draconian prison sentences, and this was soon echoed in all Anglo-Saxon and colonial societies shaped by the British Empire, from India to the West Indies, from Africa to Hong Kong. But there seems to have been little idea of a distinct type of homosexual personage as part of a binary system of classification.

The 'sodomite' cannot be seen as equivalent to the 'homosexual'. Sodomy was not a specifically homosexual crime; the law applied indifferently to relations between men and women, men and beasts, as well as men and men. And while by the eighteenth century the persistent sodomite was clearly perceived as a special type of person, he was still defined by the nature of his act rather than the character of his personality.

From the early eighteenth century, however, historians have traced the evolution of new sexual types, third and even fourth sexes. From the mid-nineteenth century 'the homosexual' (the term 'homosexuality' was invented in the 1860s) was increasingly seen as belonging to a particular species of being, characterized by feelings, latency and a psychosexual condition. This view was elaborated by pioneering sexologists who produced ever more complex explanations and descriptions. Was homosexuality a product of corruption or degeneration, congenital or the result of childhood trauma? Was it a natural variation or a perverse deformation? Should it be tolerated or subjected to cure? Havelock Ellis distinguished the invert from the pervert, Freud the 'absolute invert', the 'amphigenic' and the 'contingent'. Rather later, Clifford Allen distinguished 12 types, ranging from the compulsive, the nervous, the neurotic and the psychotic to the psychopathic and the alcoholic (Weeks 1985: 90). Kinsey invented a seven-point rating for the spectrum of heterosexual/homosexual behaviour, which allowed his successors to distinguish a 'Kinsey one' from a 'five' or 'six' as if real life depended upon it (see Weeks 1985: 89–91).

This labelling and pigeonholing energy and zeal has led historians to argue that the emergence of distinct categories of sexual beings over the past century or so is the consequence of a sustained effort at social regulation and control. Its effect was to sharpen the binary divide between the normal and the abnormal, to construct homosexuality as the despised Other, and to underwrite heteronormativity as the unspoken dominant structure.

Writers on the history of lesbianism have suggested that the development of a sexualized lesbian identity at the end of the nineteenth century and early twentieth century was an imposition by sexologists designed precisely to split women from women, breaking the ties of emotionality and affection which previously bonded all women together against men (Faderman 1981). There is clearly an element of truth in this. Nevertheless, I think it much more credible to see the uneven and often prolonged emergence of distinct identities from this period as in part the product of struggle against prevailing norms, which had necessarily different effects for men and women. Sexologists did not so much invent the homosexual or the lesbian as attempt to put into their own frequently pathologizing language changes that were taking place before their eyes. Pioneering sexologists like Krafft-Ebing were confronted by people appearing in the courts or coming to them for help, largely as a result of a new politically motivated zeal to control more tightly aberrant manifestations of sexual desire. The definition of homosexuality as a distinct form of sexual desire was one attempt to come to terms with this new reality. Krafft-Ebing found himself in an unlikely alliance with articulate defenders of their own sexualities, to explain and even justify them. This in turn produced an inevitable response in the urge to self-definition, and the articulation of new sexual identities (Oosterhuis 2000).

Sexual activity was increasingly coming to define a particular type of person. In return, people were beginning to define themselves as different, and their difference was constituted around their sexuality. One Thomas Newton was arrested in London in 1726, entrapped by a police informant in a homosexual act. Confronted by the police he said: 'I did it because I thought I knew him, and I think there is no crime in making what use I please of my own body' (Bray 1982: 114). Here we can see, embryonically, the urge to self-definition that was to flourish in the proliferation of homosexual identities in the twentieth century. In turn, the growth of the category of the homosexual at the end of the nineteenth century presaged a profusion of new sexual types, subjectivities and identities in the twentieth century: the transvestite, the trans-sexual, the bisexual, the paedophile, the sado-masochist and so on. Increasingly in the twentieth century, people defined themselves by defining their sexuality. The question we have to ask is why sexual practices became so central to individuals' definition of self and of normality.

Sexuality as the truth of our being

Sexuality, Foucault (1979) argued, is shaped at the juncture of two major axes of concern: with our subjectivity – who and what we are; and with society – with the future growth, wellbeing, health and prosperity of the population as a whole (Foucault 1979). The two are intimately connected because at the heart of both is the body and its potentialities. 'As the human body becomes autonomous and self-conscious', Lowe wrote, that is, as it becomes the object of a fully secular attention, 'as emotion recoiled from the world and became more cooped up, sexuality in bourgeois society emerged as an explicit phenomenon' (Lowe 1982: 100).

And as society has become more and more concerned with what Foucault called 'biopower', with the lives of its members, for the sake of moral uniformity, economic wellbeing, national security or hygiene and health, so it became more and more preoccupied with the sex lives of its individuals, giving rise to intricate methods of administration and management, to a flowering of moral anxieties, medical, hygienic, legal and welfarist interventions, or scientific delving, all designed to understand the self by understanding sex.

Sexuality as a result has become an increasingly important social and political as well as moral issue. If we look at the major social crises in Britain from the beginning of the nineteenth century (and this can be echoed in all the major industrializing and urbanizing societies, other things being equal) we see that in one way or another a preoccupation with the sexual has been integral to them (see Weeks 2012 for details on the following discussion).

In the crisis of the French revolutionary wars in the early nineteenth century, one of the central preoccupations of ideologists was with the moral decline which it was believed had set off the train of events leading to the collapse of the French monarchy. In the 1830s and 1840s, with the first crisis of the new industrial society, there was an obsessive concern with the sexuality of women and the threat to children who worked in the factories and mines. By the mid-nineteenth century, attempts to re-order society focused on the question of moral hygiene and health. From the 1860s to the 1890s prostitution, the moral standards of society and moral reform were at the heart of public debate, many seeing in moral decay a sign of impending imperial decline. In the early decades of the twentieth century these concerns were re-ordered in a new concern with the quality of the British population. The vogue for eugenics, the planned breeding of the best in society, although never dominant, had a significant influence in shaping both welfare policies and the attempt to re-order national priorities in the face of international competition.

Inevitably, it fed into a burgeoning racism during the first half of the twentieth century. During the inter-war years and into the 1940s, the decline of the birth-rate engendered fevered debates about the merits of birth control, selective encouragement of family planning policies, and the country falling into the hands of the once subject races. By the 1950s, in the period of the Cold War, there was a new searching out of sexual degenerates, especially homosexuals, because they were apparently curiously susceptible to treachery. This was to become a major aspect of the McCarthyite witch hunt in the USA, which had echoes in Britain and elsewhere. By the 1980s in the wake of several decades of so-called permissiveness, minority forms of sexuality, especially homosexuality, were being blamed for the decline of the family, and for the return of epidemics (in the form of AIDS), and a new moral conservatism gave energy to a revival of right-wing political forces. Yet by the new millennium, while moral fundamentalism still flourished across the globe, it had become clear that rapid social and cultural change were relentlessly undermining traditional patterns, giving rise to a heightened sexual individualism and new claims for 'sexual citizenship'.

A series of concerns are crystallized in all these crises and critical moments: with the norms of family life, the relations between men and women, the nature of female sexuality, the question of sexual variation, the instability of gender, the relations between adults and children, and so on. These are critical issues in any society. The debates about them in much of the West and increasingly in the Global South over the last few decades have been heated precisely because debates about sexuality are debates about the nature of society: as sex goes, so goes society; as society goes, so goes sexuality.

INTERSECTIONS

Sexuality and power

Issues of sexuality became increasingly important in the whole working of power in modern and modernizing societies. I mentioned earlier that one of the effects of a historical approach to sexuality was to see power over sexuality as productive rather than negative or repressive. The metaphor of repression comes from hydraulics: it offers the image of a gushing energy that must be held in check. The social and historical approach to sexuality I am advocating would stress rather the impact of various social practices and discourses that construct sexual norms, meanings, subjectivities and identities in the very process of regulating sexual behaviours.

The rejection of a repression model – what Foucault (1979) called the 'repressive hypothesis' – does not of course mean that all regimes of sexual regulation are of equal force or effectiveness. Some are clearly more harsh, authoritarian and oppressive than others. One of the important results of historical investigations of sexuality has been a reassessment of the whole Victorian period, which was classically seen as a period of unique moral hypocrisy and sexual denial. It is now increasingly apparent that this is highly misleading. Far from witnessing an avoidance of sex, the nineteenth century was not far from being obsessed with sexual issues. Rather than being the subject that was hidden away, it was a topic that was increasingly discussed in relation to diverse aspects of social life. This does not mean, however, that the Victorian period can now be seen as peculiarly liberal. In England, as we have seen, the death penalty for sodomy was still on the statute book until 1861. Restrictions on female sexual autonomy were severe and the distinction between respectable women and the unregenerates (the virgin and the whore, the Madonna and the Magdalene) reached their apogee during this period. Although the present may not have produced a perfect resolution of all conflict, for many of us it is infinitely preferable to what existed little more than a hundred years ago.

The usefulness of abandoning the repressive model, in its crude form, however, is that it does direct us towards an attempt to understand the actual mechanisms of power at work. Power no longer appears a single entity which is held or controlled by a particular group, gender, state or ruling class. It is, 'more like a process than an object' (Schur 1980: 7), a malleable and mobile force which takes many different forms and is exercised through a variety of different social practices and relationships. If this approach to power is adopted, then we need to abandon, as I have already indicated, any theoretical approach which sees sexuality moulded by a dominant, determining will – whether it be of 'society', as functionalist sociology tended to suggest, or 'capitalism', or 'neo-liberalism' as Marxists or anti-globalization theorists might argue, or 'patriarchy' or 'men', as some feminists would propose, or 'heteronormativity' or sexual binarisms, which queer theorists tend to finger. Power does not operate through single mechanisms of control. It operates through complex and overlapping – and often contradictory – mechanisms, which produce domination *and* oppositions, subordination *and* resistances, regulation *and* agency.

Conflicting dynamics

The implication of the understanding that power is multi-dimensional is that the subjectivities at the heart of sexuality are complex and potentially divided, as individuals negotiate the various discourses and forces that address them. Individual identities are shaped by, and at the intersection of, a host of often conflicting dynamics: of class, gender, ethnicity and race, and a host of other influences including nationality, faith, geography, age and generation, ability and disability. The multiple sexual discourses that call on our needs and possibilities have been shaped and are re-shaped by these dynamics, and the multiple vectors of domination and subordination, power and resistance they reveal.

The recognition of the intersectionality of social forces has become a central focus of contemporary analysis of sexuality, even though the specifics of the erotic easily become forgotten in the challenge of exploring the intersections of gender, class and race (Taylor et al. 2010). The interlocking, mutually reinforcing impact of various forms of power and domination around sexuality was first identified by Black feminists in the 1980s as it became clear that White feminist analyses could not speak to the experience of all women. Similarly, it also became clear that early gay liberationist theory was not able to address the issue of the many forms of diversity. As Nash (2008: 13–14) notes, the force of these critiques was to highlight the reality that 'identity is complex, that subjectivity is messy, and that personhood is inextricably bound up with vectors of power'. But these insights can only be the starting point of analysis. The real challenge is to grasp the diverse ways in which the 'messiness' operates in everyday practice. To help clarify this, I want now to look more closely at the three key aspects of power relationships that have been most salient in contemporary debates: class, gender and race.

Class

Class differences in sexual regulation are not unique to the modern world. In the slave-owning society of pre-Christian Rome, moral standards varied with social status. 'To be *impudicus* (that is passive) is disgraceful for a free man', wrote the elder Seneca, 'but it is the slave's absolute obligation towards his master, and the freed man owes a moral duty of compliance' (Veyne 1985: 31). What was true in the ancient world has become more sharply apparent in the modern. It has in fact, as I have already indicated, been suggested (notably by Foucault) that the very idea of 'sexuality' is an essentially bourgeois one, which developed as an aspect of the self-definition of a class, both against the decadent aristocracy and the rampant 'immorality' of the lower orders in the course of the eighteenth and nineteenth centuries. It was a colonizing system of beliefs which sought to remould the polity in its own image. The respectable standards of family and domestic life, with the increased demarcations between male and female roles, a growing ideological distinction between private and public life, and a marked concern with moral and hygienic policing of non-marital, non-heterosexual sexuality was increasingly the norm by which all behaviour was judged. 'Respectability', argues Skeggs (1997: 3) 'has always been a marker and burden of class'.

This does not, of course, mean that all or even most behaviour conformed to the norm. There is plentiful evidence that the behaviour of the working classes remained extremely resilient to middle-class manners, producing its own complex rules and rituals (Weeks 2012). Nevertheless, the sexual patterns that exist in the twenty-first century are a product of a social struggle in which class continues to be a vital element. This has resulted, not surprisingly, in distinctively classed patterns of sexual life. Kinsey's American sample of 18,000 in the 1940s suggested that whether it be on masturbation, homosexuality, the incidence of oral sex, petting, concourse with prostitutes, pre-marital or extra-marital sex, or 'total sexual outlet', there were significantly different class patterns among men. For women, on the other hand, Kinsey suggested, class differences played a relatively minor part: their age and gender ideologies were much more critical factors in shaping behaviour.

It is, however, difficult today to be as blasé in relation to women and class as Kinsey would seem to be. As the guardians and guarantors of respectable standards over the centuries, women's sexual norms and behaviours have always been seen through, and defined by, the prism of class. Despite the gradual erosion of class boundaries, the work of Skeggs and others shows the continuing salience of class assumptions about female sexuality, especially the sexuality of working class women (see Weeks 2007 for a historical perspective on this in the twentieth century). It is hardly surprising, then, that the literature abounds with images of relations between men and women (and indeed between men and men, and women and women) where class, power and sexual fantasy and desire are intricately interwoven.

Gender

Gender is a crucial divide. A number of feminist writers have seen the elaboration of sexual difference as crucial to the oppression of women, with sexuality not merely reflecting but being fundamental to the construction and maintenance of the power relations between women and men (Weeks 2016, Chapter 4). There clearly is a close relationship between the organization of gender and sexuality, as Rubin's sex-gender system suggested. Rubin herself was subsequently to revise her position, arguing that it was both analytically and politically essential to distinguish the gender system from the historically specific sexual systems that shaped subjectivities and power relations (Rubin 1984). This proved to be an enormously stimulating insight, encouraging a host of historical studies of sexual systems. It suggested, contra to a strong radical feminist analysis, that we cannot simply derive sexual subjectivities from gender. That would give it an *a priori* significance that would deny the intricacies of the social organization of sexuality. At the same time it remains vital to recognize that sexuality is constituted in a highly gendered world. The patterns of female sexuality are inescapably a product of the historically rooted power of men to define and categorize what is necessary and desirable. And it is, of course, still pursued, recast and reformulated by men. We traditionally look at the world through our concepts of male sexuality so that, even when we are not looking at male sexuality as such, we are looking at the world within its framework of reference.

This framework is of course the result of more than the contingencies of biology, or the inevitability of sexual difference. It is constituted by a historically specific organization of sexuality and gender, what Connell (2005, 2009, 2013) calls the 'gender order'. This is structured by and through shifting patterns of masculinity, in its hegemonic and subordinate forms, and femininity, also in complexly varying patterns. 'Masculinity' and 'femininity' are relational terms, given meaning only through the existence of the other. But this means that inevitably normative definitions of sexuality are structured by this relationship, and by the privileging in particular of heterosexuality.

This privileging has been variously theorized as 'compulsory heterosexuality', 'institutionalized heterosexuality', the 'heterosexual matrix', the 'heterosexual panorama', the 'heterosexual imperative', the 'heterosexual assumption', culminating in the conceptualization of 'heteronormativity' (Warner 1999). The labels reflect different theoretical positions and political positions, but they all point to a key understanding. Sexuality is, in complex but inextricable ways, locked into the structuring of gender, and both are locked together by the heterosexual norm. The binary divides between masculinity and femininity, and between heterosexuality and homosexuality (with the first term in each couplet as the dominant one), still positions sexual subjects and organizes sexual desire and gender norms in contemporary societies, in ways which subordinate women, marginalize the sexual transgressor and occlude gender non-conformity.

This structuring, of course, has never been either monolithic or unchallenged. The law, medicine, the psychological institutions, social norms, even popular opinion are often highly contradictory and change over time. Before the eighteenth century, female sexuality was regarded in Europe as voracious and all-consuming. In the nineteenth century, there was a sustained effort to inform the population that female sexuality among respectable women just did not exist. In the later twentieth century, there was a general incitement to female sexuality as an aid to all forms of consumerism. The sexuality of women has at various times been seen as dangerous, as a source of disease, as the means of transmitting national values in the age of eugenics, as the guardian of moral purity in debates over sex education, and as the main focus of attention in the debates over permissiveness and sexual liberation in the 1960s and after. Female sexuality has been limited by economic and social dependence, by the power of men to define sexuality, by the limitations of marriage, by the burdens of reproduction and by the endemic fact of male violence against women. At the same time, these contradictory definitions have as often provided the opportunity for women to define their own needs and desires. Since the late nineteenth century, the acceptable spaces for self-definition have expanded rapidly to include not only pleasure in marriage but also relatively respectable forms of unmarried and non-procreative heterosexual and same-sex activities.

The patterns of male privilege have not been broken. At the same time, the real changes of the past century and the long-term impact of feminism testify that these patterns are neither inevitable nor immutable. There is plentiful evidence of 'crisis tendencies' in hegemonic masculinity, and of major, if uneven, transformations in the position of women. Each is reflected in the shifting conceptualizations of male and female sexual subjectivities.

Race

Categorizations by class or gender intersect with those of ethnicity and race. The evolutionary model of sexuality put forward by the theorists of the late nineteenth century inevitably presented the non-white person – 'the savage' – as lower down the evolutionary scale than the white, as closer to nature. An abiding myth that has coursed through both theoretical and popular discourse throughout the past two centuries has been that of the insatiability of the sexual needs of non-European peoples and the threat they consequently pose for the purity of the white race. A fear of black male priapism, and the converse exploitation of black women to service their white masters, was integral to slave society in the American South in the nineteenth century and continued to shape black–white relationships well into the twentieth century. In apartheid South Africa, the prohibitions of the Mixed Marriages Act and section 16 of the Immorality Act designed to prevent miscegenation were among the first pieces of apartheid legislation to be introduced after the National Party came to power on a policy of racial segregation in 1948. As the regime attempted to deal with the crisis of apartheid in the 1980s by re-shaping its forms, one of the first pillars of apartheid it attempted to remove were precisely these Acts. As a result, the regime came under heavy criticism from extreme right-wing groups which argued that the whole edifice of apartheid would be undermined if the laws were repealed. That of course proved to be the case.

Behind this is a long history of the encounters between the imperial heartlands and the colonized peoples in which the latter's erotic patterns were constituted as 'other', and inferior. The process has been encoded in a series of practices, from immigration laws to birth control propaganda, from medical attitudes to the pathologizing in psychology and sociology of different patterns of family life. As Stoler argues, via the colonial encounters, an 'implicit racial grammar underwrote the sexual regimes of bourgeois culture' (Stoler 1995: 9). Western notions of racial purity and sexual virtue – that is, norms of white sexuality – were in large part constituted by rejection of the colonized Other (Nagel 2003). As Western societies themselves have become less homogeneous and more racially and ethnically mixed in recent years as a result of large-scale migration, the apparent liberalism of a number of European countries have been severely challenged as the anonymity of the other has become the face of the neighbour – a potential sexual as well as cultural threat. Yet high degrees of sexual intermingling across the racial and ethnic divides in countries like Britain (Weeks 2007) suggest that what Gilroy (2004) has been described as new forms of 'conviviality' are also developing that are transforming the meanings of difference, and the power of racism.

The categories of race, gender and class may be analytically separable but they are lived inextricably together, alongside other dimensions of difference. Ethnic minorities who are most subject to racist practices tend to be working class or poor, socially excluded in a variety of ways, while the definition of membership within the ethnic group can often depend on performing gender and sexual attributes successfully. Power operates subtly through a complex series of interlocking practices. As a result, political challenges to oppressive forms are complex and sometimes contradictory. They are enmeshed in the whole network of social contradictions and antagonisms that make up the modern world. There is, however, an important point that we can draw from this discussion. Instead of seeing sexuality as a unified whole, we have to recognize that there are various forms of sexuality: there are in fact many sexualities. There are classed sexualities and gender-specific sexualities, there are racialized sexualities and there are sexualities of struggle and choice. The 'invention of sexuality' was not a single event, now lost in a distant past. It is a continuing process in which we are simultaneously acted upon and actors, objects of change, and its subjects. We are simultaneously made by, and make, sexual history.

3

THE MEANINGS OF
SEXUAL DIFFERENCE

A TRUE SEX?

Let me start this chapter with a story, about Herculine Barbin, a nineteenth-century French 'hermaphrodite', as told by her/himself, and offered to the world by the French philosopher Michel Foucault (1980b). Herculine was born in the French provinces in the mid-nineteenth century, with an indeterminate gender – that is she had organs of both sexes. She was brought up in a largely all-female world by nuns, and known as Alexina, in a context where her ambiguous status did not seem to matter. She lived, as Foucault (1980b: xiii) comments, 'the happy limbo of a non-identity'. But this was a period in European history, the 1860s and 1870s, when identity, as man or woman, as heterosexual or homosexual, was beginning to matter in a new and forceful way. In particular, it began to matter to the authorities, and especially to the legal and medical professions, that here was someone who did not easily fit into the categories of gender and sexuality that were being newly refined and redefined. Authority wanted something more neat and tidy. Alexina was officially re-categorized as a man, Abel. After a few years of trying to live unhappily as a male, Abel committed suicide.

This sad story is in many ways a minor tale of provincial mores; the tragedy was highly personal, and made no apparent impact on the larger dramas of French or European history. And yet, for my story about gender and sexuality, it has poignant echoes. Above all, as Foucault noted, it throws light on a culture where it was becoming imperative to place people by strictly defining their gendered identities. 'Do we *truly* need a *true* sex?', Foucault asks. This is a question that, as we have seen, until recently Western societies vigorously answered in the affirmative, and the nineteenth century was a crucial moment in the elaboration of gendered categorizations. And, despite everything that has changed since then, especially the rise of transgender and intersex consciousness and activism, we are still heirs of the beliefs and behaviours that drove Herculine/Alexina/Abel to his/her death.

THE BIOLOGICAL IMPERATIVE

In our culture, whom we have sex with still matters. Gender, the term conventionally deployed to describe the social condition of being male or female, and sexuality, the cultural way of living out our bodily pleasures and desires, have over the generations become inextricably linked, with the result that crossing the boundary between proper masculine or feminine behaviour (that is, what is culturally defined as appropriate) sometimes seems the ultimate transgression – which is why transgender, which ultimately suggests the fluidity and contingency of gender, can be so challenging to orthodox beliefs.

We still find it difficult to think about sexuality without taking into account gender; or, to put it more generally, the elaborate facade of sexuality has in large part been built upon the assumption of fundamental differences between men and women, and of male dominance over women. The genital and reproductive distinctions between biological men and biological women have been read not only as necessary but also as sufficient explanation for different sexual needs and desires. They appear as the most basic distinctions between peoples, deeply rooted in our 'animal natures'.

Science has gone to extraordinary efforts to explain and justify this. It is one of the peculiarities of us humans that we seek answers to some of our most fundamental questions about ourselves by looking at the lives of animals. Researchers have found evidence and support for their wildest hypotheses about sexual difference in everything from insects and the humble worm to the seaside sparrow and rhesus monkeys. In the process, much – no doubt – has been learnt, especially about animal behaviour. But much remains inexplicable by such methods.

Unfortunately for the simplicities of research, human beings are complex, arbitrary and changeable creatures. We manipulate language constantly to reshape our perceptions of the world – and of sex. We perform in ways which defy the apparent logic of our external appearances. We blur the edges between masculinity and femininity. We can even change genders by cross-dressing, through surgery, or by simply living a new gender. We create other differences that transcend the differences of gender (of age, race, sexual need); and we construct boundaries that have little logic 'in Nature'. We even change our behaviour in response to moral, political or accidental factors. Yet all the time we like to indulge the fantasy that our genders and sexualities are the most basic, the most natural, things about us, and that the relations between men and women are laid down for all eternity, like fingerprints in concrete, by the dictates of our inborn 'nature'.

In cultures preoccupied with sexual difference, as most of the sexual cultures around the world still are, such beliefs have crucial social effects: to repeat, the ways we think about gender and sexuality shapes the way we live them. So discussions about the origins and form of the differences between men and women are much more than obscure debates. They are central to the direction of our society.

The American sexologist John Money, who did so much to distinguish 'sex', assumed to be biologically given, from 'gender', socially defined (see Downing, Morland and Sullivan 2014), has noted 'the cultural practice, taken for granted in our culture, of maximizing the differences, behavioural included, between the sexes, rather than maximizing the similarities' (Money 1980: 133). The 'science of sex' cannot be blamed for this, given the deeply embedded cultural assumptions the early sexologists encountered: in many ways they merely theorized what they believed they saw. Moreover, many of them, alive to empirical reality, were eventually anxious to assert the overlap as much as the differences. For Havelock Ellis by the 1930s, sex was 'mutable', its frontiers uncertain, with 'many stages between a complete male and a complete female' (Ellis 1946: 194). Yet at the same time the search for the essentially feminine and the essentially masculine continued, with the inevitable result that sexual differences were stressed at the expense of similarities. Sexology became a weapon in the endemic conflict over the appropriate social relationships and positionings of men and women that was accentuated in the last decades of the nineteenth century and has continued, with varying rhythms and intensity, ever since.

The very definition of the 'sexual instinct' was essentially one derived from male practices and fantasies. Just consider some of the metaphors deployed in early writings on sex: overpowering forces, engulfing drives, gushing streams, uncontrollable spasms. Such imagery has dominated the Western discourse on sex. Early sexologists drew on this imagery even as they attempted to put it on a more scientific basis. So sex was defined as a 'physiological law', 'a force generated by powerful ferments', a drive 'which cannot be set aside for any sort of social convention', and most graphically of all, 'a volcano that burns down and lays waste all around it; . . . an abyss that devours all honour, substance and health' (see Weeks 1985: 80–85; Lancaster 2003). The Darwinian revolution in biology, which demonstrated that 'man' (that is, men and women) was part of the animal world, encouraged the search for the animal in man, and found it in his/her sex.

Female sexuality was inevitably a problem – an enigma, a 'dark continent' in Freud's famous words – for such views. In the West, from the ancient world to the eighteenth century, medical theory taught that there was but one sex, with the female body simply an inverted version of the male (Laqueur 1990). Simultaneously, popular cultural tradition held that female sexuality was voracious, all-devouring and consuming. This has had a significant recent revival in comments (by men) that modern feminism has exhausted and enfeebled men by encouraging female sexual demands. Such an argument probably tells us more about male fears and fantasies than it does about women, but it has to be noted nonetheless as a fanciful and persistent myth. But since the eighteenth century the more conventional view has been to treat female sexuality as fundamentally different but basically complementary to male sexuality: reactive, responsive, brought to life only through some sort of 'reproductive instinct', or kissed into life by the skill of the wooer, the male, as Havelock Ellis put it. Lesbianism was particularly problematic for theorists of sex precisely because it was an autonomously female sexuality in which men played no part.

The idea that there is a *fundamental* difference between male and female sexual natures has been a powerful one. Even the abundant evidence, building on the observational work of Kinsey and colleagues (1948 and 1953) and Masters and Johnson (1966), that there is a fundamentally similar physiological response among men and women, has not undermined the belief in basic psycho-sexual differences elsewhere. The idea that there are differences between peoples is not in itself dangerous. What is peculiar about the gender/sexuality nexus is that certain differences have been seen as so fundamental that they become divisions and even antagonisms. At best there is the argument that though men and women may be different they can still be equal. At worst, assumptions about the forceful nature of the male sexual drive have been used to legitimize male violence and domination over women, and to affirm the female destiny of reproduction.

We might think that such beliefs have been sufficiently undermined in recent decades, especially through the critiques of modern feminism, to have little credence. But we would be mistaken. Take the views of some writers influential on what became known as the 'New Right' in Britain and North America during the 1980s.

Roger Scruton, an English Conservative philosopher, counterposed what he vividly described as the 'unbridled ambition of the phallus', eschewing all obligation, to the nature-given role of women to 'quieten what is most vagrant'. For George Gilder, a fervent defender of traditional values, it was only the claims of marriage and the family that could channel the man's 'otherwise disruptive male aggression' into social obligation to fend for his wife and offspring (Gilder 1973; Scruton 1983, 1986). Such ideas have coloured, and served to justify, socially conservative views of gender, sexuality and the family well into the twenty-first century.

For both Scruton and Gilder, there is a belief in a refractory (male) human nature, threatening disruption unless constrained by moral will and social orthodoxy. Views such as these found a justification in the 'new synthesis' of sociobiology, through which biological determinism enjoyed a revival in the 1970s and 1980s, and in its sibling, evolutionary psychology, which to some extent had superseded it in influence by the millennium.

EVOLUTIONARY DIVERSIONS

Both sociobiology and evolutionary psychology have made an important impact, and not only on the conservative thinkers. The new prestige enjoyed by the genetic revolution has been deployed by a number of would-be liberal sources to explain the intractability to change of social institutions, and the inevitability of certain givens (such as male/female differences), and some aspects of it have even been used to argue for greater freedom for homosexuals on the grounds of their biological functionality (compare Wilson and Rahman 2005). We need, therefore, to be alive to the appeal of the new evolutionism – as well as to the dangers I believe to be inherent in it.

Sociobiology was defined by its founding father, E. O. Wilson, as 'the systematic study of the biological basis of all social behavior' (Wilson 1975: 4). It aimed to bridge the gap which had opened up between traditional biological theories on the one hand and social explanations on the other by attempting to demonstrate that there was a key mechanism linking both. This mechanism, in the words of one of the best-known popularizers of neo-evolutionism, was 'the fundamental law of gene selfishness' (Dawkins 1978: 7). The gene is the basic unit of heredity, defined as a portion of the DNA molecule which affects the development of any trait at the most elementary biochemical level. It carries the code which influences future development. So much may be generally agreed. Where many latter-day evolutionists go further is by arguing – going enthusiastically beyond Wilson's initially more tentative positions – that genes exist for every social phenomenon, so that the random survival of the genes could explain all social practices from economic efficiency and educational attainment to ethnic and racial differences, gender divisions and sexual preference.

In this mode of thought the fundamental unit is no longer 'the individual', as in classical liberal theory; nor is it 'society', as in the great alternative tradition. The individual is now viewed as little more than a vehicle for the transmission of genes, 'a selfish machine, programmed to do whatever is best for his genes as a whole' (Dawkins 1978: 71). If this is true, then the great conflict between individual and society can be simply dissolved: a continuum exists between the timeless energy of the gene, and the most complex social manifestations, with society and nature working in harmony. So what about apparently social institutions like marriage, parenting, social bonding? They were 'adaptive', in a key term of evolutionary theory, products not of history or social development but of 'evolutionary necessity'. And what about ideas, ideals, values and beliefs? They are no more than enabling mechanisms for survival.

So, certain aspects of human sexual behaviour, such as male philandering and female coyness, the argument goes, are biological adaptations selected in the infancy of the human race, 100,000 to 600,000 years ago, and have become universal features of human nature, ensuring the propagation of our ancestors' genes. Similarly, rape can be seen as an adaptive strategy, by which otherwise sexually unsuccessful men propagate their genes by mating with fertile women who might otherwise reject them; or parental love can be reduced to a means of successfully ensuring gene survival (Wilson 1978: 3; Thornhill and Palmer 2000).

Given this certainty, the existence of but two sexes is paradoxically a problem for sociobiology. Sex, E. O. Wilson (1975) argues, is an antisocial force in evolution, for it causes difficulty between people. The male/female relationship is one of mutual mistrust and exploitation. Altruism, necessary for gene survival, is more likely when everyone is the same.

So why is human reproduction not carried out through parthenogenesis, as it is with some primitive creatures? And why are there two – not three, four or five – sexes? 'To be perfectly honest', Cherfas and Gribbin (1984: 4) cheerfully admitted, 'nobody knows'. Which is why, they decide, sex is such an enigma. The most likely reason for sexed reproduction, they ultimately decided, is that it promotes diversity, the ability to shuffle the genetic pack to hedge bets against an unpredictably changing environment. Two sexes are just enough to ensure the maximum potential genetic recombination. Two sexes also ensure health and hardiness, by mixing the chemical constituents sufficiently to produce immunity against disease. So men's job 'is to provide the means by which females can fight off disease': far from being 'redundant', men are still essential for the future of the human race (Cherfas and Gribbin 1984: 178).

Whatever the intricate (and sometimes metaphysical) speculations, one outstanding conclusion flowed from all this: 'with respect to sexuality, there is a female human nature and a male human nature, and these natures are extraordinarily different . . .' (Symons 1979: 11). These differences begin and end with the evolutionary characteristics of the ova and testes. Because males have an almost infinite number of sperm (millions with each ejaculation), while women have a very restricted supply of eggs (around 400 per lifetime), it is deduced that men have an evolutionary propulsion towards spreading their seed to ensure diversity and reproductive success, and hence towards promiscuity, while women have an equal interest in reserving energy, an instinct for conservation, and hence a leaning towards monogamy. From this can be deduced the explanations for all the other supposedly fundamental differences: greater competition between men than between women, a greater male tendency towards polygamy and jealousy whereas women are 'more malleable' and amenable, and a greater sexual will and arousal potential in men than in women.

There is clearly a great intellectual attraction in such evolutionary explanations: they provide clarity where social scientists may see complexity, certainty where others recognize only contingency. There is also a certain political logic in the vogue for evolutionary theories: they provide an explanation for certain apparently unsolvable social problems in a conservative cultural climate, for example, why men are so reluctant to change, why gay men are apparently more promiscuous than lesbians. Such theories also – and this is a prize attribute – seem to speak to widespread, commonsense beliefs about the naturalness of sexual divisions. They go with, rather than against, the grain of popular prejudice. But if they can claim to explain some things (love at first sight may simply be the powerful response of the body to the scent of a very different set of histocompatibility antigens; homosexuality may be necessary to encourage altruistic concern for the offspring of siblings), they cannot generally or convincingly explain others (why there are variations between different cultures, for example, or why history frequently undergoes rapid social change, with new attitudes towards gender and sexuality emerging).

Evolutionism such as this is also ultimately deeply conservative in its implications, for if the explanation of what we do, socially and sexually, lies in the haphazard collision of genes, then there is little we can do to change things: bend the twig a little here, unbend it there, but not too much either way in case the whole branch breaks off. If, as H. J. Eysenck and Glenn Wilson reaffirmed, there is 'a strong, underlying biological source for the widely differing sexual attitudes we observe when we look at men and women' (Eysenck and Wilson 1979: 9), then feminist demands – or even liberal reforms – are utopian.

Some or all of this may of course be true. The problem is that while evidence from biology, natural history, or the postulated early history of mankind may be suggestive, it cannot be conclusive. It may be impossible finally to disprove a sociobiological or evolutionary psychology hypothesis – who knows what 'science' will turn up? – but it is equally difficult to prove it. In the real world of sexuality in which we live, things are a little more complex than the high priests of the 'sexual tradition', including some contemporary evolutionists, like to think (but see Jones 2002).

BIOLOGICAL MODES OF ARGUMENT

The most ardent advocates of biological determinism generally display three characteristic modes of argument:

argument by analogy; a reliance, amounting almost to an intellectual tyranny, on 'average statements'; and finally what I shall call, for want of a better phrase, the 'black hole' hypothesis. They are all fraught with difficulties.

1. Argument by analogy

This assumes that by observing animals in the wild – notably in recent arguments, penguins – we can crack the code of our civilization. A new emphasis on observing animals in their natural habitat during the inter-war years was one of the roots of sociobiology. E. O. Wilson devoted most of his first attempts at a synthesis to insects and birds. The trouble here is that despite all efforts at neutral observation, human prejudices insensibly creep in. As Rose et al. put it:

> Again and again, in order to support their claims to the inevitability of a given feature of the human order, biological determinists seek to imply the universality of their claims. If male dominance exists in humans, it is because it exists also in baboons, in lions, in ducks, or whatever. The ethological literature is replete with accounts of 'harem-keeping' by baboons, the male lion's domination of 'his' pride, 'gang-rape' in mallard ducks, 'prostitution' in humming birds.
>
> (Rose et al. 1984: 158)

It should hardly need saying that what is happening here is the attribution of highly coloured social explanations to animal behaviour. Why should groupings of female animals be seen as harems? They could equally well be seen, for all the counter-evidence available, as prototypes of feminist consciousness-raising groups. To say that perhaps evokes a smile. But so should the circular argument by which explanations drawn from human experience are attributed to animals and then used to justify social divisions in the present.

Evolutionary psychology partly recognizes that by moving away from explanations rooted in animal behaviour – in favour of evidence provided by our genetic inheritance, and by theorized originary Adams and Eves on the prehistoric savannah. But this narrative is itself disrupted by dogmatic assumption that explanations lie in 'reproductive strategies' to ensure gene survival. Such theorizations deny human agency and creativity in favour of a hypothetical evolutionary meta-history.

2. The tyranny of averages

Explanations based on averages provide another seductive but dangerous approach. On *average*, men may be more sexually active than women. Male homosexuals *may* be more promiscuous than female homosexuals. This *may* have something to do with the genes. It may equally have something to do with culture: greater opportunities for male sexual expression, and for choice of partners, for example, as a result of prohibitive historical constraints on women's freedom of action. More fundamentally, to say that on average men have more sexual activity than women is tantamount to saying that some women are more sexually active than some men. Average statements are both true and not particularly useful.

Yet they carry an enormous weight, in part at least because we prefer clear-cut divisions to ambiguity. Nature herself, however, can be very ambivalent, as the very idea of 'averages' suggests. Why aren't we?

3. The 'black hole' hypothesis

The 'black hole' hypothesis – the assumption that if there are mysterious effects, there must be something unknown but determinate out there which can explain them – is the final resort for those who can find no other explanation for sexual differences. If all else fails to explain human phenomena, then a biological cause, even if as yet it is undetected, must exist. If more men than women are in top jobs, then biology surely explains it. If society is resistant to the politics of feminism, then it must be because it goes against human nature. If the causes of homosexuality can be explained neither by sociology nor psychoanalysis, then biology (hormones, instincts, a 'gay gene' or the 'gay brain') must explain it. Biology provides the default explanation.

There is a classic example of this at the conclusion of the final report of the Kinsey Institute on homosexuality, *Sexual Preferences* (Bell et al. 1981: 191–92). The authors carefully explore the lack of evidence for a single cause of homosexuality, and conclude that there is no evidence for one in sociology or psychology. But instead of then testing the hypothesis (which Kinsey himself had endorsed) that homosexuality was not, therefore, a unitary condition, with single roots or causation (and in any case was no more worthy of aetiological explanation than its supposed opposite, heterosexuality), the authors conclude that there must be a biological explanation. This, in the context of the book, is empty speculation. The 'solution' owes more to the continuing prestige of biological sciences than evidence. It positively invited a further generation of search for the gay gene or gay brain (LeVay 1991; Hamer et al. 1993; Wilson and Rahman 2005). The so-called discovery of both seemed to justify the search – only for the evidence to crumble when subject to detailed interrogation. But as ever, biology is called on to fill a gap which social explanations have been unwilling, or unable, to fill.

I have no desire to minimize the importance of biology. Biological capacities clearly provide the potentiality out of which so much that is human is shaped. The body, in its full corporality, provides the locus, and sets the limit for social activities. On the body are inscribed our differences as men and women. Copulation, reproduction, nurturance and death are clearly biological in origin and provide the parameters of human existence. Less cosmic biological factors equally have social effects. Genetic differences (among men and among women, as well as between them) can affect physical appearances, size, strength, longevity, the colour of hair and eyes. Differential production of hormones can affect sexual maturation, distribution of body hair, fat deposition and muscular development. These are not unimportant as they are elaborated in complex cultural codes which lay down the appropriate or inappropriate physical appearance and behaviour of each gender. But it is, ultimately, the social meaning that we give to these differences that is of real importance. If the biological differences between the sexes are actually minute when compared with the similarities, and in fact, only one gene out of 100,000 needed to make up each person distinguishes men from women, then the critical markers that we conventionally use to demarcate difference need to be re-evaluated.

Anatomical differences are apparently the most basic of all. It is on the presence or absence of the male or female organs that gender is immediately assigned at birth. Yet, the possession of a penis or vagina cannot be a universally applicable standard, even in animals. In birds, the male does not have a penis; other animals have only 'intromittent organs', such as claspers in sharks and dogfish (Archer and Lloyd 1982: 47–8). Even among us humans the meanings of these very real organs are not transparent. The vagina can be conceived of as passive, or as all-devouring. The clitoris has been conceptualized as no more than a 'vestigial phallus', and as the site of women's multi-orgasmic potential. The penis has an even more supercharged symbolic value in our culture. Its 'thrusting', 'forceful', 'penetrative' nature has been seen as the very model of active male sexuality. But there is a marked discrepancy between this symbolism and the way the penis is often experienced:

> Male genitals are fragile, squashy, delicate things . . . penises are only little things (even big ones) without much staying power, pretty if you can learn to see them like that, but not magical or mysterious or powerful in themselves, that is, not objectively full of real power.
>
> (Dyer 1985: 30–31)

The significance we give to the male and female organs is important both socially and psychologically. If we follow the insights of psycho-analysis, then the existence or absence of the male penis (that is, the fear or fantasy of castration) is critical for the negotiation of the Oedipal crisis, and for the acquisition or non-acquisition of psychological masculinity and femininity, the very organization of sexual difference. But the critical meanings we assign to them are, according to Freud, demanded by culture and do not arise straightforwardly from the biology alone. The same potential ambiguity exists over two other, less obvious markers: the chromosomal make-up of men and women, and hormonal patterns.

The existence, firstly, of chromosomal differences is well known. The distinction is the one made in international sporting competitions for defining the sexes, where competitors, in women's athletic events particularly, have to undergo a sex chromosome test where there appears to be ambiguity regarding their gender. Human beings have in the nucleus of every cell in their body 46 chromosomes: twenty-two pairs, and two sex chromosomes. In females these sex chromosomes are identical (XX); but in males one is an incomplete structure, carrying little genetic material (the Y chromosome: men generally have an XY pairing). The difficulty is that these are not absolute markers. Sometimes chromosomes do not separate during cell division in the usual way, giving rise to XXY, X, XXX, or XYY patterns: are they male or female?

Sometimes there are individuals whose chromosomes say one thing, and their appearance another: males in that they have XY chromosomes, and possess testes which secrete the male hormone; but ambiguous in that they have not, through congenital androgen insensitivity, become externally masculinized. Many individuals are intersexed and in the contemporary world affirm their beings as part of the hyphenated coalition of sexual rights bearers – LGBTQ – and I.

Similarly, and second, the importance assigned to hormones, the chemical messengers secreted by the glands, has been exaggerated. The main hormone produced by the testes is testosterone; this, together with hormones of the same general type, are called *androgens*, the 'male hormones'. The main hormones produced by the ovaries are oestrogen and progesterone (the 'female hormones'). These hormones are undoubtedly important for development: testosterone produces important changes at adolescence, including a deepening voice and the appearance of body hair. The rise of oestrogen levels in girls at puberty encourages breast development, fat redistribution and the beginning of the menstrual cycle. But even so, we are not talking of uniquely male and female possessions. Ovaries and testes each produce all three hormones, and the adrenal glands secrete androgens in both sexes. What differs is the ratio.

Again there is no absolute divide. As Kinsey himself put it some time ago:

> The fact that hormones are produced in the gonads is, without further evidence, no reason for believing that they are the primary agents controlling those capacities of the nervous system on which sexual response depends.
>
> (Kinsey et al. 1953: 728–29)

Hormones, no more than chromosomes, are decisive in shaping social and psychic sexual differences.

SEXUALITY AND SOCIAL RELATIONS

Biological determinism insists on the fixity of our sexualities and genders, on their resilience in the face of all efforts at modification. Social and historical explanations, on the other hand, assume a degree of fluidity and flexibility in 'human nature', in its potentiality for change – not overnight, not by individual acts of will, but in the long grind of history and through the complexities and agencies of social interaction. The evidence of other cultures, and of different periods of our own, shows that there are many different ways of being 'men' and 'women', alternative ways of living social and sexual life. The experience of our own recent past has shown the powerful ways in which energetic social movements – of feminism, of same-sex activism, or of trans and intersex people – with little institutional support can influence and in many cases transform gender and sexual relations. Imagine the power of the *long durée* of social change in the past, and the transformative impact of revolutionary moments. Our growing awareness of other cultures necessarily make us more attentive to alternative forms of interaction – not least because through the perspective of cultural difference and change we can begin to reflect on the historical contingency of our own 'human nature', and question the supposed fixity of our own positions as 'men' and 'women'.

The overwhelming evidence suggests that sexual meanings are subject to an enormous degree of sociocultural moulding, to the extent that, as Plummer suggested, 'sexuality has no meaning other than that given to it in social situations' (Plummer 1975: 32). But to put it like this does not, of course, resolve difficulties; it merely pushes them along a rather different path. For if sexuality and sexual differences are social in form, we still need to know where we can set the limits of purely social explanations, what the boundaries against cultural moulding are. Is sexuality entirely a matter of social naming? Is there a complete inter-changeability of roles between men and women? Are our sexual natures infinitely plastic, 'unbelievably malleable' in the famous words of Margaret Mead?

In addressing such questions there is a real danger of confronting an inadequate biological essentialism with an equally inadequate sociological essentialism, in which the malleability of sexuality is always at the bidding of deterministic social imperatives. For the enormously influential social anthropologists of the inter-war years that we encountered earlier it was not human nature but the 'cultural configuration' that was the main object of concern. This was a real gain in that it forced a rethink of many cherished sociological 'truths'. But there were, nevertheless, real problems with the cultural relativism that emerged. Each culture presented itself as a necessary and inexplicable set of differences from others. History, development and change were not issues high on the agenda. Each society, moreover, was seen as imposing itself on its inhabitants as a totality in which all social positions were *necessary* responses to societal demands. This type of argument was taken up by many later writers to argue for the functionality of differentiated sex roles. Individuals 'accept and reproduce', Weinstein and Platt (1969: 6) wrote, 'the patterns of behavior required by society', with the family as the main conduit for this social moulding, and neatly complementary 'social roles' as the necessary result. There does not seem to be much room for manoeuvre in this.

Not only is society seen as the prime mover, but individuals, we must presume, are blank sheets, *tabula rasa*, on which are imprinted the required characteristics needed to make that society function adequately. Society organizes a binary sexual division of labour to fulfil its demands – in reproduction, nurturance, employment, household activities and sex. It even creates deviant social roles – for example, a stigmatized 'role' for homosexuals in certain cultures (McIntosh 1968) – both to provide slots for those who cannot quite fit in, and to act as a warning to the rest of society of the awesome effects of stepping out of line.

Such arguments obviously have an appeal. They offer an elegant explanation for the obvious differences and divisions we see around us. But there is a problem with any theory which endows 'society' with a conscious will, and which believes that all the parts fit together like a marvellous clockwork: where do people and their subjective wills and agency come in? Moreover, there is a curiously paradoxical result of this stress on social moulding. In emphasizing the social as the prime mover, certain characteristics of 'nature' are not questioned. More specifically, in most socially deterministic accounts the necessity for a sexual division of labour along lines of anatomical differences is not challenged but reaffirmed.

MULTIPLE REALITIES AND DIVERSE
SOCIAL WORLDS

I would argue that neither is 'society' as unified and total in its impact as such theories suggest, nor are the lines of difference so clear-cut and decisive. In practice it is difficult not to recognize the complexity of social relationships, the multiple realities and diverse social worlds through which we negotiate our everyday lives. 'Society' is not a whole governed by a coherent set of determinants, but an intricate web of institutions, beliefs, habits, ideologies and social practices that have no necessary *a priori* unity and whose actual relationships have to be unravelled rather than taken as read. If we transfer this view of 'the social' to sexual activities, we will see that far from 'society' moulding 'sexuality', in any straightforward way, what we describe as sexual is constructed through a complexity of social relations, each of which has a different view of what constitutes sexuality and appropriate sexual behaviour. The modern Western apparatus of sexuality, Michel Foucault suggested, is heterogeneous, including: 'discourses, institutions, architectural arrangements, regulations, laws, administrative measures, scientific statements, philosophic propositions, morality, philanthropy, etc.' (Foucault 1980a: 194). All of these together make up what we define as sexuality, but they clearly do not and cannot all say the same things, or address us in identical ways. There exists in the world of sexuality a variety of different and often contradictory accounts of what it is to be sexual: organized sets of meanings ('discourses'), narratives and scripts, articulated through a variety of different languages, and anchored in a dense network of social activities.

Traditional Christian concepts of sexual behaviour, for example, relied on certain assumptions about human nature – that it is unregenerate or corrupt, that the relations of the sexes was pre-ordained, that sexual activity is only justified by reproduction or love. These beliefs are laid down in a set of statements – biblical interpretations, commentaries, canon law, sermons. They are generalized through a language of certitude and morality, which divides the sinners from the saved, the moral from the immoral. These meanings are embodied in institutions which work to reinforce beliefs and behaviours: churches, the privileged position of parenthood, the practices of confession or testimony before God, the existence of religious schools, the sacraments of baptism and marriage, even, in many countries, the legal system. The totality of these discourses and practices constructs 'subject positions' in which the moral elite can recognize themselves as truly among the chosen, and the sinful as beyond the hope of redemption. Individuals are shaped, and shape themselves, in relationship to such pre-existing sets of meaning. In the example given here they are Christian; they could equally be Islamic, Hindu, Judaic, or even secular, as in the twentieth century Soviet effort to create the new 'socialist man', which seek to regulate and control their behaviour according to firm and consciously and unconsciously imbibed rules.

It is here that the idea of the 'script', used by some interactionist sociologists to account for the way we take our sexual meanings, provides a powerful, if inevitably ambiguous, metaphor. 'Scripts specify, like blueprints', John Gagnon (1977: 6) suggested, 'the whos, whats, whens, wheres and whys for given types of activity . . . It is like a blueprint or roadmap or recipe, giving directions . . .' In this sense, scripts act in rather the same way as the earlier sociological concepts of roles. We do not, of course, follow absolutely these guidelines, or we would all be the same, and 'immorality', deviance or transgression would scarcely exist. But the 'scripts' laid down in certain social practices set the parameters within which individual choices are available; and there are oppositional as well as regulatory scripts, various forms of agency as well as blind obedience. Sexual scripts can be improvised. They overlap and contradict one another. There are, as a result, a variety of possible sexual meanings coexisting at any one time.

   In the West people have been subjected to a host of conflicting and often contradictory definitions. Science since the nineteenth century has worked hard to displace religion as the major force in the regulation of sexuality. Its language speaks less of morality and more of the 'natural' and 'unnatural', healthy and sick sexualities; its institutional focus is the clinic, hospital or psychiatrist's couch (Michel Foucault was not the first to suggest an analogy between the confessional mode and the talking cure of psychoanalysis: Freud himself made the same connection). Then there are the languages of law, medicine, education, anthropology, sociology and politics, all of which speak in carefully differentiated tones about sexuality: is it a product of criminality, nurture, cultural variation, political choice? And of course there are the counter-discourses, the reverse and often militant languages, the new 'sexual stories' of the new sexual movements and communities organized around sexual identities and practices (Plummer 1995, 2015). We live in a world of rival and often contradictory descriptions and definitions.

The emergence of clear-cut sexual differences is therefore a prolonged process for each individual subject, learned in all the complexities of social life. Family life provides models, though these are by no means clearcut. Schools convey clear messages, though not always in the same direction. Peer group assessment guards the barricades against social unconventionality. Rituals of courtship, sexual initiation, even sexual violence affirm divisions and fix sexual stereotypes. Desires and choices of partner secure the path of normality or the road to unorthodox behaviour. Media representations construct the images of desirable identities. Religious and moral and political involvements help organize adult ways of life. Even chance brings its wayward influence. It is in response to all these influences – and many more – that we shape our subjectivities, our sense of who we are, our positionality in relation to others, how we came to where we are, where we want to go. Our individual and collective identities as men or women, heterosexual or homosexual, straight or gay/lesbian/bi/trans, queer or whatever, are a product of complex processes of definition and self-definition in a dense and intricate arrangement of social relations.

On the surface, at least, this suggests that male and female gender identities, far from being fixed for all eternity by natural attributes, are rather fragile and haphazard,

subject to a variety of influences and often torn by contradictions. For instance, children have traditionally learned
early on in Western societies that to be a 'real man' one
must cast away any homoerotic feelings. Male homosexuality has been stigmatized through several centuries as
effeminate, an inversion of gender, precisely 'unmanly'.
Yet we also know that many 'real men' do see themselves
as homosexual, and that from the 1970s there was a general reaction in the male gay world, in Western countries
at least, against an automatic association of homosexuality with effeminacy. In non-Western cultures it is often
assumed that men can indulge in homosexual practices
as long as they do not take the female ('passive') role.
Conventional views about what it is to be a man often
conflict with sexual desires and (probably) sexual activities: yet for many gay men the two are held in tension.
Women have been traditionally defined as having a sexuality which is responsive, nurturant and closely associated
with reproduction. But over the past few decades, wom-
en's bodies have been increasingly sexualized in the media
and through representations generally. The same woman
can be addressed in the media both as an efficient home-
maker, caring and domestic, and as a *femme fatale*, sexual
and alluring, with no sense that the different definitions
may be in conflict or may have confusing effects. And, of
course, women have sought to take control of their own
sexualities, to define themselves as autonomous erotic
beings. We hold together in our minds and in our sexual make-ups a host of changing – and often warring –
accounts of ourselves, our motives, our wishes and desires
and our needs.

PERFORMING IDENTITIES

'Masculinity' and 'femininity' are fraught with conflicting and contradictory messages, and they have different meanings in different contexts. They do not mean the same thing in formal social documents or legal codes as they do in popular prejudice. They mean different things in different class, geographical and racialized milieu. And yet, whatever the qualifications we make, they exist not only as powerful ideas but as critical social divides. We do it in different ways at different times but we all the time divide people into 'men' and 'women'. More than this, we are not speaking of simple, meaningless differences: we are in fact referring to power differentials and to historical situations where, socially and practically, men have had the power to define women. Maleness and male sexuality remain the norms by which we judge women. This does not mean that male definitions are simply accepted; on the contrary, there are constant battles over sexual meanings at individual and collective levels, and there are different types of masculinities – hegemonic, subordinate, marginalized – which shift over time, as they respond to changing pressures and struggles (Connell 2005, 2009). But the battles are against, and within the limits set by, the dominant norms. These in turn have traditionally been encoded via a social privileging of particular relationships – in marriage and family arrangements and a host of other social institutions and activities, through which gender and sexual identities are constructed and constantly reaffirmed and performed.

Gender and sexuality, therefore, are less the expressions of some underlying truths about human nature. They are social practices we enact in defined situations, things we do over and over again, often small acts incessantly repeated, cultural productions which, as Judith Butler has suggested, 'create the effect of the natural, the original, and the inevitable' (Butler 1990: x; see also Butler 1993). If we accept this radical view of the performativity of sexuality and gender, then there is nothing out there which explains everything: there is no 'there' there. There are only the repetitive acts, imitations of imitations, through which gendered and sexualized identities are performatively produced and reproduced. From this perspective, hetero-sexuality and homosexuality are not emanations of the genes or hormones or anything else: they are regulative fictions and ideals through which conformities are gener-ated, reinforced and normalized by constant reiterations. That does not mean that the body is a fiction. The norms are inscribed on the body in a variety of ways through the relations and rituals of power which prescribe and pro-scribe appearance, physicality, who and what is desirable, and so on. The point is that while sex could not exist with-out the body, sexuality does not emanate effortlessly from the body.

Perhaps most of this takes place on a level where its subtleties escape our conscious notice. But its weight can be determining. Researchers have shown the extreme pressures to conform to accepted sexual divisions and heterosexual arrangements that exist and are constantly reinforced among children, adolescents and adults alike through language, ritual and interaction. Differences are institutionalized and reaffirmed throughout social life – through parental practices, the education processes, peer pressures, work practices (such as sexual harassment) and street conventions ('wolf whistles'), to routine rituals in bars and other social activities (for example, see Hearn et al. 1989; Adkins 1995; Witz et al. 1996). The question of male sexual violence against women can from this perspective be seen as an extension of a pervasive culture. Such violence is endemic, enacted in a series of sexualized situations from adult rape to child abuse, from sexual harassment at work to domestic violence. But it is not the inevitable by-product of an inherently aggressive masculinity, rather, 'the ritualistic enactment of cultural meaning about sex' (Coward 1984: 239).

Males, in *becoming* men, take up positions in power relations in which they acquire the ability to define women. That does not mean these power relations cannot be challenged, nor that gendered sexual relations are fixed for all time. But it does mean we have to start by recognizing the entrenched patterns that continue to delimit the domains of sexuality.

SEXUALITY AND THE UNCONSCIOUS

Gender and sexual identities are not pre-given, automatic or fixed. They are on the contrary both socially organized *and* contingent. They are also relational. Masculinity and femininity each exist only because of the existence of the other. They are shifting and changing definitions, locked together in an apparently inevitable but all the time changing dance of life and death. At the same time it remains difficult to escape our strong investment in sexual difference, and the considerable power it continues to give to men in the gender order. Advocates of the existence across all cultures of structures of patriarchal power would see this as a sufficient explanation. It cannot explain, however, either the deep commitment many have to sexual difference, or the strain that is evident in many people's lives, men and women, as they strive to maintain it. Sexual difference is apparently necessary *and* precarious, fundamental yet provisional. How then do we recognize ourselves in these social categories? Why do we invest so much in what appears to critical sexual theory so ephemeral? Why are sexual differences apparently so inessential yet so permanent and resilient? It is at this point that many have sought insights from another theoretical approach, that of psychoanalysis, the theory of the dynamic unconscious and of desire.

Psychoanalysis has made a critical contribution to the theorization of sexuality during the past century or so, though its impact has often been ambiguous and contradictory. Like so many other of the great intellectual preoccupations of the past century (Marxism, democracy, nationalism, even feminism spring to mind), it has different meanings in different contexts. Freud's own work provides a treasure chest for varying interpretations, while the work of the many who claim to be his legitimate successors takes us down many highways and byways, often to a destination that bears little relationship to what Freud said, or meant, or wanted to believe. It is therefore hazardous in the extreme to venture to describe a 'true Freud'. A more interesting and adventurous route is to look at the way in which recent reinterpretations of Freud have offered a challenge to the orthodoxies of the sexual tradition. Here the critical contribution has come from two distinct, largely femi-nist, appropriations of psychoanalysis. The first, drawing initially on the work of the French analyst Jacques Lacan (no feminist he), and subsequently on the French feminist theorists of sexual difference influenced by him, if only by rejection, such as Luce Iragaray, Julia Kristeva and Hélène Cixous, led to a fierce psychoanalytical/philosophical cri-tique of the phallic order and a celebration of the female body (Bristow 2011). The second built on the investiga-tions of infancy by female analysts such as Karen Horney and Melanie Klein, and focused on the significance of parenting and social interaction in shaping and reproduc-ing distinctions between men and women, especially in relation to care (Chodorow 1978).

For such thinkers, the importance of psychoanalysis lay in the fact that, despite a long feminist hostility towards Freud and his followers, it precisely did not assume sex-uality or gender as unproblematic categories (Coward 1983). Rather, psychoanalysis offered a way of challenging the rigid distinctions between men and women, and prob-lematized the pre-given nature of sexual difference, while recognizing the power of unconscious meanings and the psychic investment in sexual difference. Freud himself was very clear on the dubious nature of concepts of masculin-ity and femininity and of sexuality, believing them to be among the most difficult known to science.

There are three key elements in the attempted 'recov-ery' of Freud. First, there is the theory of the unconscious itself, the very core of psychoanalysis. The psychoanalytic tradition proposes that individuals are not predetermined products of biological imperatives, nor are they the effects simply of social relations. There is a psychic realm – the unconscious – with its own dynamic, rules and history, where the biological possibilities of the body acquire meaning. Chodorow put this clearly:

> We live an embodied life; we live with those genital and reproductive organs and capacities, those hormones and chromosomes, that locate us physiologically as male and female. But . . . there is nothing self evident about this biology. How anyone understands, fantasizes about, symbolizes, internally represents, or feels about her or his physiology is a product of development and experience in the family and not a direct product of the biology itself.
>
> (Chodorow 1980: 18)

The unconscious is a sphere of conflict: between ideas, fantasies, wishes, and desires – above all sexual desires – denied access to conscious life by the force of mental repression, yet 'returning' all the time to disrupt consciousness in the form of dreams, slips of the tongue, jokes, neurotic symptoms or 'perverse' behaviour. What fundamentally constitutes the unconscious are those wishes and desires which are repressed in the face of the demands of reality, and in particular the repressed, incestuous desires of infancy: 'What is unconscious in mental life is also what is infantile' (Freud 1916–17: 210).

This leads to the second point: to a theorization of sexual difference. Identities, as men and women, and the organization of desires and object choices, as heterosexual, homosexual, or whatever, are not laid down automatically at birth. They are a product of psychic struggle and conflict as the initial 'blob of humanity', with its undifferentiated, polymorphously perverse sexuality, and bisexual nature (object choice is not pre-given), negotiates the hazard-strewn path to a precarious maturity. The child negotiates the phases of initial development where different parts of the body become focuses of erotic excitement (the oral, anal, phallic and genital phases), advancing through the dawning recognition of 'castration' (the presence or absence of the male organ) to the drama of the Oedipus crisis, in which the young person struggles with incestuous desires for the mother and the father, to an eventual identification with the 'appropriate parent' of the same sex. Through this 'epic' struggle the undifferentiated infant finally becomes a little man or a little woman. This is of course a schematic description which does little justice to the subtle intricacies of Freud's final accounts. There is no inevitable progress to the altar of proper behaviour. If the process 'worked' automatically there would be no ambiguity about gender, no homosexuality, transgender, fetishism, and so on. For Freud, attaining sexual identity, and the soldering together of identity and desire (who we are, and what we need and lack), is a struggle that we all have to enter and that by no means ends in a victorious capture of the position allotted to us by reason of our anatomy, or the demands of culture.

On the other hand, as Freud notoriously wrote, 'Anatomy is destiny' (Freud 1916–17: 178), and this is the core of the objections to Freud's theories from the first and ever since. The phrase appears to underpin the resilience of our social arrangements, to justify sexual division, to impose a tyranny of the body over the mind. There is, however, an alternative way of seeing the importance of anatomy: as symbolically important, representative of sexual differences, which acquire meaning only in culture. In post-Lacanian psychoanalytic writings, the penis, or rather its symbolic representative, the phallus, is seen as the prime marker in relation to which meaning is shaped. It is the mark of difference, representing power differences existing in the 'symbolic order', the realm of language, meaning and culture, and of history (and therefore, potentially, of change) (Mitchell 1974). What the child acquires in its access to the order of meaning at the Oedipal moment is a growing awareness of the *cultural* importance of the male organ for subsequent sexual difference and social position.

Thus the threat of castration to the boy, or the culturally produced belief in a 'castration' that has already taken place for the girl, becomes of decisive psychic significance. The terror of castration propels the young boy and young girl *differently* through the crisis. Both have to break with the primal connection with their mother, but they break with it differently: the boy through an identification with his father and eventual transference of his love for his mother into a desire for other women (this is what a man is, and does); the girl in a much more difficult and long-drawn process to confirm her identification with the mother and transform her desire to have a penis into a desire to receive the favour of the penis from another (that is, to be a woman receptive to a man).

What matters in this is not so much the detail – which in its crude outline can seem risible – as the attempt it reveals to show how sexed identities are shaped in a complex human process through which anatomical differences acquire meaning in unconscious life. Our destinies are shaped not so much by the differences themselves but by their meaning, which is socially given and psychically elaborated. But a third point emerges from this: that identities are not only precarious acquisitions, they are provisional ones, 'imaginary closures', which are subject to disruptions all the time, through the eruption of unconscious elements, repressed desires not fully or finally extinguished by the Oedipal drama. For Freud, to be human was to be divided, to be constantly 'decentred', swayed by forces outside conscious control. And at the heart of this fractured subjectivity are the ambiguous meanings of masculinity and femininity:

> For psychology, the contrast between the sexes fades away into one between activity and passivity, in which we far too readily identify activity with maleness and passivity with femaleness, a view which is by no means universally confirmed in the animal kingdom.
>
> (Freud 1930: 106, note 3)

At this point Freud can clearly be seen as a precursor of those theorists who have sought to question the fixity of our human nature and the rigidity of gendered divisions. Psychoanalysis sought to promote universal explanations that transcended different cultural histories. But surely what is really enduring is the recognition that the Freudian tradition offers a way of thinking of psychic connections and emotional investments that can be applied to many and varied histories and cultures without imposing a transcendent ideal of a true human nature (Alexander and Taylor 2011).

AFFECT, AND THE STRUCTURING
OF EMOTIONS

We now have two terms with which to challenge the rigidities of biological determinism: 'the social', a web of institutions, relationships and beliefs; and 'the unconscious', which in many ways mediates between social imperatives and biological possibilities, while having a complex history of its own.

The attraction of psychoanalysis has been that it offers an explanation of the psychic and emotional investment that individuals have in the structures of gender and sexuality. Feelings, emotions and affects have been a crucial part of the thinking on sexuality since the nineteenth century. Psychology was a critical contributor to early sexology, and as we have seen, psychoanalysis opened up new ways of thinking of sexuality. But there have been other significant attempts to think of the swirls of emotionality that make sexuality so potent a personal and social presence, without surrendering to the assumption of overwhelming inbuilt instincts. The pioneering critical sociology of sexuality from writers such as John Gagnon, William Simon and Ken Plummer, with its emphasis on symbolic interaction, multiple social worlds and sexual scripts, was underpinned by a social psychology derived from George Herbert Mead. More recently there has been a renewed interest in theories of affect and the emotions (see Love 2007; Wetherell 2012)

The question of subjectivity, the relationship between social structures, concepts, discourses and sets of belief on the one hand, and the individual sense of self and identity and the feelings attached to them on the other, has been central to this debate. Discourses, located in the realm of language, were central to Foucault's contribution to theories of sexuality. They work to address and constitute the subject, subjectifying and subjecting the individual simultaneously, creating 'docile bodies'. But critical sexual theorists have become increasingly aware that they cannot guarantee how the subject will identify with and take up different subject positions. Both in relation to gender and sexual identities, the individual subject is never wholly captured by a unitary model of who and what they are. In the multiplicities of desires and possible identifications lies the possibility of refusing identity (Moore 2011).

The idea of cultures as made up of intense emotions as well as social institutions has generated a renewed interest in what Raymond Williams (1977) called 'structures of feeling', the patterning of emotions and ways of seeing that shape distinct ways of being. Other sociological concepts such as 'habitus', after Norbert Elias and Pierre Bourdieu, (Weeks 2011: 77–9), 'desiring machines', following Gilles Deleuze and Felix Guattari (Beckman 2011) or 'assemblages', popularized by Jasbir Puar (2007) are similarly concerned with the structuring of distinct patterns of emotions that become psycho-social realities. The work of Eve Kosofsky Sedgwick (2003) on 'touching feeling', heavily influenced by the work of the American psychologist Silvan Tomkins, stimulated new explorations of the complexity of feelings around the sexuality-gender matrix, in the present and in the past.

In part this new concern with affect and emotions was a recognition that there was a danger of a certain aridity in simply focusing on the social or the psychic without reflecting on the intensity of people's commitments to their subjectivities and identities. But equally important was a new awareness that debates on sexuality and gender aroused intense and growing public feelings, that opposition to sexual change was not epiphenomenal or false consciousness but deeply rooted. This became ever more critical as the optimism that pushed the agenda of feminism and gay politics in the 1970s gave rise to a sense of impasse in the 1980s and 1990s. The divisions within feminism as revealed in the so-called sex wars, the apparently irresistible rise of social conservatism, especially in the USA, and the massive impact of the HIV/AIDS epidemic, contributed to a much darker mood, and led to a growing interest in such topics as memory, loss, trauma, insult, shame, guilt, anger, mourning, abjection and melancholia often at the expense of the more optimistic perspectives of hope, pleasure and radical change of earlier periods.

PHOBIAS AND NORMS

It is surely no coincidence that this period also saw the widespread acceptance and deployment of concepts of homophobia, biphobia and transphobia as explanatory modes, which suggested a visceral and internalized fear and hatred of those who are different. Irrational feelings policed the boundaries of the normal, excluding or punishing the different. The very roots of the concept of homophobia do indeed lie in the search for a psychological explanation for hostility towards homosexuality, as a response to widespread beliefs that homosexuality was itself a pathological manifestation. In its original formulation, as popularized by George Weinberg (1972), homophobia was in effect simply a reversal of the traditional terms. Over time, the concept had broadened to embrace not only hostility towards bisexuality and transgender but also wider cultural and political hostility towards sexual and gender diversity and non-conformity (Bryant and Vidal-Ortiz 2008; Weeks 2011: 82–3). Political homophobia has become an effective weapon of state policy in many parts of the globe, as elites both in post-colonial Africa and post-Soviet eastern Europe exploit fear of sexual change to underpin authoritarian nationalist agendas (Weiss and Bosia 2013).

From this perspective the phobic anxieties are more than individual irrationalities. They are manifestations of wider cultural anxieties concerning sexual and gender difference which can be exploited through moral panics and channelled into socially conservative or reactionary political movements (Herdt 2009). For some queer theorists they are manifestations of heteronormativity, where fears, anxieties and panics are consolidated in normative structures that affirm the centrality of heterosexuality not simply as a set of practices but as a sexual and gender structure.

It is tempting to see concepts such as homophobia, biphobia, transphobia or heteronormativity as having a universal significance, providing an explanatory tool for the persistence of the fear of difference in diverse cultures. But that would be to perpetuate the errors made by the other disciplinary explanations we have explored, whether biological, social or psychic determinism. To my mind they are better seen as cultural patterns that vary across time, and even within particular societies (Robinson 2008), and require an appropriate historical and social exploration and understanding. The meanings of sexual difference will not be found in supra-historical tropes but in detailed historical and social scientific studies of sexual cultures and gender norms, such as those that gave rise to the tragedy of Herculine Barbin, and countless people since.

4

THE CHALLENGE OF DIVERSITY

THE LANGUAGE OF PERVERSITY

Two words

If the way we think about sex shapes the way we experience it, then words are tiny marks of those thoughts, haphazard signs scribbled on the page or floating in the air, which we charge with meaning. Let us take two words that are common in discussions about sexuality in the Anglophone world. The first is 'perversity', the state of being 'perverse' or 'perverted', a turning away from what is proper and right. The second is 'diversity', the condition of being 'diverse', concerning 'difference' or 'unlikeness'. The two words are clearly related, each of them suggesting a move away from a strict 'normality' (another key word). *The Shorter Oxford English Dictionary* acknowledges the link by recording as one meaning of 'diversity' the word 'perversity', a usage it dates back to the sixteenth century. There is clearly a common history. Yet when applied to sexuality, the implications of these words have been quite distinct. Perversity and diversity may appear to refer to the same phenomenon. In reality a chasm has opened between them signifying a major shift in the languages of sexuality and the way we think about our needs and desires. For while all the terms relating to 'perversity' suggest a hierarchy of sexual values and practices in which 'the perversions' are right at the bottom of the scale, 'diversity' hints at a continuum of behaviours in which one element has no more fundamental a value than any other.

The perverse

The language of the perverse has always had a strongly moral accent, implying a turning away from what is right, an indulgence in wrong. It is laden with opprobrium. The utilization of terms like 'perversion' and 'pervert' in the sexological writings of the late nineteenth century therefore carried a powerful charge. These terms arose, according to Havelock Ellis (who had himself shown no small skill in deploying them in his earlier writings), at a time when 'sexual anomalies were universally regarded as sins or crimes, at the least as vices' (Ellis 1946: 126). As a result, prohibitions which were rooted in ancient Christian codes were transferred, willy-nilly, to the ostensibly scientific language of the sexological textbooks. Here they became the framework in which clinical investigation of individual sexual lives was conducted, providing definitions, Kinsey sharply commented, nearly identical with 'theologic classifications and with moral pronouncements of the English common law of the fifteenth century' (Kinsey et al. 1948: 202). Homosexuality, transvestism, fetishism,

voyeurism, kleptomania, sadism and masochism, copro-
philia, undinism, frottage, chronic satyriasis and nymphomania, necrophilia, pederasty . . . the list was endless. Each
perversion was investigated with dispassionate care and its
causes were endlessly speculated upon. Was it a degeneration or a harmless anomaly, congenital or acquired, the
result of tainted heredity or the effects of moral corruption, a product of psychic trauma or free and wilful choice?

Krafft-Ebing offered a distinction between a *perversion*
and a *perversity*, the latter a product of vice, the former
a psycho-pathological condition. Havelock Ellis distinguished between *inversion*, a more or less random biological 'sport', and *perversion*, which sprang from moral
indulgence. Magnus Hirschfeld and his followers separated *perversions* from *anomalies*. But whatever the
speculations about precise demarcations or aetiologies
(causes), there was no doubt about the result. Walking
out of the pages of these sexological writings, speaking in
authentic tones of self-confession (even if their more out-
rageous memories were carefully censored, accompanied
by lines of dots, or rendered in Latin) were real individual beings, marked or marred by their badges of sexual
unorthodoxy.

The result of what Foucault (1979) described as the 'perverse implantation' was twofold. On the positive side, the
description of these new types of sexual being consider-
ably expanded the definition of what could be considered
as 'sexual'. Freud opened his *Three Essays on the Theory of
Sexuality* in 1905 with a discussion of homosexuality and
other 'sexual aberrations' precisely because he believed
that their existence transformed conventional views as to

what constituted sex. He used them, as Laplanche and Pontalis (1980: 307) put it, 'as a weapon with which to throw the traditional definitions of sexuality into question'. The new definition extended backwards to include even the most modest whispers of infantile sexuality (attachment to the breast, contraction of the bowels, manipulation of the genitals, a generalized sensuality, as well as less overt but more significant Oedipal anxieties) and outwards to the farthest reaches of human behaviour, to embrace not only common or garden variations but also esoteric manifestations that had little obvious connection with orgasm or even pleasure at all. Here were the seeds of a modern view of an infinite sexual variety. But the negative side of this classificatory enthusiasm was a sharp reinforcement of 'the normal'. There was little discussion of heterosexuality as such (there still isn't that much in comparison to our obsession with the 'abnormal'). The term itself emerged, almost reluctantly, *after* homosexuality and originally referred to 'psychic hermaphrodism', what we now call bisexuality. But the very absence of speculation about its fundamental nature reinforced its taken-for-granted status, part of the air we breathe, the silent assumption which shapes everyday life.

Moreover, the debates over the causes of the perversions and the would-be scientific descriptions of scandalous examples worked to emphasize their pathology, their relationship to degeneracy, madness and sickness, and helped to reinforce the normality of heterosexual genital relations. This served to reinvigorate that disease model of sexuality which enormously influenced twentieth century ways of thinking about sexual behaviour.

Freud and perversion

Yet there was sufficient ambiguity in these labelling and taxonomic efforts to open alternative ways of seeing sexuality. Take, for instance, Freud's attempt to argue for the broadening of the meaning of sexuality. Perversions, he argued in the *Three Essays*, are simply acts which either *extend* sexual practices beyond those regions of the body conventionally designated as appropriate (that is the genitals of either sex), or *linger* over activities that may be proper if they ultimately lead to genital sexuality (the so-called forepleasure, such as kissing, caressing, sucking, biting), but which become perverse if they remain as ends in themselves (Freud 1905). This may be a fair working definition, and it is more generous in its inclusiveness than many others on offer. It is, however, difficult to avoid the conclusion that there is, in Freud's mind, a model of what sex should be, a goal towards which sexual practices ought to be directed, and hence a prescription of how we must live.

Freud was an interesting example of the ambivalence of these early scientists of sex for the very reason that he went further than anyone else in incorporating the perverse within the acceptable range of sexuality. The effect of the *Three Essays* was to suggest that perversions, far from being the unique property of a sick or immoral minority, are the common property of us all. Their negative was revealed in neurotic symptoms, which were displaced representations of repressed sexual wishes. Their positive presence was demonstrated in forepleasures, and by the social existence of obvious perverts walking the streets, filling the hospitals and the courtrooms. These perversions – 'deviations in respect of sexual object', including homosexuality and bestiality, and 'deviations in respect of sexual aim', whereby pleasure extended beyond genitality – represented the re-emergence of component instincts to which we are all heirs. In the universal poly-morphous perversity and bisexuality of infancy, Freud was able to find roots of what later sociologists were to label as 'our common deviance':

> No healthy person, it appears, can fail to make some addi-tion that might be called perverse to the normal sexual aim; and the universality of this finding is in itself enough to show how inappropriate it is to use the word perversion as a term of reproach.
>
> (Freud 1905: 160)

But if this is the case, why retain the concept? The attitude of psychoanalysis to homosexuality is revealing here for the very reason that for Freud it was, as he put it, 'scarcely a perversion'. The real interest in Freud's discussion of the topic, in various forms over many years, is his very real ambiguity and reluctance to do this.

On the one hand, Freud carefully examines and rejects contemporary sexological views on the subject. He argues that the reduction in the choice of partner to one of the same sex in homosexuality parallels a similar reduction in heterosexuality. As a result, he suggests, 'from the point of view of psycho-analysis the exclusive sexual interest felt by men for women is also a problem that needs elucidat-ing . . .' (Freud 1905: 146, note 1, added 1915). Homosex-uality could not be regarded as a thing apart. In the fact of object choice and genital organization of sexual activity it was often continuous with heterosexuality. Moreover, he wrote in his essay on Leonardo, everyone is capable of homosexual object choice, as the evidence of dreams and fantasies reveals. And homosexual feelings, 'blocked and rechannelled', sublimated into more amorphous emotions of solidarity, brotherhood and sisterhood, were an important element in understanding group psychology. All single-sex institutions, from the sanctity of priestly orders and peace of monasteries and nunneries, to the masculine ethos of military discipline, might in some sense be seen as resting on sublimated homosexuality (Freud 1910: 99, footnote; 1921: 67–143). Freud therefore distanced himself from any idea that homosexuality was a sign of 'degeneracy' – a favoured nineteenth-century term – on the grounds that this was no more than 'a judgement of value, a condemnation instead of an explanation'.

He also rejected the distinction, favoured by Havelock Ellis among others, between 'acquired' and 'congenital' homosexuality as being 'fruitless and inappropriate' (Freud 1905: 138–39; 1920: 154). Homosexuality, like its sibling form heterosexuality, can only be understood in relation to the working of the psychic apparatus as a whole. Its roots were to be found in the universal bisexuality to which we human animals are born, and in the mental processes by which each individual negotiated the hazards of castration anxiety and the Oedipus crisis to obtain a precarious 'sexual identity'.

So, homosexuality was not a disease. It needed no 'cure'. It was widespread. It was continuous with heterosexuality in many of its forms. And like this, it was not a single condition, but more a grouping of different activities, needs and desires:

> What we have thrown together, for reasons of convenience, under the name of homosexuality, may derive from a diversity of processes of psycho-social inhibitions.
>
> (Freud 1905: 146)

Here, apparently, once and for all, we see homosexuality demystified. No longer need it be hidden under a stone like worms and other disturbing creatures. It was a more or less ordinary phenomenon, part of the life of us all, and now subjected to the light of scientific reason. And yet, that is not quite how it has been seen within psychoanalysis, nor was it in practice how ultimately Freud himself was able to leave the subject. The problem lay in that little word 'inhibitions'. For while on the one hand we have this rational deconstruction of homosexuality, on the other we are offered a model of sexuality which assumes a normal pattern of development, and which therefore makes homosexuality highly problematic as a life choice. In his famous letter to the mother of a young homosexual, Freud assured her that homosexuality was no vice or degradation, nor was it an illness: it was nothing to be ashamed of. But, he added: 'We consider it to be a variation of the sexual function produced by a certain arrest of the sexual development' (E. Freud 1961: 277). Therein lies the difficulty. A 'development' assumes an appropriate end result, and 'arrest' an artificial blockage. For Freud the growth of each individual from infancy to mature adult sexuality repeated the (hypothetical) development of the race as a whole from primitive sexual promiscuity and perversity to monogamous heterosexuality. This was not a product simply of evolution but of cultural imperatives. It was the tragic destiny of humankind to forgo as a matter of necessity the infinite range of the desires in order to ensure survival in a world of scarcity. Each individual, like the race itself, had to attain the 'tyranny of genital organization' in order to survive, while appropriate object choice became less an act of volition and more a cultural demand. In the end, therefore, a heterosexual and reproductive imperative is reinserted into Freud's account. Once a goal-directed version of sexuality is introduced, however surreptitiously, then the whole laboriously constructed edifice of sexual variety begins to totter.

For Freud, the term 'perversion' had a precise technical meaning, as an aspect of all our lives we could not escape. It was a problem only when it became an end in itself and inhibited the road to 'mature sexuality'. But it was very difficult to separate that meaning from the wider moral and political meanings attached to it. A crack was left in the door which allowed judgmental values to re-enter a supposedly neutral clinical discourse. Many post-Freudians eagerly pushed the door wide open. So, for example, Ernest Jones, one of Freud's most loyal supporters and his biographer, criticized him for an over-tolerant attitude toward his lesbian patient and commented that 'much is gained if the path to heterosexual gratification is opened . . .' (Jones 1955: 299). Later Freudians, in their haste to abandon the idea that homosexuality itself was not a pathology, even junked Freud's central concept of universal bisexuality. For Socarides, heterosexuality was the natural state from which homosexuality was a deviation. He observes that one of the curious resistances of his patients lay in their assumption that their disorder was 'a normal form of sexuality', and suggests that 'these views must be dealt with from the very beginning' (Socarides 1978). For Elizabeth Moberly, heterosexuality is the goal of human development (Moberly 1983).

In such comments we can see a return to a pre-Freudian moralism. Freud himself can scarcely be blamed for this. Nevertheless the seeds of such positions are sown by the ambiguities of Freud's own writings. He speaks, at various times, of homosexuality as an abnormality, a disorder, as pathological, and in the male case a 'flight from women'. Indeed, occasionally he even described it without ambiguity as 'a perversion'. Nor is this ultimately surprising. In the last resort, whatever the qualifications in the statement that the germ of perversion is present in us all, the notion of development must imply a norm.

Categorizing sexualities

The founders of sexology – and here Freud, one of its most radical figures, was no exception – constructed a model of sexuality from which it has been difficult to escape. On the one hand, we were offered a norm of behaviour, which was heterosexual, procreative and largely male, in which female sexuality has almost invariably been defined as secondary or responsive to the male's. This applied, it must be added, even to the concept of perversion itself. As Plummer (1984: 219) put it, the field of 'sexual deviation' was mainly demarcated by the issue of male desire.

Female breaches with the norm were fitted into a dichot-omized picture of male activity and female passivity. Not surprisingly, the most commonly recognized female sex-ual deviations included servicing men in prostitution or pornography, or 'provoking' men, as in accounts of rape; and lesbianism, the most common form of female sexual variation, was generally speculated about in terms which derived entirely from the male (but see Beccalossi 2012).

On the other hand, there was an ever-growing cata-logue of 'perversions', 'deviations', 'paraphilias' or 'sexual disorders' which inevitably marginalized and in the last resort pathologized unorthodox sexualities. The language of perversion divided the sexual world into the normal and the abnormal, the elect and the damned, and rarely did they meet.

THE DISCOURSE OF DIVERSITY

Theoretical challenges

A 'perverse dynamic', Dollimore has argued, lies at the heart of western constructions of sexuality (Dollimore 1991). The striving to produce and regulate the norm inevitably produces the Other, the feared and execrated or merely despised, who simultaneously denies and confirms the norm. The political and sexual ordering is always internally disordered by the very perversities it produces and sets up against itself. That disorder, of course, provides the elements of resistance, subversion and transgression, and ultimately the notion of a pluralism of sexualities, of diversity as a fact of life. In two critical areas, one theoretical, the other political, a 'discourse of diversity' has arisen over recent generations, and it has had significant cultural effects.

The first area is that of sexology itself. On one level it is little more than a cosmetic terminological change, signalled as early as the 1930s by Havelock Ellis himself. The term 'perversion', he suggested, 'is completely antiquated and mischievous and should be avoided' (Ellis 1946: 127). He offered as a replacement the less fevered (if still ideologically laden) term, 'sexual deviation', and this phrase became commonplace in sociological discussions in the half century or so afterwards. Latent in such shifts of terminology was a more important change: the recognition of sexual pluralism and the emergence of what Gayle Rubin described as the concept of a 'benign sexual variation' (Rubin 1984).

The seeds of this new approach were clearly planted by the investigations of the founding sexologists themselves, and the delicate plants were nourished by an appropriation of the Freudian advocacy of a common infantile polymorphous perversity. The celebration of desire as many-sided and many-shaped by some modern writers has taken this position to its logical, often morally anarchic, conclusion. The key figure in transforming the public debate, apart from Freud, was Alfred Kinsey. Coming close, as he rather reluctantly admitted, to Freud's speculations, he suggested that there was an important idea that rarely featured prominently in either general or scientific discussion, that sex was a normal biological function, acceptable in whatever form it appeared. He wrote to a boy struggling with homosexual feelings: 'Biologically there is no form of outlet which I will admit as abnormal.

There is no right or wrong biologically' (cited in Pomeroy 1972). Such statements were clearly still in the naturalistic framework of the sexual tradition and in that form must be taken with a pinch of scepticism. Yet the underlying message has become crucial to contemporary debates. Few sexologists in the mainstream would feel relaxed at using a term like 'perversion' to describe the varieties of sexual patterns today. For Robert Stoller, perversion was 'the erotic form of hatred', defined not so much by the acts, *the* perversions, but by the content, hostility, while the term 'pervert' for describing a particular type of person is banned completely from sexological debates. There was even a new and welcome modesty abroad, admitting that '. . . it is crucial to remember that we still know very little about the mechanisms or causes of human sexual behaviour . . .' (Stoller 1977: 45). Such modesty worked against categorical positions.

But if we know little about the causes, we do know increasingly about the forms and frequent occurrence of sexual diversity, and this rather than his questionable biologism is Kinsey's real contribution. The two vast volumes he largely wrote, *Sexual Behavior in the Human Male* and *Sexual Behavior in the Human Female*, and the others he inspired, may have had methodological problems and insufficiently representative or rigorous samples, and are suffused with unconscious biases of their own. Some contemporary critics, for example, have sharply critiqued his casual attitude towards inter-generational sex. But the thousands of subjects he and his colleagues interviewed provided an unparalleled insight into American sexual life, and by extension into other cultures too. When it became possible to say, on the basis of what was then the most thorough investigation ever done at that date, that 37 per cent of the male sample had had sexual contact to orgasm with another male, then even if the sample was unrepresentative and the percentage figures were exaggerated, homosexual activity could no longer be seen as a morbid symptom of a tiny sick minority. At least among a significant section of American men it was a fairly common occurrence. And if this was true of homosexuality, then it was potentially true also for a wide range of other sexualities, from bestiality to paedophilia, from sado-masochism to a passion for pornography.

Kinsey was fascinated by the range of variations in human sexual behaviours. He cited with glee the example of two men who lived in the same town, met at the same place of business, had common social activities, and yet experienced enormously different sexual lives. One individual he interviewed had had one ejaculation in thirty years; another had thirty a week, a difference of 45,000 times. This was just one example for Kinsey of the vast variety that existed, across the divide of class, gender and race. From this flowed a profoundly important and influential sociological – and political – point. He wrote:

> The publicly pretended code of morals, our social organization, our marriage customs, our sex laws, and our educational and religious systems are based upon an assumption that individuals are much alike sexually and that it is an equally simple matter for all of them to confine their behavior to the single pattern which the mores dictate.
>
> (Kinsey et al. 1948: 197)

But what if people were in fact different, had different needs, desires and behaviour? Then a yawning gap would appear between moral codes and sexual behaviour, throwing into confusion the absolutist certainties of the sexual tradition. This was the favoured point of departure for subsequent critiques of normative regulations.

Sexual minorities

If transformations within mainstream sexology provided a theoretical framework for a recognition of diversity, the political energy came from a different source, that of the 'sexual minorities' themselves. I noted earlier that since at least the nineteenth century most industrial societies have witnessed a sustained effort to articulate and develop distinct lesbian and male homosexual identities in the context of extending subcultures, networks and social communities. By the mid-twentieth century a new concept was emerging in the USA and parts of Europe, that of the 'sexual minority', articulating new claims to recognition, rights and ultimately social inclusion and full citizenship. At first this was largely an expression of a growing homosexual consciousness, but in its wake other assertions of minority sexual identities have emerged. The example of homosexuality, as Gayle Rubin argued, has provided a repertoire of political strategies and organizational forms for the mobilization of other erotic populations (Rubin 1984). Transgendered people, bisexuals, sado-masochists, fetishists, man-boy lovers, sex workers and others vocally emerged, clamouring for their right of self-expression and legitimacy, with varying degrees of successful recognition.

The hesitantly speaking perverts of Krafft-Ebing's medico-forensic pages, confessing their most intimate secrets to the new sexual experts, have walked out of the clinical text and onto the stage of history, the living proof of sexual diversity.

These new sexual and social identities may have publically emerged on the terrain first mapped and carefully articulated by the sexologists themselves. But as Kinsey himself forcefully observed, it is only the human mind which invents categories and tries to force facts into separate pigeonholes; and the facts constantly subvert.

Same-sex identities

Sexology was important in establishing the language by which these miscreants were described and analysed. Through their symbiotic relationship with the medical profession (many of them, like Ellis and Hirschfeld, were trained doctors, though other influential figures were not) these early sexologists helped construct a very influential disease model, the effects of which are still with us. But the poor creatures they described were not their inventions: they were products of very complex social processes, of social definition and of self-definition in which sexology played an important but not decisive part. Moreover, the language of sexology could itself be used to challenge the certainties of the sexual tradition.

I started this chapter with words. Several other words symbolize the movement both of language and everyday life (as far as they can be distinguished): 'sodomite', 'homosexual', 'gay', 'queer'. The universal adoption of the term 'gay' in all Anglophone countries from the early 1970s can be seen as a new stage in the public expression of a positive personal identity, by creating a clear *social* identity organized around sexuality. In the same way, the gradual spread of terms such as 'invert' or 'homosexual' from the late nineteenth century marked a significant breach with the traditional terminology of the sin that could not be named among Christians, that of sodomy. 'Sodomite' was a term suffused with heavy tones of mediaeval morality. It was also ambiguous. It signified someone who committed a particular type of sexual *act*, that of buggery or anal intercourse. The homosexual, on the other hand, as Foucault and others argued, was a particular type of sexual *person*, given not only a name but a personalized history (weak father, strong mother, or sometimes overbearing father and submissive mother), physical characteristics (wide hips and high voice if a man, masculinized figure and hair on the upper lip if a woman), and indicative failures (inability to whistle, dislike of children). Many thus described by the clinical discourse might not recognize themselves fully or at all in such descriptions; but they were able to validate their existence, affirm that others like them existed by their naming, and that, far from being unique creatures, they could re-enter the canons of recognized, if perverted, sexualities. A new language of self-description emerged – 'invert', 'uranian', 'third' or 'intermediate' sex – that marked the embryonic stirring of an affirmative, and modern, sense of sexual self.

The search for valid sexual identities has characterized the history of same-sex love, male and female, since the nineteenth century. Different groups of people have found different ways of doing this: there is no pre-ordained goal. Gender, geographical and racial differences have produced differentiated identities. The widespread use of the word 'gay' today in many parts of the Global South cannot be taken to mean, as some have concluded, that there has been a universalization of Western meanings. On the contrary, a common language can conceal a huge range of sexual patterns. There is no necessary link between sexual practices and social identity. But for many, establishing a firm sense of sexual identity has remained critically important. Categorization and self-labellings, that is the process of working out a social identity, may control, restrict and inhibit, as many critics have argued, but at the same time they provide, as Plummer noted, 'comfort, security and assuredness' (Plummer 1980: 29). And a precondition for attaining a secure sense of personal identity and belonging has been the development of wider social networks, of finding a collective way of dealing with sexual differentiation, of establishing sexual communities and social worlds, of telling stories in ways which could make for mutual recognition and support (Plummer 1995, 2015).

Finding voice

The emergence of distinctive sexual subcultures and communities is part of a wider process that has marked the modern world, that of ever-growing social complexity and social differentiation, producing a new pluralism of class, ethnic, racial and cultural forms as well as a diversity of gender and sexual experiences. This process of differentiation has of course produced not only complexity but new forms of social conflict and antagonism. It is in the context of continuing struggle over appropriate behaviour that politicized sexual identities also emerged, articulated since the late nineteenth century (hesitantly at first) in a series of homosexual rights groupings and other sex reform movements throughout the industrialized world (Paternotte and Tremblay 2015). These have been an important way of sexual outsiders responding to the changing patterns of sexual regulation and of challenging sexual norms.

Sociologists have suggested a number of factors that are necessary for this successful emergence: the existence of large numbers in the same situation; geographical concentration, especially in cities; identifiable targets of opposition; sudden events or changes in social position; and an intellectual leadership with readily understood goals (Adam 1978, 1995). Each of these was present in the history of homosexual movements at various times, which explains its significant social presence compared to other sexual minorities. Already by the late nineteenth century there were groups of men who saw themselves as 'homosexual', emerging from and increasingly constructing their own social worlds. Lesbian groupings were more embryonic; nevertheless, in many North American and European cities both an identity and social networks were developing. These were the seedbeds of support for such organizations as Magnus Hirschfeld's Scientific-Humanitarian Committee in Germany, founded in 1898, and the smaller sex reform organizations in Britain and elsewhere, founded on the eve of the First World War. The organizations fluctuated in their fortunes as political circumstances changed. The German homosexual movement, at one time the largest in the world, was effectively destroyed by the Nazis during the 1930s. By the 1950s nevertheless there were new initiatives, especially in Scandinavia, the Netherlands, France and Britain, with a strong impetus also now from the USA. Organizations like the Mattachine Society and the Daughters of Bilitis in the USA were founded partly in the wake of the McCarthyite witch hunts against sexual deviants in the early 1950s, but also in the context of expanding subcultures of male homosexuals and lesbians during the post-war decade (D'Emilio 1983). It was the juncture of the increasingly sophisticated gay communities of cities like New York and San Francisco with a newly politicized movement of 'gay liberationists' in the late 1960s that provided the energy for the emergence of mass gay and lesbian movements in the USA in the 1970s and 1980s (Weeks 2015). This provided a model which other countries followed wherever local conditions permitted. 'Gay', as I have suggested, has now become a universal signifier, though acquiring subtly different meanings in different cultures (Altman 2001).

Conditions that made it possible for homosexuality to find a voice have not always been present for other groupings. The intense stigma attached to inter-generational sex, and its inevitable overlap with child sex abuse has made it very difficult for its advocates to develop a substantial subculture, find a common voice or group together over long periods in stable organizations. Characteristic organizations that developed in the 1970s, like NAMBLA (North America Man Boy Love Association) in the USA and PIE (Paedophile Information Exchange) in Britain, soon experienced social obloquy and constant police attention, and

the mainstream gay and lesbian movement sharply dis-
sociated themselves. Perhaps more crucially, it is not an
activity that lends itself easily to the establishment of stable social communities (whatever the public perception of
conspiracies of abusers), given the social hostility and the
transient nature of adult-child relationships.

On the other hand advocates of sado-masochistic sex or
the now more commonly used acronym BDSM (covering
bondage, discipline, submission, sadism and masochism),
have developed support networks and subcultures in various cities across the globe, as sexualities have become, in
Giddens' (1992) not altogether happy phrase, more 'plastic'.
BDSM became an issue of major sexual political controversy in various radical movements, with both the feminist
and gay and lesbian movements sharply divided about the
merits of such activities in the 1970s and 1980s. But to an
unexpected degree the iconography of BDSM has entered
the public arena, diluting its political threat and mobilizing energies. Issues related to transgender activities have
also been controversial, though debates in these cases have
not been so much about sexual activity as about whether
transgender confirms or radically subverts assumptions
about gender. Sex work (on the streets, in brothels, in
pornography, strip clubs, on the web) have posed different problems again for political organization: about the
validity of working in the commercial sexual field, about
women servicing male fantasies, which often involve the
playing out of desires for violence and degradation, and
about the international trade in women and children.

But although the conditions for the emergence of powerful political organizations on the model of gay and

lesbian groupings may vary, the fact is that through an increasingly globalized, mediatized and digitalized world new networks and communities have emerged around sexual issues, and through these a range of sexual identities have been both affirmed or challenged, generalized or particularized. In cyberspace, especially, new opportunities have exploded for exploring who or what you are with no necessary juncture between material bodies and erotic fantasies and play, offering ever growing opportunities for both pleasure and danger, political and cultural mobilization and spaces for exploitation.

In this new erotic economy, there no longer appears to be a great continent of normality surrounded by small islands of disorder. Instead we can now witness huge clusters of islands, great and small, which seem in constant motion one to the other, each with its own unique vegetation and geography. New categories and erotic minorities have emerged. Older ones have experienced a process of subdivision as specialized tastes, specific aptitudes and needs become the basis for proliferating sexual identities. The list is potentially endless as each specific desire becomes a locus of political statement and possible social identity.

A number of questions inevitably arise: Is each form of desire of equal validity? Should each subdivision of desire be the basis of a sexual and possible social identity? Is each claim for identity of equal weight in the debates of sexual politics? What about the heterosexual identity, which is rarely articulated but provides the master discourse? Is identity indeed an appropriate category for thinking of the flux of erotic experience? Does identity not delimit, constrict and constrain free choice? Aren't identities simply narrative devices to provide a sense of security and stability, ultimately fictions, if 'necessary fictions' (Plummer 1995; Weeks 1995)?

Queering the pitch

Earlier I signalled that the term 'queer' is part of the complex history of sexual identity. For decades a term signalling both external opprobrium and subcultural self-description in the world of homosexuality, gay liberationists decisively abandoned it in the 1970s because of its connotations of self-loathing. By the 1990s, however, it had been adopted again by sex radicals, as a mark of rejection of binary systems of classification (male/female, heterosexual/homosexual) and of identities. Queer activism challenged 'regimes of the normal' and the heteronormative structuring of sexuality and gender (Warner 1993; Jagose 1996; Brown 2015). Its origins were in the radical activism of AIDS Coalition to Unleash Power (ACT UP) and similar groups appalled by the abject neglect of the AIDS crisis, and the general moral conservatism of the USA in the 1980s and early 1990s, but it overlapped with new (or at least newly rediscovered) theoretical tendencies that stressed difference and non-identitarian perspectives against what was seen as the growing conformism of the mainstream gay movement. Queer theory opened challenging new perspectives, largely building on earlier constructionist debates while incorporating critical insights from literary theory and cultural critiques. Now the perverse, far from being a signifier of sickness, or a condition requiring apologetics, was seen as a position from which the norm could be challenged. Transgression becomes the defining characteristic of a politics of subversion.

The American queer scholar Lisa Duggan (2003) saw in the identity politics of the USA, with its obsession with legal reforms and same-sex marriage, a symbiotic entanglement of gay activism with social conformism, giving rise to what she described as 'homonormativity'. Jasbir Puar (2007), going further, proclaimed the existence of 'homonationalism', signalling the white lesbian and gay alignment with the excesses of what was seen as a neo-colonialist and Islamophobic human rights discourse. For many radicals a straightforward identity politics was no longer enough. In some ways it was the problem. A celebration of diversity had its limits, not least because it chimed with neo-liberal free market ideology, and could not be detached from wider issues of race, poverty, globalization, inequitable power and the meanings of social justice (Haritaworn 2012).

And yet, of course questions of identity keep returning. 'Queer' itself can become the basis for a non-identity identity. A self-description such as 'I am queer' is rich in ambiguity, but also is a clear positioning in the politics of identity. And political and cultural identifications emerge all the time in this age of identity politics. Two relatively new examples illustrate graphically the limits of sexual categorization, one suggesting an obsessive individual preoccupation with sex, the other a rejection precisely of the culture's obsessions: sex addiction and asexuality.

Sex addiction emerged as an individual disorder just as previously medicalized categories such as homosexuality were being challenged, and speaks to a culture that requires therapeutic explanations for what comes to be regarded as aberrant behaviour, in this case compulsive sexual activity, usually with multiple partners. It subsumes in some respects what used to be known in earlier sexological times as priapism, 'Don Juanism' and nymphomania, moralistic or medico-moral terms that carried heavy cultural condemnation. Sexual addiction, contrariwise suggests a personal problem that can be addressed by clinical treatment, or two-step self-help programmes, in what has become a multi-million dollar therapeutic industry. It has nevertheless interpellated thousands of the famous and not so famous (up to 6 per cent of the American population by some estimates) as ready subjects of this would-be scientific classification (Carnes 2001; Reay et al. 2015). It suggests above all that in a world of unparalleled sexual choice many find comfort in a category, even an identity, that suggests excessive sex is a burden.

The asexual category, like sex addiction, has clinical antecedents, notably in the concept of frigidity, but has developed a more positive flavour as an identity category for many who reject the burden of sexualized definitions and classifications. It has been defined as a 'sexual orientation' marked by a lack of sexual attraction towards any gender. It is not equivalent to celibacy or deliberate or involuntary abstinence. Nor, for some self-defined asexuals, does it necessarily preclude some sexual activity. It's just, according to Asexuality Archive.com (2012), that asexuals are not attracted to anyone, and that is not a problem. Like many newly defined sexual categories, asexuality has developed a growing literature, an endorsement of diversity, numbers of people affirming their self-proclaimed subjectivity and identity and a simultaneous queering of the category. It is marching out of the textbooks into people's lives, opening new possibilities of self-recognition (Carrigan et al. 2014; Cerankowski et al. 2014).

The proliferation of sexual categories, and invention of sexual identities, is apparently never-ending, shifting the boundaries, confusing the classifications, intersecting various subjectivities, subverting and refreshing the languages of sexuality.

DECONSTRUCTING THE CATEGORIES

Acts and context

To affirm the existence of diversity does not answer difficult questions: it merely raises new ones. The first point to make is that the admitted *fact* of sexual diversity need not lead to a widely acceptable or accepted *norm* of diversity. The efforts made by social moralists and fundamentalist groupings over the past 50 years to encourage or enforce a return to 'traditional values' suggests that some people at least have not given up the hope of a revival of a universal moral standard. There are also powerful tendencies among quite disparate radical groups to search for a new morality in which the corrupt elements of a liberal/capitalist/bourgeois/Western/imperialist/patriarchal/heteronormative society – the language varies – could be finally eliminated. The problem here lies in the fact that even among the sexually marginalized and vocal sexual minorities there is often little agreement, indeed sometimes there is passionate and sometimes fierce disagreement. Is pornography constitutive of male violence, a reflection of a generally sexist society, or harmless? Is bisexuality a challenge to rigid binarism or a refusal to make up your mind? Is inter-generational sex a radical challenge to arbitrary divisions of age, or is it child sex abuse? Is transgender a rejection of the tyranny of gender or is it a surrender to such sexual divisions and stereotypes? Does BDSM involve a submersion in dangerous fantasies – or worse – of violence, or is it a more or less harmless playing out of eroticized power relations? These questions, and many others, are important because they challenge us to rethink the criteria by which we are able to decide between appropriate and inappropriate behaviour and practices.

The sexual tradition for a long time basically offered only two positions: either sex is fundamentally dangerous, acceptable only when channelled into appropriate channels (generally, marital procreative sex); or sex is basically healthy and good, but it has been repressed, distorted and denied by a corrupt society. A third approach, which is the one I have advocated in this book, argues that sexuality only attains meaning in social relations, which implies that we can only make appropriate choices around the erotic by understanding its historical, social, cultural and political context. This involves a decisive move away from the morality of 'acts', which has dominated sexual theorizing for hundreds of years, and in the direction of a relational perspective which takes into account context and meanings. Many still take it for granted that sin or salvation, morality or immorality, normality or abnormality reside solely in what we do. This was enshrined in the Christian codes of the Middle Ages, in the tables that declared that heterosexual rape was higher up the scale of value than masturbation or consensual sodomy, because the former was procreative and the latter were barren. There, the priority given to reproduction dictated the hierarchy of value.

In the twenty-first century we are ostensibly more tolerant (though that is not always apparent in those fundamentalist or ultra-nationalist regimes which believe that homosexuals or female adulterers deserve being stoned to death in the name of religious values), but many still take for granted the assumption that some practices are inherently better than others. Now, however, we tend to give more credit to nature, biology or the science of sex rather than blind faith for revealing this hierarchy. Anal intercourse is no longer the worst crime known to Christians – though until a 2003 Supreme Court decision it was still illegal in some parts of the USA, and remains so in a majority of countries in the former British Empire. Masturbation is no longer the gateway to horrors among young people, and is encouraged by books, magazines and newspapers on every station bookstall or street corner, and one of the pleasures positively incited by the internet.

Sometimes changes are the result of scientific reassessment. More usually they are the result of moral and political shifts helped by well-organized campaigns. It was the militant organization of lesbians and gays, not any scientific breakthrough, that led to the removal of homosexuality from the list of disorders in the *Statistical and Diagnostic Manual* (DSM) of the American Psychiatric Association in 1974 (Bayer 1981). Subsequent revisions of the DSM, culminating in a thorough revision in 2013, trace a major shift in the diagnosis of sexual disorders and their treatment which sceptics would say owe little to science (APA 2013). Similarly, passionate campaigns by feminists, social purity men and women, and reformers of various persuasions over the past 100 years, not advances in knowledge, have shifted perceptions of sexual abuse, the international sex-trade, pornography and sex work, birth control and abortion in various directions. But the unconscious belief that some acts are better than others still exists, even if, in a pluralistic world, we cannot always agree what that order ought to be.

A relational perspective attempts, on the other hand, to understand all these sexual activities as social practices and as aspects of wider social relations, in order to unravel the context in which acts become meaningful. This in turn involves attempting to understand the power relations at play, the subtle coercions which limit the possibilities of choice, the likely impact of a particular sexual activity on the self and others, as well as the possibilities of pleasure and personal autonomy that may be encouraged. There are very difficult issues at stake in such an endorsement of radical sexual pluralism, and I shall attempt to explore these later. The point that needs underlining here is that such a perspective must involve breaking with any moral system based on acts as such.

If we do this it is no longer possible simply to condemn a sexual practice because it is 'homosexual' or 'heterosexual' or 'sado-masochistic'. Instead we should begin to ask: what makes this particular activity valid or invalid, appropriate or inappropriate? What are the social factors that make these practices meaningful? What are the power relations at work? If we take a few current examples we will see the type of factors that might be taken into account.

Heterosexuality and its discontents

The first example is of heterosexuality. Heterosexuality is so much taken for granted as the norm across all cultures that it is rarely questioned. It has been the given of sexual theorizing, the natural form by which we judge others. Until quite recently, there has been little attempt to theorize it, or trace its history (Katz 1995). Some feminist critics of its current form have ended up rejecting all forms of heterosexuality because it supposedly perpetuates male dominance. For writers such as Adrienne Rich, 'compulsory heterosexuality' is the key mechanism of control of women, and hence institutionalized heterosexuality is the master discourse that shapes and defines the sexual order (Rich 1984; see also Jackson 2000). Theorists have discussed this issue in various terms: the 'heterosexual matrix', the 'heterosexual panorama' the 'heterosexual imperative', and so on, while queer theorists have spoken of 'heteronormativity' (Warner 1993). All are attempts to explain the defining, normalizing power of the heterosexual assumption, which marginalizes other sexualities at best, and invalidates them at worst.

But while recognizing the power of the institutionalized form, we also need to be aware of different contexts and meanings. Heterosexuality may well be an institution which locks men and women into relations of power, domination and subordination, and creates and excludes the Other, but it is also a series of practices, not a single sexual phenomenon (Segal 2015). The term embraces loving relationships as well as rape, choice as well as coercion. It covers a multitude of sexual activities from intercourse in the missionary position to oral and anal intercourse. As a term it obscures differences of age, of gender, of culture and even of the fantasies of the partners involved. A relational perspective would start out not with the object choice or the act (genital intercourse) which is taken as its most characteristic form, but with the host of factors that shape its significance. Is the sexual act itself one means of perpetuating relations of domination and subordination? If so, what are the alternatives? Does the possibility exist for equal relations between men and women? Is change necessary, desirable, possible? And perhaps most profound of all is the underlying question: how stable and unchanging are the structures of heterosexuality, and behind them the fixity of gender?

Bisexuality

Bisexuality has been often ignored by sociologists of sexuality who have focused more on the binary divide of heterosexuality/ homosexuality (Monro 2015). Yet it is simultaneously one of the basic ideas of sexuality, and one of the most ambiguous and challenging. It has been a familiar idea at least since the Ancient Greeks, who speculated on the fundamental bisexual basis of both gender and the erotic. From the late nineteenth century, meanings extended not only to refer to the constitutional make-up of an individual and the nature of the embryo, but also to a person's object-choice and sexual practices.

In more recent times this shifted into a description also of sexual orientation and identity: not simply that 'everyone' was constitutionally bisexual at birth, as Freud suggested, but that the 'bisexual' was a particular type of person (Angelides 2001).

Though the idea of bisexuality pointed to the arbitrariness of the distinction between heterosexuality and homosexuality, which was emerging at the same time as the concept of bisexuality, it was often seen as a failed heterosexual identity, or a half-way house to a homosexual identification. Bisexuality was in danger of being a limbo category. This has changed since the 1970s with the emergence of sexual rights and liberation movements, where new identities began to proliferate. Now bisexual became a self-proclaimed identity in its own right. Bisexuals constructed their own communities and social worlds, with campaigning groups, social facilities, newsletters, books, and websites, chatrooms and all the facilities of a distinctive social group. Bisexuality emerged as a separable sexual orientation, with its own form of hostility, denigration and prejudice – biphobia. Bisexuality had come out as a fully formed way of being. For many in the gay liberation movement of the early 1970s bisexuality was seen as a cop-out, a failure to face the full consequences of coming out. For many women involved in second-wave feminism, bisexuality offered a transition to lesbianism, or an exploration of a fuller female sexuality. But for many self-declared bisexuals their identity was as valid, and clear cut, as more firmly established lesbian or gay identities, an essential aspect of the challenge to discrimination and prejudice, and the claim to human rights. This has been reflected in the political labelling that developed in the 1990s, where bi or bisexual was firmly wedded to a broad coalition of sexual activists.

Such a common identification, however, carries its own contradictions. Some bisexual activists, for example, felt that the rise of same-sex marriage as a key lesbian and gay issue undermined sexual radicalism and any challenge to heteronormative values – for example through polyamory – and threatened to consolidate an ethnic-type lesbian and gay identity (Klesse 2006). Garber (1995) sought to recover the radical implications of Freudian thought by arguing that society has depended on the repression of bisexuality for its very definition of civilization. The subversive return of the repressed through the celebration of bisexual desire can queer the settled order and conventional sexual categories, and open up new possibilities for pleasure, without the fixity of identity. Other critics have also argued that there has been a commodification of bisexual desires in a fashion 'ideally suited to, and thoroughly complicit with, the postmodern ethos of consumer capitalism' – though in this it is no different from other forms of sexuality (Storr 2003: 159). Against this, activists have argued that bisexuality, alongside transgender, should be seen as a part of the struggle against the rigidities of traditional categorizations, and a vital aspect of the fluidity of sexuality and gender.

There is no reason to think that the practice of bisexuality in and of itself, is any more transgressive than any other sexual practice. Context is all. At the same time, the concept of bisexuality has always had within it the ability to disrupt dichotomous ideas of sexuality, to go beyond binarisms, and to suggest the multiple possibilities of sexual desire, or polysexualities (Beckman 2011). The history of bisexuality suggests the uncertainties at the heart of the idea of sexuality, and the complexities and multiplicities of lived sexual experience.

The transgender challenge

Gender practices that decisively break with the naturalness and stability of conventional assumptions about masculinity and femininity fundamentally undermine any ahistorical notions about the fixity of gender and the naturalness of heterosexuality. Transgender practices, including cross-dressing, cross-living, gender fluidity and physical transitioning, subvert the very notion that there is an original true nature which underpins compulsory heterosexuality and heteronormativity (Rubin 1999: 184).

Since the turn of the millennium transgender has had an ever-growing public presence, to the extent that as I write it is being touted as one of the most significant social movements of our time. This is largely a result of the self-activity of trans people over a long period, resulting in significant political, legal and social advances in many jurisdictions in the Global North and South (Stryker 2008). This has been accentuated by the global publicity given to the transitioning of several prominent public figures, often associated with sporting achievement. But the transgender challenge has a central ambivalence. Transgender as a category embraces both a move towards the essentializing of traditional gender, and a profound unsettling of gendered beliefs. It is the first element that has attracted the most heated controversy, especially from some feminists who see both cross-dressing and transsexuality as a surrender to the most stereotyped gender imagery (most famously Raymond 1979), an all too easy acceptance that there is a true gender that trans people want to live. It is also, ironically, a critical and necessary stance for many pre-operative trans people in a number of countries who have to convince the authorities before they can receive access to medical intervention not only that they passionately believe that they are currently living in the wrong gender, but also that they can live in the other gender. The acceptance in many jurisdictions that trans people can claim certain new rights, for example to medical treatment and to change their birth certificates, is based on the assumption that they have been trapped within the wrong body, and have now transitioned to a new self. This, Morgan (1999: 234) argued, is the 'transsexual dilemma'. In order to obtain basic rights trans people must present a coherent, essentialist identity without ambiguity.

But at the same time, the emergence of the broader category of transgender or trans as a central motif in the struggles over gender and heteronormativity since the 1990s reflects a radical challenge, which has been widely taken up within queer theory and politics. 'Gender fucking', transgressing gender norms in dress and behaviour, had been a key element in Gay Liberation since its stormy birth at the now nearly mythic Stonewall riots in New York in 1969, where a number of trans people were militant participants (Playdon 2004; Weeks 2015). The subversive and transgressive emphasis of the contemporary transgender moment represents a further shift, in which 'transgender' becomes an umbrella for all cross-living and cross-dwelling people, a whole gamut of 'gender complex' people (More and Whittle 1999). The public emergence of trans people as a collective presence represents the emergence of new forms of agency. In the process, the trans person has become an iconic figure for boundary crossing, for challenging fixity, and the transgender experience has 'increasingly come to be seen as a privileged vantage point from which it is possible to observe how sexed and gendered bodies are conceived and enacted in everyday life' (Kulick 1998: 259; Namaste 2000). Drag queens, drag kings, transmen, transwomen, bi-gender persons, cross-dressers, gender queers, gender ambiguous, intersexed and gender fluid people – all suggest that the gender constellation is not binary but multi-polar, polyvocal and subversive (Halberstam 1998, 2005; see discussion in Elliott 2009).

Yet the queer celebration of transgression can obliterate the ordinariness of transition, and erase crucial distinctions, for example between the butch queer lesbian and a transperson, or the specific experiences of pre- and post-operative transsexuals (Rubin 1999: 189). Prosser has spoken of transition as a journey not an event, but a journey that has its own specifications and location, not a post-modern celebration of mobility (in Rubin 1999: 91, 110). This is well put. Journeys across boundaries, migrations, are a common feature of the contemporary world. They are not mythic adventures, they are not necessarily transgressive. They are part of a life-long process of negotiating identity, difference, marginality, the right of exit, and the right to voice (Ekins and King 2006; Hines and Sanger 2012; Hines 2013).

The play of power: BDSM

BDSM has in recent years emerged from the shadows (Moore 2010). Consensual BDSM has become for many the basis of a viable personal and collective identity, focused on the eroticization of power itself. As an early advocate of consensual BDSM put it: 'we select the most frightening, disgusting or unacceptable activities and transmute them into pleasure' (Califia 1979: 19).

For the theorists of the sexual tradition, sado-masochism had its roots in an exaggeration of the normal relations intrinsic between men and women. For Krafft-Ebing, sadism was 'nothing else than excessive and monstrous pathological intensification of phenomena – possible too in normal conditions, in rudimental forms – which accompany the psychical sexual life, particularly in males . . . Masochism is the opposite of sadism . . .' (Weinberg and Levi Kamel 1983: 27). But even Krafft-Ebing had to recognize that a pathologized description of this sexual phenomenon was insufficient. One of his early case studies, from whom he apparently learnt a great deal in an ongoing dialogue, was an articulate advocate of sado-masochism (Oosterhuis 2000). Over the past century there have been various attempts to articulate SM as a benign sexual variation and choice.

Consensual BDSM is a catch-all label which embraces a range of activities, including 'all sexual identities and practices involving pain play, bondage, dominance and submission and erotic power exchange' (Langdridge and Barker 2007: 6). Not all practitioners would wish to see these activities as the basis for identity, nor would even those who go public on their activities and identities see them as necessarily radical or transgressive. It is simply an aspect of their sexual life. Yet for many advocates of BDSM from within the sexual cultures of the West, there is a larger agenda. Consensual BDSM, it is argued, provides unique insights into the nature of sexual power, therapeutic and cathartic sex revealing the nature of sexuality as ritual and play (Linden et al. 1982; Samois 1982; Mesli and Rubin 2015).

New sexual stories around BDSM have proliferated in recent years, and these stories are clearly expressing new needs and a wider sense of identification around once outlawed and execrated sexual activities. On one level there is no necessary link between the various possible practices, iconographies, uniforms, fetishisms and sexual pleasures that huddle under the general label. BDSM is as arbitrary a sexual category as any other we have discussed. But its growing public profile may also be seen as indicative of a wider shift: as a logical extension of severing the link between reproduction and sexuality, which is a characteristic feature of the contemporary sexual world. What the advocates of consensual BDSM effectively do is pose very dramatically the question of where the limits of sexual experimentation and pleasure can be drawn. If pain, domination and submission, ritual and power play are not in themselves intrinsically wrong, and are all enacted in the context of informed choice, then we need to think again about the relationship between context and choice, subjectivity and consent in talking about sexuality. Should people have the right to consent to activities that are conventionally regarded as painful and potentially harmful? What are the conditions that make such choices valid? Is there the same possibility of free choice between say a man and a woman as there is between people of 'the same caste' (gay, two women)? The activities of the 'sexual fringe', among which proponents of BDSM may be seen as radically transgressive members, may remain marginal to the mainstream of most people's sexual lives, but they do in fact ask major questions about what are the limits of normality, what are the boundaries of valid sexual activity, and what are the extremes to which we can go in the pursuit of pleasure.

The limits of consent: Paedophilia

The power relations that sex can involve are most dramatically illustrated by the question of sex between adults and young people, broadly known as paedophilia. Few topics arouse such fear and anxiety in contemporary societies. The 'paedophile' has become a symbol of predatory evil, a synonym indeed not only for child sex abuser but also in many cases for child abductor and even murderer. The peculiar horror invoked by the abuse of innocence, by the imposition of adult desires on the vulnerable, powerless child, speaks for a culture that is profoundly anxious about the boundaries and differences between adults and children, and has become increasingly concerned with protecting the young as long as possible. Yet this has not always been the case.

In the late nineteenth century paedophilia was lauded by some for its pedagogic possibilities – the so-called Greek love justification. In the passage from childhood dependence to adult responsibility, guidance, sexual and moral, of a caring man can be invaluable, it was argued (Angelides 2004a). It was further legitimated in the twentieth century by the supposed facts of childhood sexuality: sexology itself revealed the wide extent of childhood sexual potentiality including the existence of infantile masturbation (Egan and Hawkes 2010). If something is so natural, and omnipresent, should it be as rigidly controlled as childhood sexuality is today? And again, if it is natural, then surely it cannot be harmful even if it takes place with adults. As Tom O'Carroll, a militant supporter of inter-generational sex (who ended up in prison for his pains) wrote '. . . there is no need whatever for a child to know "the consequences" of engaging in harmless sex play, simply because it is exactly that: harmless' (O'Carroll 1980: 153).

Such comments have aroused fierce condemnation. For the vast majority of people, sex with children is not harmless play, it is simply child sex abuse, involving powerful adults using their experience and wiles to gain satisfaction from exploiting children. The growing sensitivity to abuse is the result of long campaigns, often led in Western countries by feminists, or by campaigners who experienced abuse themselves (Angelides 2004b). This has become a global phenomenon, with international campaigns to end the traffic in children and the worst abuses of sex tourism. This without doubt marks an advance in society's awareness of the reality of exploitation, and the power of adults over children. Yet there is something rather odd in the ways in which various late modern societies, from Australia to Europe to the USA, have focused on the figure of the anonymous paedophile rather than on the hard reality that most abuse of children is carried out by a close relative or family friend, or perhaps by a priest, as a wave of scandals from the UK and Ireland to Australia and the USA has underscored over the past two decades (Loseke et al. 2003).

Despite, or perhaps because of, the emotiveness of the issue, it is important to be as rational and dispassionate as possible in looking at what is involved. Age is an ambiguous marker. Is there an ideal age at which consent becomes free, rather than abusive, and a relationship becomes consensual, rather than coercive? Certainly the vast majority of people could agree that it should not be 3 or 8, but what about 12 or 14 or 15 which are the ages of consent in various European countries? The DSM-5, the latest version of the American Psychiatric Association's *Diagnostic and Statistical Manual of Mental Disorders*, makes an uneasy distinction between paedophilia, defined as sex with pre-pubescent children, and hebephilia, an erotic preference for pubescent children, which it appears to suggest is less worrisome (American Psychiatric Association 2013). Critics would point out that this clinical classification still ignores power imbalances between adults and young people. The reality is that attitudes and practices are quite inconsistent across cultures. Laws vary enormously, and sometimes affect boys and girls quite differently. Brian Taylor pointed to the existence of eight possible subcategories of inter-generational sex, depending on the age of those involved, the distinction of gender, the nature of the sexual proclivity, and the interaction of all three (Taylor 1981). This suggests that there are paedophilias, not a single paedophilia, and the social response should be sensitive to these distinctions, even as it focuses rightly on protecting the young and vulnerable.

MAKING CHOICES

The categories I have selected for discussion here have different social weights and implications. Their histories may be intertwined but they have had, and continue to have, distinctive historical trajectories. But the fact we can analyse them now as changing historical and sociological phenomena, and not as natural givens, indicates how far we have come in our understanding of human sexualities. And this is not simply a privilege of the academic few. At the end of the nineteenth century, when these issues began to be aired in the discreet pages of the new sexology, the appetite for knowledge may have been substantial, but the audience was relatively limited. Today, we live in the midst of a discursive explosion, a vast efflorescence of sexual stories (Plummer 1995, 2003). Some individuals may be too shy or modest to confess their secret desires to their partners or closest friends but appear to have no difficulty in telling all to millions of television viewers in reality shows, or in indulging their fantasies across the anonymous spaces of the internet.

We have come a long way. But the fact that we can tell our stories so insistently does not obviate the fact that stories have different weightings, embody diverse values, and impact differentially on people. We still need to make distinctions. Deconstructing the unitary categories of the moralists and the early sexologists has the inestimable value of opening up crucial debates about the parameters within which valid decisions and choices can be made.

Two final points need to be made. First of all, the acceptance of the idea that there are benign social variations should not imply an abandonment of distinctions. There are certain classes of act connected with sex that can find universal condemnation as malignant, especially those involving deliberate acts of violence, whether in the form of sexual murder, rape or child abuse. This is the class that Stoller appears to be addressing in his attempt to theorize perversion as the erotic form of hatred. It is a potentiality in all of us, in his view, which relates to the tensions and anxieties produced by the necessity of attaining particular gender identities. The issue that needs stressing is that, even here, it is not the act itself which constitutes the problem but the whole context – social and psychic – that gives rise to it, and from which it takes its meaning; factors such as family circumstances or male anxiety and power. In other words, if the perversion in this sophisticated psychoanalytic approach is in fact a revolt against the limits imposed by culture, a means of eluding, in Chasseguet-Smirgel's phrase, 'the fatal character of the Oedipus complex', a life-denying leap away from reality, then it is still that culture, that reality which can help us to understand the individual activity (Chasseguet-Smirgel 1985: 26). The traditional concentration on the aetiology of the individual's act can no longer be sufficient.

This leads to the second point, concerning the real meaning of the concept of diversity. As Plummer wrote in the fairly early stages of this debate:

> however neutral and objective talk about sexual diversity appears to be, it is also talk about power. Every culture has to establish – through both formal and informal political processes – the range and scope of the diversities that will

be outlawed or banned. No culture could function with a sexual free-for-all, but the pattern of these constraints is exceedingly variable across time and space.

(Plummer 1984: 219)

The vital point here is that the distinctions we make are in the last resort ethical or political ones, dependent less on the rational weighing of evidence than on cultural traditions and the political balance of forces. It is for this reason that questions of sexuality are inevitably, inescapably, political questions.

What is ultimately wrong with the traditional use of the term 'perversion' is that its ostensibly scientific terminology obscures moral and political judgements. It forecloses discussion. The advantage of embracing the idea of 'diversity' is that it leaves the important questions wide open – to debate, negotiation and political choice.

5

SEXUALITY, INTIMACY AND POLITICS

SEXUALITY ON THE FRONT LINE

Sexuality as a battleground

All civilizations and cultures have to be concerned with the regulation, organization and ordering of sexuality and gender. In the West a preoccupation with sexuality has been at the heart of its concerns since before the triumph of Christianity. It has been a matter of political debate for something like two hundred years. Already, by the last decades of the nineteenth century, many of the preoccupations of second-wave feminism in the 1970s were on the agenda: concerning male power over women, sexual exploitation, the differences between men and women and the meaning of consent and choice. By the 1920s and 1930s, with the rise and fall of a world sex reform movement, the apparently irresistible rise of social authoritarianism and fascism, and a greater willingness even in

Western democracies to intervene in personal life, the intricate connections between sexual values and political power, especially in institutionalizing normative heterosexuality, were clearly visible (Canaday 2009; Herzog 2011). It was during this period, through the writings of such people as Wilhelm Reich, that a concept connecting sex and politics – 'sexual politics' – first came into being.

It is fair to say, nevertheless, that only since the 1960s has the idea of sexual politics had an overwhelming impact and resonance, moving from the periphery to the centre in terms of policy, and moving from the original heartlands of modernity to the rest of the globe in terms of geo-political resonance. Today we take the centrality of sexuality to political discourse for granted as a powerful contemporary reality. Moreover, it is no longer a politics confined to what can broadly be called 'the left' or 'progressive' circles. Since the 1970s some of the most skilful and influential developments of a politics around sexuality and personal life have come from conservative forces, whether the moral traditionalists of Western cultures, the 'fundamentalists' of Christianity, Islam, Hinduism or Judaism across the globe, or a new authoritarian nationalism in parts of Africa and eastern Europe. To an unexpected and unusual degree, sexuality has become a battleground for contending political forces, a front-line of contemporary politics. It seems that for many the struggle for the future of society must be fought on the terrain of contemporary sexuality.

We are, I have argued, in the midst of a long, unfinished revolution in sexual and erotic life, which has gone beyond its Western starting points and has global implications. Since the 1950s there has been a 'great transition' in the relations of sexual and personal life (Weeks 2007). The transition has worked its ways through different cultures at different speeds and rhythms, meeting varying opportunities, challenges and oppositions, and the ramifications and implications are still working their way through particular histories. At its heart is a crucial, if uneven, revolution in the relations between men and women, profoundly unsettled by rapid social change and by the rise of modern feminism, accompanied by a wide ranging destabilization of traditional concepts of gender. This has contributed to, and in turn been shaped by, what Anthony Giddens has described as a 'transformation of intimacy' (Giddens 1992), marked by a decline in the traditional family, the rise of many different ways of sexual life, and the growth of more democratic patterns of relationships.

Alongside this we have seen a series of other dramatic shifts: a challenge to the fixity of the heterosexual/homosexuality binary, and the coming out of LGBTQ ways of life; an explosion of sexual diversity, and a proliferation of new sexual narratives and meanings; and the growth of sexual and intimate citizenship. Together these have defined the politics of sexuality in the contemporary world. We are in the midst of a struggle over the present and future of sexuality, sexual and gender differences, and intimate life, a struggle which has at its heart the aspiration towards egalitarian relations and social justice. But this in turn feeds an ongoing sense of uncertainty about the place we give to the erotic in our lives and relationships, about identity and pleasure, obligation and power, choice and consent. The fixed points which seemed to organize and regulate our sexual beliefs and morals – religious, familial, heterosexual, monogamous – have been radically undermined during the past half-century. And far from abating, the rate of change is gathering speed as the forces of globalization ensure that no sexual culture can escape the challenge of dramatic transformation.

Under the uniformity propounded by religious or national traditions there always lay the devil of diversity. Nevertheless, the recognition of sexual and social diversity as a spectacular fact of the contemporary, increasingly globalized, world has sharpened the dilemma of how to cope with it. Increasing numbers no longer look to tradition to find their moral and ethical anchors. They are forced by the juggernaut of change to find their lodestars in themselves, in their individual judgement and choices. This can be liberating; it can also face individuals with the loneliness, the terror, of moral choice (Elliott and Lemert 2006).

Nostalgic longings

Rapid change often breeds a profound nostalgia, a melancholic longing for the pieties and simplicities of a lost era. It seems to be one of the characteristics of people faced by social change to yearn for a return to a supposed 'golden age' of order, decency, discipline and propriety. The difficulty is that the more we search for it, the more we seem to find ourselves locked into an endless maze where the goal is always just around the next corner. Traditionalists in many Western countries have ventured various historical possibilities. Was this 'golden age' in the 1950s, before the supposed descent into 'permissiveness' during the 1960s, with what the former British prime minister Margaret Thatcher (in a speech of 27 March 1982) called its denigration of 'the old virtues of discipline and self-restraint' (Marwick 1998: 4)? Or could it be found in the years between the great world wars, when writers like the pioneering British advocate of birth control, Marie Stopes, looked forward to a 'glorious unfolding' in relations between men and women (Weeks 2012)? Or perhaps we may find traces of it in the last great flowering of peace and social hierarchy in Europe before the outbreak of the First World War, if we ignore its imperialist assumptions, materialist excesses and upper-class hypocrisy, and widespread social unrest? Each of these periods has had its advocates as a 'golden age' – but, more important, each also had its own prophets of decline and doom, looking yet further back. Yet they of course have an air of provincialism when put into a global perspective. Many post-colonial regimes have looked back to an idealized age before imperial depredations and the imposition of Western sexual norms and legislation (Weeks 2016, chapter 6). And then there are the world-historic certainties and grand perspectives of eternity offered by the fundamentalist prophets, who see modernity itself as the enemy (even as they exploit its scientific breakthroughs to create transnational movements for moral regeneration) (Bhatt 1997).

The historical accuracy of a reference point in the past is, of course, irrelevant to its contemporary power. It provides a yardstick with which to judge the present, usually revealing more about our current discontents than past realities. More particularly, the glorification of the past enables people in the present to pinpoint the imagined movement of decline. And for social conservatives, the 1960s has regularly been portrayed as the period when it all began to go wrong. The changes which the decade has come to stand for – a liberalization of attitudes, heightened individualism, greater freedom of sexual discussion, reforms of the law governing sexual behaviour, and so on – have become symbolic of wider transformation in our relation to traditional values. As Hawkes (2004: 6) has written

> Sexual liberation was a double-edged sword. Certainly it alleviated the embarrassed secrecy that fed ignorance and discouraged open discussion about sexual matters. But it also fed campaigns by conservative movements about promiscuity, the disintegration of the family and the corruption of youth.

It matters little that the impact of the changes of the 1960s were limited at the time. They can be seen as harbingers of much wider transformations.

BEYOND TRADITION

Secularization

A number of underlying historic processes have profoundly and irrevocably undermined traditional ways of being. The first is the secularization of sexuality, by which I mean the progressive detachment of sexual values from religious values – even for many of the religious. This has a long history, but possibly the key feature of its development was the process, beginning in the mid-nineteenth century, whereby the initiative for judging sexuality passed from the Churches to the agents of social and mental hygiene, primarily in the medical profession, and to science more generally. This has been an unfinished revolution in the sense that moral and medical matters remain inextricably linked. You can still be singled out as sick and immoral if you offend our often unspoken norms. Nor, of course, do I intend to imply that the religious have given up their attempts to regulate sex. We only have to observe the rise of religious fundamentalism tied to moral authoritarianism in the Christian and Islamic worlds alike to counter that argument. More broadly, we are in the midst of a global revival of religion which challenges any easy assumption about the inevitable triumph of secularization.

Faith-based movements rail against secularization, and campaigns on sex education, marriage, abortion and same-sex relations are suffused with religious claims and imagery. Yet the fact that these challenges focus on the secular nature of sexual change is a backhanded tribute to how far secularization has gone. Formal demarcations of what is right and proper, appropriate or inappropriate, have become increasingly the province of non-religious experts – in sexology, psychology, medicine, welfare services and social policy. Even in the most traditional of churches, such as the Roman Catholic, many of the faithful routinely ignore their leaders' teaching on birth control, homosexuality or celibacy. From America to Australia, Austria to Ireland, the Church hierarchy itself has been devastated by accusations of paedophilia in the priesthood. Similarly, the puritanical moral codes of the Arab world and its current turmoil have not stopped the growth of a new grass-roots openness about sexuality, while the young people of the Islamic Republic of Iran have started their own sexual revolution within the absolutist codes propounded by their religious leaders (see Mahdavi 2009; El Feki 2013). The fundamentalist emphasis on a rigid sexual code can be seen as, in part at least, a reaction to the dissolving impact of secularization. We reassert the value of that which is most threatened. But today we can reinvent the past and try to capture the future with the most advanced skills of the present. The new theocracies of the Islamic world may be resisting the whole thrust of modernity, but are doing so with the panoply of late modern technology which itself is contributing to the decline of the sacred.

For the non-religious, attitudes have largely floated free of religious sanctions altogether. The process of secularization has gone further in some countries (for example, Great Britain, despite having national churches, and most parts of Western Europe) than in others (especially the USA, despite a formal separation of church and state). In all of them, however, the effect has been to place on sexual relations themselves a greater burden of expectation than ever before. In the absence of any alternative world outlook to that of religion, sexuality itself has become an arena for thinking about personal destiny and belonging.

Individualization

The new surge of expansive energy of world capitalism from the 1980s, which is linked to the wider process of globalization, has served to speed the dissolution of traditional structures, and to encourage the process of 'individualization', which has had a profound effect on family and sexual norms (Beck and Beck-Gernsheim 1995). There is a great historical irony in this. Some of the most prominent proponents of 'setting the individual free' to exploit the new market forces (Margaret Thatcher in Britain, Ronald Reagan in the USA) were moral conservatives and social authoritarians with regard to personal life (at least the personal lives of the masses). However, the very success of their economic ideologies served to fundamentally undermine their moral traditionalism. If you extol individual choice in economic matters, how can you resist the tide towards individual choice in matters concerning intimate life?

Individualization is a social process which dis-embeds the individual from the weight but also from the protection of traditional structures. New opportunities but also new uncertainties are the inevitable result. One significant effect of these major social developments is the drawing into commodity relations and relations of exchange of growing areas of 'private life' (Hennessy 2000; Hawkes 2004). A spectacular example of this has been the vast growth of the market for pornography on a global scale since the 1950s. It has become a multi-billion-dollar industry, completely resilient to various efforts to eliminate it whether from traditionalists or feminists.

There has been a 'mainstreaming' of sexuality in Western culture (Attwood 2009), with female bodies a particular focus. Sex – especially female sexuality – has become a central feature of advertising, a vital element in the selling of everything from cars to central heating. At the same time, new markets for sexualized products have constantly been discovered or created – among adolescents in the 1950s, women in the 1960s, gays and lesbians in the 1980s and 1990s, and pre-pubescents in the present, not least through the marketing of popular (and often sexually inciting) music. These changes have obviously increased the possibilities for exploitation, and their ill-effects can be seen in the form of degrading and objectifying imagery of women, in the seediness of the sex areas of major cities across the globe, in a romanticization of sexual violence, and the commercialization of sexual pleasures. Sex tourism has become one of the least appealing aspects of globalization, a new face to sexual colonialism and exploitation. Prostitution is a huge international industry, with sex workers often becoming commodities to be traded – 'trafficked' – as part of the vast international flows of migration (e.g. O'Connell Davidson 1998; Altman 2001; Seabrook 2001).

Liberalization and the growth of sexual toleration

It is easy to outline the negative effects of sexual change. But it is important to signal too the enormous gains as a result of a wide-spread *liberalization* of attitudes throughout the industrialized West and in parts of the Global South, and an accompanying growth in toleration of individual difference, and acceptance of sexual diversity – especially among and by the young. What was once tabooed has become increasingly taken for granted. Across the world, people are generally more accepting of birth control, abortion, divorce, pre-marital sex, cohabitation of non-married partners and divorce, and of same-sex activity and gender non-conformity. There has been a new recognition of the legitimacy of female autonomy. This does not mean there are not major areas of difficulty, or even plain authoritarianism. The Roman Catholic hierarchy throughout the West has continued its opposition to non-marital sex, artificial birth control, abortion and divorce, even as its congregations have in their millions ignored it. Abortion has been a major divisive cause in the USA. In some Western countries, and more generally across the globe, the law continues to treat homosexuality and heterosexuality differentially, especially in the recognition of same-sex marriage or civil partnerships.

Attitudes to teenage sexuality, and to enlightened sex education also vary enormously, with sometimes disastrous results. Countries like the USA, where sex education has become a significant political divide, and the UK, where attitudes to teenage sex remain ambivalent, have tended to have much higher rates of teenage pregnancy than European countries like The Netherlands, where sex education is efficient and taught early – though recent data suggests the differences are diminishing (BBC 2015). Above all, perhaps, the changes of recent years have differentially affected men and women. There have indeed been greater opportunities for women to express their sexuality, a major encouragement of female sexual fulfilment. But in a culture in which the 'male in the head' continues to hold sway in many circumstances, this has often been in situations defined by men, for the benefit of men (Holland et al. 1998). Outside the highly developed countries, especially in those parts of the world which seek to define themselves against a corrupt or decadent West, the law of male dominance and of (often invented) tradition remains rampant, with violent abuses of the human rights of same-sex people, women and children all too common (Bamforth 2005).

In such a context the concept of toleration seems a feeble barque, and it is perhaps not surprising that the idea of sexual tolerance has been highly contested. The American philosopher Wendy Brown (2006) has argued that the idea of tolerance can hide the historical and power sources of difference, displace ideas of justice and equality, reduce differences to individual experiences, and point to an agenda of individual emotional and behavioural change rather than political and social transformation. This is the 'tolerance trap' that Suzanna Walters has described, where apparent changes in attitudes and public practices in relation to homosexuality in a number of mainly Western countries, and especially the USA, obscure deeper realities of continuing inequality hidden under the warm blanket of toleration.

This points to a fundamental problem with the liberal concept of toleration. It is frequently a stance based on anxiety rather than full acceptance, on acquiescence rather than commitment. For millions across the globe still subject to various forms of sexual oppression and exploitation, tolerance might seem a glorious gift. The problem is that tolerance is always subject to the arbitrary permission of authority and the fickle waves of public opinion, and stops short of full recognition of the validity of different ways of life.

The distinction that Rainer Forst (2013) makes between a 'permission' concept of toleration, and a 'respect' concept offers a useful alternative approach. The first is concessionary and conditional, the second is about mutuality and recognition, and a positive understanding of what toleration can be. A more radical 'respect' version of toleration requires doing more than leaving other people alone. It is based on positively supporting people to seek control of their lives, and on the full validation of different ways of being human.

Despite all the horrors that persist in large parts of the world, a concept of toleration based on mutual respect has been advancing on a global scale. At the very least on all standard measures of opinion, attitudes, if not universally non-authoritarian or non-exploitative, are certainly more varied and open than they were even a generation ago. This has been accompanied by an explosion of discourses around sexuality, a new willingness, and compulsion indeed, to speak about sex, to tell sexual stories in ever more inventive ways, resulting in an unprecedented profusion of sexual speech in everything from self-help literature and internet chat rooms to confessional and explicit television reality programmes. Homosexuality, the love that once dared not speak its name, has assumed an unprecedented volubility, and in its wake a profusion of sexual dissidents have spoken of their needs and rights in a new vocabulary of sexual desire. 'Sexuality' now speaks in many languages and modes, to and for many different types of people, offering a cacophony of alternative values and possibilities.

Cybersex

The internet has provided an explosive and amazingly efficient means of distribution of these proliferating sexual flows. It is revolutionizing sexuality more generally, in ways that are still working their way through the erotic world. Cybersex offers multiple forms of erotic excitement, entice-ment and entanglement, with a proliferation of new forms of interaction. We now have cybersex, cyber-stalking, cyber-rape, cyber-victims, cyber-porn, cyber-voyeurism, compu-sex, sex chat rooms, sex news groups, sex bulletin boards, camcorder sex, virtual sex, cyborgs, online dat-ing sites and apps, social networks, blogs, vlogs: a 'cyber-sexual smorgasbord' in Plummer's evocative phrase. The list is potentially limitless as the power and use of the internet expands and our erotic imagination finds new virtual nooks and crannies (Plummer 2003: 9–12). The internet has become a site for sexual cruising, courtship, chat, confession, dating, self-affirmation, experiment, fantasy, masturbation, friendship, networking, fashion, marketing, embodiment and dis-embodiment and virtual community – and for potential exploitation, violence and threat (Weeks 2007: 158–61). It also has potentially signif-icant political possibilities. It has become a site of feminist and queer spaces and possibilities as well as for the mobi-lization of conservative values and the re-invention of tradition. More radically, it has become a site for new pos-sibilities of individual agency, as ever new spaces open up for human contact and the re-making of subjectivities and identities, on a global scale. Your virtual connection may be with a physical neighbour or with peoples the other side of the world. Cyberspace is now an everyday reality of social interaction and erotic exploration for millions of people beyond the restrictions of borders, cultures, lan-guages and traditional values.

The technological fix

These cyber-phenomena can be seen as part of a wider aspect of the technologization of the erotic as the scientific revolution explodes old certainties, and opens new possibilities. New technologies have shaped various aspects of personal life, from sex aids to reproductive technologies and designer drugs. If science has promised to free us from reproductive inadequacy, it also promises us freedom from sexual inadequacy. Sex may no longer be necessary to reproduction, and reproduction no longer the sole goal of sex, but this has only served to ensure that pleasure and performance can be technologically enhanced. If the Pill was the technological fix of the 1960s, Viagra and its kin chemicals became the fix for the early twenty-first century. Sex in America, said Meika Loe, author of *The Rise of Viagra*, 'will never be the same again' (Loe 2004: 5). But this is not just an American story. Since Viagra was launched by the Pfizer pharmaceutical company in 1998, it has become a global boom story. The little blue pill that 'changed sex in America' has now been joined by others, Cialis and Levitra, that compete for a multi-billion-dollar market, with 'a female Viagra' joining the market in 2015. The wonder pills are now freely available over the counter in many countries as well as illicitly, on a massive scale, through the web. They have ceased to be simply medical alleviators of genuine medical problems. They have become happiness pills offering an instant fix.

In the process, there is an acute danger that anything less than a hyper performance will be pathologized (Tiefer 2006: 273–94). All the science is just window dressing for an industry, Tiefer argues, and the most dangerous aspect of this is the invention of a new medical problem for women, for which the female Viagra may be the solution: 'female sexual dysfunction' (FSD) (see essays in *Sexualities* 2006). The problematization of individual sexualities, and the invention of new problems, is deeply revealing of underlying cultural anxieties. As the old categories of sexual inadequacy are challenged, new ones proliferate. The invention since the 1980s of 'sex addiction' provides a revealing contemporary example: it nods to the sexualization of the culture by pathologizing those who succumb to it (Reay et al. 2015).

Science, as such examples suggest, is no better guide today to sexual dilemmas than it was in the late nineteenth century. Yet for many millions of people escaping from social privation and sexual authoritarianism, the sexual freedoms opened by secularization, individualization, growing social tolerance and science have offered vast new possibilities. The changes of the past generations have acted like a solvent on old certainties and inherited values.

Relationality and the intimate revolution

The effects of all this on actual *behaviour* are more difficult to gauge. There have, clearly, been significant changes in key life choices, particularly in the devaluation of marriage as the only legitimate gateway to adult sexual activity. Yet surveys also demonstrate that despite significant shifts, individual behaviour remains fairly traditional. The high divorce figures (40 per cent of marriages in Britain) can be seen as a sign of the decline of marriage, but also as a desire to end failing relations in the hope of a better one. A high proportion of divorced people remarry – and remarry again if necessary. There is no great surge of polyamorous relationships, despite the growing attention devoted to them (Barker and Langdridge 2010). Serial monogamy, not promiscuity or multiple relationships, is now the norm. Despite the higher profile of same-sex relations, the percentage of the population who see themselves as homosexual, or perhaps more accurately are willing to be open about their sexuality and declare themselves to opinion surveys, appears (at 1 to 2 per cent) much smaller than many believed (or feared). And while the young may be having sex at an earlier age, their sexual practices remain hidebound by fairly traditional beliefs about the right thing to do in male–female relations. Behaviour has lagged behind attitudes (Laumann et al. 1994; Wellings et al. 1994; Johnson et al. 2001).

People on the whole hold fast to values of intimate life, even as the family as we once knew it (or believed we knew it) is no longer so dominant. Western cultures remain suffused by familial values, to the extent that the language of family still provides the dominant vocabulary of truly lasting relatedness that we have. It is surely significant that as lesbians and gays moved from a politics of identity in the 1970s to a politics of relationships and partnership rights in the 1990s and beyond, it was the language of 'families of choice' that emerged (Weeks et al. 2001).

The reality of course is that there is no longer such a thing as 'the family'. Many sociologists now talk about 'relationality' rather than the family as such, recognizing that the need for mutuality and caring relationships at various levels cannot any longer (if they ever could be) be confined within a narrow institutional form (Smart 2007). The traditional connection between marriage, the family and sexuality has been largely severed; but in its place we have no obvious single alternative – rather a plurality of forms. For many this is a grave danger; for others it is the supreme challenge: to move from simply recognizing diversity as a fact to be endured, to seeing it as a value to be cherished.

By the first decade of the twenty-first century, key elements of the great transition had become the settled habits of millions. There was an increasing separation of sex and reproduction, with more effective birth control the norm in Western countries and a major challenge in the Global South. The traditional link between sexual activity and marriage was manifestly crumbling. The link between marriage and parenting was dissolving in the lives of many people. The heterosexual/homosexual binary was visibly fraying, despite many efforts to reassert it. The pillars of traditional gender were under assault, with the growing recognition of the trans experience as the most visible sign of this. The separation of marriage and heterosexuality, especially through same-sex marriage, was high on the political agenda, and the reality in a number of jurisdictions. And above all, new forms of everyday agency were apparent on a global scale as people in their millions adapted to changing possibilities of sexuality and intimate life.

LIVING WITH UNCERTAINTY: HIV/AIDS

Moral panics

The changes described above, while important, have not of course rid the world of sexual hazards and risks. Claims either of 'sexual liberation' or of 'moral decline' would seem to be wide of the mark. Yet the very subtlety and ambivalence of change has contributed to a climate of uncertainty and (for some) confusion. In such a climate, deep currents of feeling come to the surface and find expression in anxiety, fear and panic. It was a tragedy of historic proportions that somewhere in the middle of a huge, messy, confused and uneven transition in sexual values and practices, a crisis emerged that threatened all that had been achieved – AIDS.

A characteristic feature of the popular response was a generalized moral panic. Moral panics are flurries of social anxiety, usually focusing on a condition or person, or group of persons, who become defined as a threat to accepted social values and assumptions. They arise generally in situations of confusion and ambiguity, in periods when the boundaries between legitimate and illegitimate behaviour seem to need redefining or classification.

Classic moral panics in the past have often produced drastic results, in the form of moral witch hunts, physical assault and legislative action. Since the Second World War, there has been an apparently endless series, many of them focusing on moral and sexual issues: over venereal disease, prostitution, human trafficking, homosexuality, child sex abuse and paedophilia, teenage sex, pornography and so on. A significant feature in many of them has been the connection that has been made between sex and disease, disease becoming a metaphor for dirt, disorder and decay. Not surprisingly, panics have emerged over the social and moral connotations of genital herpes, cervical cancer and most dramatically of all, HIV and AIDS.

Epidemic

Particularly in the early 1980s, when the first signs of an unprecedented epidemic emerged among the male gay population of the USA, the reaction to AIDS illustrated the characteristic signs of a classic panic. More important for our discussion here, it revealed also the wider anxieties abroad about the changing place of sexuality in modern culture. The resulting crisis threw light on many dark corners, condensing a number of social stresses into a recognizable symbolic target (Weeks 2000). As the epidemic raged worldwide in the decades that followed, taking millions of people to a premature grave, and even threatening a fundamental breakdown in economic life in some parts of the world, the dangerous connection of sexuality, disease and death has put the erotic to an unprecedented trial.

One of the most striking features of the HIV/AIDS crisis at the start of the epidemic was that, unlike most illnesses, at first the people who were affected by it, and had to live and die with it, were chiefly blamed for causing the syndrome, whether because of their social attitudes or sexual practices. And as most people presenting with HIV/AIDS at the beginning of the epidemic in Western countries were gay men, this was highly revealing about current attitudes and feelings towards unorthodox sexualities. From the earliest identification of the disease in America in 1981–82, AIDS was addressed as if it were a peculiarly homosexual affliction, and the term 'gay plague' became the common description of it in the more scabrous parts of the media.

In fact it was clear from the beginning that other groups of people were prone to the disease: Haitians (in the USA), intravenous drug abusers and haemophiliacs (the latter because of their dependence on other people's blood). It soon became apparent, too, that in large parts of central Africa, where the disease may have originated, and where it seemed to be endemic, it was the general population that was afflicted and it was therefore clearly transmittable through heterosexual intercourse. But it was the apparent connection between unorthodox sexual activity and the disease that chiefly fuelled the major elements of panic in the industrialized West, and for long coloured responses across the globe.

In the normal course of a moral panic there is a characteristic stereotyping of the main actors as peculiar types of monsters, leading to an escalating level of fear and perceived threat, the taking up of panic stations and absolutist positions, and a search for symbolic, and usually imaginary solutions to the dramatized problem. In the case of AIDS there was a genuinely appalling disease, which devastated the lives of many people, for which there was no cure, and which at first seemed unstoppable in its rate of spread. By mid-1985 it had already become the largest single cause of adult male deaths in New York City and was widespread elsewhere. Anxiety was legitimate. However, the form that the anxiety took was a search for scapegoats, and here gay men were peculiarly vulnerable. Certain sexual practices (for example anal intercourse) and social habits (multiple partners) generally (though often misleadingly) associated with male homosexuals were given a prime role in the spread of the disease, and it became easy to attribute blame to people with AIDS. From this a slippage readily took place: between the idea that homosexuals *caused* 'the plague' (itself without any backing in evidence) to the idea that homosexuality itself was a plague. Manifestations of what Susan Sontag called 'practices of decontamination' against the vulnerable soon appeared (Sontag 1983, 1989): restaurants refused to serve gay customers, gay waiters were sacked, dentists refused to examine the teeth of homosexuals, rubbish collectors wore masks when collecting garbage from suspected victims, prison officers refused to move prisoners, backstage staff in theatres refused to work with gay actors, distinguished pathologists refused to examine the bodies of AIDS patients, and undertakers refused to bury them.

The scientific evidence already by the mid-1980s was clear: AIDS was carried by a virus, which was not in itself exceptionally infectious. It was only possible to catch it through intimate sexual contact or interchange of blood. It was not a peculiarly homosexual disease, and most people in the world with the disease were in fact heterosexual. Moreover, its spread could, in all likelihood, be hindered by relatively small changes in lifestyle, particularly the avoidance of certain sexual practices (such as anal intercourse without protection). All this suggested that what was needed was a public education campaign which both allayed fears and promoted an awareness of safer sexual activities. Eventually, across the rich and highly developed world, this is what happened (Altman 1994; Haour-Knipe and Rector 1996; Moatti et al. 2000). But not before fear and ignorance produced a fervour of punitive responses. And as the pandemic spread inexorably across the globe, the pattern of fear, blame, wilful neglect and inconsistent response followed – with a vital difference: whereas in the richer parts of the world, safer sex practices slowed the spread of HIV and from the mid-1990s expensive cocktails of drugs proved effective in slowing down the impact of multiple illnesses, in the majority of the world the epidemic was inextricably linked with poverty and a web of other diseases.

The global impact of HIV/AIDS

As in the West the reaction to the HIV/AIDS epidemic shone a revealing light on deep-rooted anxieties and a prevailing climate of uncertainty, so in the rest of the world, the epidemic revealed structural inequalities, exploitation and the hazards of unprecedented sexual change. Vast disruptions of population in response to rapid industrialization, moves from country to city, migrations across borders, flight in the wake of war, eased the spread of sexual and blood-borne infections. Ignorance (for example, the apparent widespread belief in southern Africa that sex with a virgin would cure sexual infections) or prejudice (against condoms on the grounds that they were unmanly) helped rapid spread. Transnational travel carried the epidemic from continent to continent.

By 2015 there were an estimated 40 million people in the world living with HIV and AIDS, of whom half were women. There were nearly 2 million new infections a year. Thirty-four million people had died. The majority of new infections and deaths were in sub-Saharan Africa, where 26 million were living with HIV/AIDS. But from South

America to South-east Asia, from Eastern Europe to China and India, HIV was a potent threat, portending economic and social collapse, population decline, and ever greater numbers of orphaned children, if the new treatments such as anti-retroviral drugs were not deployed fast and effectively (often much a matter of money and commitment as availability).

In the face of so much horror it seemed difficult at first to find resources for hope. And yet they could be found. Starting in the gay communities of Western cities, but spreading throughout the globe, there was an unprecedented mobilization of community-based responses to HIV and AIDS, ranging from self-instruction in safer sex to advocacy, campaigning and treatment activism. Those most affected often took the lead in combating the epidemic. In the face of disease and death, many people found means of living their lives well. The international mobilization against HIV and AIDS, whether through official bodies like UNAIDS or in proliferating non-governmental organizations (NGOs), helped to develop an international discourse around sexual risk and sexual health – though frequently against the backdrop of state ignorance and neglect. Haphazardly and hesitantly at first, Western expertise and drugs began to alleviate some of the worst suffering. By 2015 some 15 million people were receiving anti-viral treatment in low- and middle-income countries. An unprecedented development of local research studies in Africa, Asia and Latin America as well as the richer countries of the West cast a dazzling light on the diversity of sexual patterns. Sexual practices and identities that had been hidden in shame or ignorance began to find their voice, and open themselves to history, and therefore change. HIV/AIDS, an unprecedented crisis in sexual behaviour, had an uncanny way of revealing the risks, contradictions, confusions, ambiguities, cruelties and opportunities in our relationship to the sexual. It is perhaps not surprising that the initial reaction was fear and panic. All one can say is that combating HIV/AIDS required much more than that: medical commitment, community mobilization, national and international funding – and an understanding of the significance of sexuality in contemporary cultures, and an ability to face its challenges openly and honestly.

SEXUAL AND INTIMATE CITIZENSHIP

Intimacy matters

There has been a proliferation of sexual stories since the eighteenth century, but only in the late twentieth and early twenty-first centuries have these stories gained a mass audience. The sexual stories we tell are deeply implicated in moral and political change, and shifting stories of self, identity and relationships carry the potential, as Plummer has argued, for radical transformations of the social order (Plummer 1995, 2003). They are circulated in and through social movements, communities and networks, and become the focus for thinking through and re-orientating the needs and desires of everyday life. Over the past generation we have seen a change in the forms and organization of the stories we tell each other, and late modern stories reveal and create a multiplicity of new projects, new constituencies, new forms of agency and new possibilities for the future. These are stories of human life chances, of emotional and sexual democracy, of pluralistic forms of sexual life, opening the way for a new culture of intimacy. Issues that were typically wrapped in the discretion of the private sphere have become public, giving rise to a wider concept of citizenship and recognition, what has become known as sexual or 'intimate' citizenship (Evans 1985; Weeks 1998; Plummer 2002 and 2015; Correa et al. 2008).

Citizenship and belonging

Sexual/intimate citizenship, like all forms of citizenship, is about belonging, about rights and responsibilities, social exclusion and social inclusion. It is concerned with equity and justice, and about the implications of claiming full recognition as social and human beings. Traditionally, claims to citizenship have been based on ensuring civil, political, social and economic rights. Since the 1970s the rights discourse has expanded rapidly, embracing gender, race, and a host of other issues, including sexuality. In a global sense the traditional battles for full equality in civil, political, social and economic rights have yet to be fully won, but there is now a widespread recognition that these cannot be separated from issues of intimate life. The international movement for reproductive rights put sexuality and sexual rights at the centre of a nexus of intersecting lines of power, demonstrating the variety of local, national and global forces, and conflicting aspirations, which shape women's claims to self-determination in relation to their bodies. In the same way, the LGBTQ movement has become global in scope, taking on different local preoccupations, adapting to different configurations of oppression/suppression/opportunity. In both cases, the claim to full citizenship necessarily embraces new claims for rights.

The recognition of the intersection of various forms of discrimination, prejudice, exclusion and oppression has become central to rights claims, though it has proved easier to state their interaction than to tease out their intricacies. Various forms of exclusion and oppression, such as those around class, race and ethnicity, are not experienced additively, one after another, but simultaneously in the density of lived experience. Material disadvantage and the experience of racism inevitably configure and limit the opportunities open to full sexual citizenship. But other dimensions of exclusion from full citizenship have also become more visible as new voices open up further perspectives on injustice.

Disability, Alison Kafer (2013) has argued, needs to be recognized as a category of analysis alongside gender, race, class and sexuality. Since the 1970s there has been a growing awareness, led by people with disabilities themselves, that people are largely disabled by society, not simply by their bodies. This approach has been enormously influential, especially in pinpointing the barriers to full citizenship. A traditional deficit model of disability remains influential, however, in relation to the sexual needs and desires of disabled people (Shakespeare et al. 1996). Their sexuality continues to be seen as a problem rather than an opportunity for a rich and fulfilling life. A study by Kulick and Rydström (2015) of attitudes towards sexual practices amongst severely disabled people in Sweden and Denmark vividly illustrates how different perspectives on what constitutes justice can shape policy and practice, even amongst two apparently similar, progressive social democratic, sexually liberal neighbours. In Denmark, the sexuality of people living with disabilities is acknowledged, discussed and facilitated, to the extent that care workers are allowed to intervene to support and help them achieve sexual pleasure. In Sweden, on the other hand, the sexual needs of disabled people are played down, and workers tend to see any facilitating efforts as sexual abuse. In this example, the idea of full sexual citizenship has different meanings and implications, with little common ground.

Age, generation and temporality are further critical dimensions of difference. Sexuality, as Plummer (2010) has argued, is lived differently in different generations, and re-shaped during the life course. At the same time, particular generations are always criss-crossed by other differences, so we do not march through history in phalanxes of age-cohorts. Halberstam (2005) famously spoke of 'queer-time' shaped by different rhythms of LGBTQ experience from the family/reproductive patterns of the heterosexual majority. In her book, Kafer (2013) analogously suggests the significance of 'crip time' as a way of problematizing and challenging concepts of normality. She aims, as she says, to make people wince, to shake things up, to jolt people out of their everyday understanding of bodies and minds.

More broadly, the distinctive demographic patterns of different countries are revealing powerful generational distinctions. We are familiar with the impact of the post-war baby-boomers in carrying new sexual values into the 1960s and 1970s and beyond, with spectacular impact on Western mores. In a similar way, the explosion of populations in many post-colonial countries of the Global South are producing a huge cohort of young people eager for jobs, opportunities, migration – and sexual experience. In the older industrialized nations of the Global North the young population is dwarfed by the baby-boom generation, living to unprecedented old age with needs never before fully articulated.

These generational factors are reflected in struggles within faith communities over sexual ethics and sexual identities (Shipley 2014). It is notable that in Western countries opposition to same-sex marriage on religious grounds increases substantially amongst older men particularly. Contrariwise, the appeal of fundamentalist, sexually conservative values in many parts of the Global South appears to be particularly acute amongst militant young men. At the same time, Christian or Muslim faiths can be a source both of struggle and of an enabling and positive identity for young queer people in various parts of the West (Taylor and Snowden 2014; Taylor 2016).

The politics of sexual and intimate citizenship are today played out in daily struggles over what can be said or performed by whom in what circumstances in a multitude of battlegrounds, institutional, cultural, political and spatial (Bell and Valentine 1995; Binnie 2004). As befits a long revolution, two steps forward are often followed by one step backwards. There is uneven development across various jurisdictions. Yet, as I have tried to indicate throughout this book, the past couple of generations have seen an unprecedented and almost certainly irreversible shift in values and practices, which in turn is being reflected in the achievement in many parts of the world, especially but not only in Western countries, of rights related to the body and sexual choice.

The claim to sexual citizenship has not gone unchallenged, even by supporters of radical sexual change. Some critics of neo-liberalism have argued that the emphasis on individual choice is itself a new form of regulation and control. The social theorist Zygmunt Bauman (2003, 2005) has railed against the frailty of human bonds in new 'dark times', dominated by 'liquid love' and 'liquid life'. The self-reflexive person central to the new individualism is, Adkins (2002: 123) has argued, the ideal subject of neo-liberal discourse, and 'reflexivity is constitutive of new forms of classification, hierarchies, divisions, struggle and forms of contestation'. An emphasis on individual rights and responsibilities, and the importance of self-surveillance and self-regulation for the individual who has internalized the norms and goals of neo-liberal forms of governance, is central to the new global world, Richardson (2004, 2015) has forcefully suggested. We are never more imprisoned, it seems, than when we believe we are most free (see Walters 2014).

Arguments such as these, I believe, seriously misunderstand the real gains of the long transition. Whatever the undercurrents of uncertainty that undoubtedly exist, most people have negotiated the rapids of change without recourse to a transcendent value system, or tradition, in ways which have enhanced their individual choices and freedom, especially in relation to their everyday lives. Most people in the West are not particularly interested in politics or the politics of family and sexuality in particular. They do not have grand visions of new ways of living, even as at an everyday level they do engage in 'experiments in living'. There is pragmatism in the adaptation to changes in everyday life, and a new contingency as people have, in a real sense, to create values for themselves. Most individuals muddle through. People's liberalism may well be limited to a form of live and let live morality. There is no positive endorsement of different ways of life. Yet there are very few households across the richer parts of the world which are not touched by the transformations of everyday life.

Most people know single parents. Most people know a member of their family who may be lesbian or gay. Most households have experienced divorce, remarriage, cohabitation, broken or reconstituted families. In a country like Britain there is a high incidence of sexual partnerships across racial and ethnic divides. We are in the midst of a genuine social transformation where what was once unspeakable has become ordinary.

This has been a grass-roots revolution. Dramatic changes in family and sexual life have not been led by the political elite but by everyday agency. Governments, of course, have to respond, but they inevitably do so in a variety of different ways, depending on political traditions, the prevailing balance of cultural forces, the nature of the political institutions, the day-to-day crises which force some issues to the fore, and the pressure from below, whether from conservative or fundamentalist resistance to change, or from radical social movements, rooted in everyday life. Social movements characteristically veer between 'moments of transgression' and 'moments of citizenship' (Weeks 1995: 108–23). The first highlights the factors that make for social exclusion, and the drama of difference. The second makes the claim for social inclusion, for recognition, for full belonging. In practice, the two moments constantly flow into each other, reinforcing one another. When they do work together the effects can be dramatic – as in the case of same-sex marriage.

Same-sex marriage

The debate over same-sex marriage illustrates some of the tensions and ambiguities that claims to sexual or intimate citizenship inevitably involve. Is same-sex marriage necessary because it will mark the full integration of lesbians and gays into society, as gay conservatives long argued? Or desirable because it mimics, undermines and transgresses the heterosexual institution, as some activists suggested? Is it simply, as many queer theorists stated, an accommodation to the existing order, nothing more than assimilation which drains any challenge to the existing sexual order? Or is it a simple matter of justice?

Whatever the controversies, same-sex marriage or recognized same-sex civil partnerships have rapidly spread. Since Denmark pioneered the legal recognition of same-sex unions in 1989, most Western European countries have followed suit, the majority since the millennium. Even Catholic Italy, long resistant to recognition of same-sex relational rights, adopted a form of equal marriage in 2016. Worldwide, at the time of writing fourteen countries had legalized full same-sex marriage, including Argentina,

Belgium, Brazil, Canada, France, the Netherlands (the first country to promulgate it in 2001), Sweden, South Africa and the United Kingdom (apart from Northern Ireland). Ireland endorsed it in a referendum in 2015. The United States Supreme Court declared the constitutionality of same-sex marriage in the same year. The campaigns for the recognition of partnership rights up to and including equal marriage had taken many forms, and followed various national patterns, from traditional parliamentary battles through mass mobilization to constitutional reform, but within a relatively short period remarkable change had happened (for interim commentaries see Kollman 2007; *Sexualities* 2008).

This has been a major and unexpected transformation. In the 1970s, with the rise of gay liberation ideas across most Western countries, but especially in the USA, very few – whether inside or outside the movement – advocated same-sex marriage. It seemed beyond the horizon of possibility and even of desirability in the context of fierce feminist and LGBTQ critiques of the family and heterosexual marriage (Chauncey 2004). But by the turn of the millennium it had become a hot, divisive political issue throughout Western democracies and more widely.

The salience of the issue signals two important, intertwined changes: shifting priorities within the LGBTQ world itself, and important changes within the national cultures that were clearly liberalizing their attitudes and laws. Kollman (2007, 2013) sees in these shifts the rise of a human rights–oriented network of LGBTQ activists committed to the recognition of 'love rights', and of cross-national political elites educated in new rights discourses and prepared to seize the initiative, even in the absence of high-profile campaigns. A defining characteristic of the remaking of sexuality since the 1950s has been those every-day experiments that happen at a grass-roots, sub-political level, often at first outside and beyond the visibility of historians and sociologists. Surely what is striking about the current prominence of same-sex relations is that it crept up on commentators and theorists unawares, though there were important signals.

The growing interest during the 1990s and early 2000s in families of choice and queer families was a sign of a new emphasis on the importance of relationships within the non-heterosexual worlds (Weston 1991, Weeks et al. 2001). The AIDS crisis had dramatized the absence of legal recognition of partnership rights amongst gay men. At the same time there was growing concern over parental rights especially among lesbians, who were often denied access to their own children, and amongst the growing number of queer men as well as women who wanted to be gay parents but found the law and social attitudes inhibiting or hostile (Rivers 2013). The felt need for same-sex relationship rights grew from the ground upwards. Governmental interventions, influenced as they were by skilful lobbying, were from this perspective a response to changing social realities, not an anticipation of them (Nicol and Smith 2008; Smart 2008).

Whatever the common patterns and underlying trends, however, each country has taken its own path, reflecting its own sexual culture, cultural bias and political balance. The original PACS legislation in France, for instance, which allowed civil unions short of marriage to heterosexuals and homosexuals alike, followed classic republican traditions by refusing to recognise the separate cultural identities of lesbians and gays (Johnston 2008). PACS was clearly distinguished from marriage, whose legal status was not affected: no new legal entity was created, and no challenge was offered to the permanence of sexual difference (the 'symbolic order') or the legitimacy of kin relations ('filiation'). It was opposed by conservatives of left and right, but bedded down as a normalised and widely accepted reform, favoured in fact more by heterosexuals than by LGBTQ people. It paved the way for equal marriage fifteen years later. In the Netherlands radical changes came about through a gradualism which fitted in easily with the tradition, originally rooted in conflicting religious affiliations, that assumed the coexistence of different rights claims, and was committed to recognizing them. The legalization of same-sex civil partnerships, and then of marriage, therefore seemed a logical next step in the Netherlands' institutionalized toleration.

The experience of the United Kingdom shows another variant. For a long time, it was classically hesitant in pursuing the legalization of same-sex partnerships – or indeed any liberalization of attitudes towards homosexuality. Yet within a very short period at the beginning of the new millennium a bundle of legal reforms belatedly modernized British sexual law, culminating in the Civil Partnership Act in 2004. From notoriously in the 1950s having the most authoritarian legal regulation, and moral censure, of sexual unorthodoxy in the Western world, by 2005 it had among the most liberal laws and attitudes. Yet the approach adopted by-passed many of the controversies which arose elsewhere. Instead of a principled debate about the merits of same-sex marriage, the UK simply reproduced marriage law wholesale but called it something else, thus avoiding much religious opposition. It was a classic case of 'liberalisation by stealth', and a very British compromise, which effectively paved the way for full equality. When same-sex marriage was enacted (in England and Wales, and separately in Scotland) ten years later, it was promoted by a Conservative Prime Minister who earlier had been publicly hostile to legal reforms (Weeks 2015).

The USA was the epicentre of controversy about the politics of same-sex marriage. As the most neo-liberal of cultures, it also produced the most fervent and fundamentalist opposition among Western democracies. As the society with the most affirmative LGBTQ identities and communities, it generated both the most energetic campaigns for same-sex marriage and the most sustained critiques from the heart of those communities. Because of the historic exclusion of African-Americans from marriage under slavery and later, and the close association of marriage with access to social entitlements, same-sex marriage, some critics argued, made claims to racially constructed ideas of sexual respectability and the naturalization of a racially stratified welfare state (Brandzel 2005; Kandaswamy 2008). Given the heat of the debate, it was surely relevant that the USA is also the most religious of Western societies. That largely explains the degree of opposition to same-sex marriage from conservative Christians. It might also help explain the fervour with which activists in the USA stood out for full recognition of same-sex marriage, compared to the more secular

British or Scandinavians who were originally more willing to compromise on civil unions (and actually achieved full same-sex marriage earlier).

Same-sex unions and marriage clearly touched powerful chords in their national cultures. But at a deeper level what we see in the new narratives about same-sex relationships is the wish for recognition for what a person is and wants to be, for validation, not absorption, a desire for the ordinary virtues of care, love and mutual responsibility. This is a wider question than the rights of queer-identified people alone. The reality is that across the world, with differing rhythms and paces, many thousands were making choices about how they wanted to live on a day-by-day basis, and making claims for full citizenship, including equal relational rights. Most of them were not particularly preoccupied by theoretical or theological disputes. They wanted to live ordinary lives (Heaphy et al. 2012). They were concerned with living their chosen lives with openness, recognition and legitimacy – as full and equal citizens.

GLOBALIZATION AND HUMAN SEXUAL RIGHTS

Global flows

The debates over same-sex marriage have become global in scope. Even those countries bitterly opposed have invoked it as a mark of the Western decadence they wish to avoid. For its supporters it has become a mark of modernity and liberalization. What is significant is the evidence it provides for a far denser and faster system for diffusing ideas, values and perceptions than ever before, 'so that a certain self-consciousness about and understanding of sexuality is arguably being universalized in a completely new way' (Altman 2001: 38). It has become necessary to think globally in order to understand social change and its impact on issues of sexuality (Waites 2005: 40–41).

The world of sexuality is being transformed by global connections and flows. Here are some elements of these flows (after Weeks 2007: 206–8):

- Flows of men and women leaving their traditional homes seeking work and new opportunities, moving from country to towns and cities, which disrupt settled family and sexual patterns and open the way to new opportunities and forms of exploitation.
- Flows of war, with soldiers crossing countries, causing disruptions, committing sexual abuses and rape, and possibly transmitting STIs; people fleeing war and extreme violence; the disruption of families, economies, cultures; 'the intimate violence' of genocides and civil wars.
- Flows of people escaping from persecution for their sexualities, or seeking access to reproductive choice.
- Flows of sexually transmitted infections, including HIV, of community-based organizations to combat them, and of international mobilization.
- Flows of pornography and sexually explicit materials in a multi-billion-dollar global industry.
- Flows of drugs with erotic connotations, both illicit and licit.

- Flows of tourism, transforming economies, transporting millions to once exotic and mysterious foreign places, and the explosion especially of sex tourism (O'Connell Davidson and Sanchez Taylor 2005).
- Flows of media that make sexual information, news, gossip, styles, scandals, personalities, stereotypes, role models, personal dramas, legal changes, reactionary pronouncements, crimes and misdemeanours instantly known everywhere.
- Flows of popular culture: in films, television, games, music, social media.
- Flows of consumption, of everything from clothes and gadgets to sex toys – with China the biggest supplier of sex toys to the West.
- Flows of religion, and their associated moralities, especially of neo-traditionalist or fundamentalist leanings (Bhatt 1997; Ruthven 2004).
- Flows of sexual stories that circulate sexual secrets and confessions, desires, practices, hopes, fears, identities and aspirations, and through their interaction shape new meanings, communities, and possibilities (Plummer 1995, 2003).
- Flows of science that try to interpret and categorize the sexual world, and increasingly to re-make it via new technologies, especially reproductive techniques (Lancaster 2003).
- Flows of social movements, such as global feminist and lesbian, gay, bisexual and transgender movements (Threlfal 1996; Adam et al. 1999).
- Flows of identities and ways of being, for example, the globalization of lesbian and gay and transgendered

subjectivities offering forms of self-realization that can shift the terms of being sexual.

- Flows of concern about children – their exploitation, their protection, their rights – and flows of children themselves, through displacement, migration, adoption and sale (O'Connell Davidson 2005; Waites 2005: 40–59).
- Flows of campaigns – from NGOs, international agencies, lobby-groups, grass-roots organizations – on everything from sexual abuse and sexual infections to human trafficking.
- Flows of conferences, seminars, academics, activists, experts, medics, psychologists, therapists, all adding to the flow of words, the proliferation of stories, the shaping of discourses and new subjectivities.
- Flows of literature: ancient, contemporary, mandarin, populist, pornographic, educational, instructional, academic, scientific, religious, moralistic, scandalous, titilating, biographical, historical, political – in millions of books, magazines, journals, pamphlets, in print, online.
- Flows through cyberspace – in ways already too vast to enumerate and list.
- Flows of reproductive necessities, to prevent and promote births: the Pill, condoms, sperm, donated eggs, adoption, surrogacy.
- Flows of regulation: on the exploitation of children, marriage rights, sex work, trafficking crimes, sexual health, medicines, drugs, pornography, internet posting or downloading.
- Flows of discourse around rights: human sexual rights, reproductive rights, relational rights, love rights (Petchesky 2000).

- Flows of transnational friendship and relationships, and diasporic flows, as younger people mainly (but not exclusively) migrate across the globe, in search of pleasures, partners, employment, wealth, freedoms, justice, home (Patton and Sanchez-Eppler 2000).
- And then there are flows of mourning and loss, as with HIV/AIDS – a reminder of the costs as well as the gains of global connectedness.

Sexual wrongs and social justice

These massive flows and intricate connections across distance and difference, a complex mixture of opportunities and threats, shape the context in which sexual norms and values are being rewritten, and new subjectivities develop. But they also highlight sexual injustice, sexual wrongs. Some of these are the results of prejudice, deliberate discrimination, historically weighted oppressions. Others are the inevitable consequences of other injustices.

International organizations such as the International Monetary Fund (IMF) and World Bank impose policies that may have dramatic effects on intimate life. Global religious organizations like the Roman Catholic Church shape policies towards abortion and birth control, and even HIV-prevention, because of its opposition to the use of condoms. NGOs – concerned with children, women, trafficking, HIV/AIDS, LGBT issues, reproductive rights, human rights – develop international campaigns which can focus world attention on sexual issues, and shape national and international strategies. The weight of mobilization is often impressive. Three thousand NGOs were accredited to the 1995 World Conference on Women in Beijing, and 40,000 delegates attended the parallel NGO forum (Altman 2001: 125). Transnational bodies like the European Union and other European institutions such as the Court of Human Rights are increasingly involved in shaping sexual norms and regulation, in relation to homosexual or transgender rights, working practices, and the cross-national trade of sexually explicit materials. The UN has intervened in relation to the role of women and children, and less successfully on homosexuality.

The various forces in play in a globalizing culture all pose once again, but now on a global scale, the fundamental question posed by living in a complex, diverse world: how to find agreed common standards by which to measure individual and particularist needs and to find ways of living harmoniously with difference. This is, for Beck (1999, Chapters 1 and 2, Beck 2002) the challenge that the cosmopolitan perspective can meet, by offering 'an alternative imagination, an imagination of alternative ways of life and rationality, which includes the otherness of the other' (Beck 2002: 18). This implies a breakaway from a perspective that freezes and reifies different cultures, identities and ways of being, and that welcomes the conviviality of intermingling. The cosmopolitan citizen is someone who is capable of working across different national traditions, communities of fate and alternative ways of life, and of engaging in dialogue with the discourses of others in order to expand the horizons of meanings that trap us in our own prejudices, anxieties and fears (Plummer 2015). But these aspirations have to confront the harsh realities of continuing – and in some contexts accentuating – disparities of power, and the difficulties of living them amidst complex multi-cultural and multi-faith societies. That is not to say, however, that there is no point in trying.

Cosmopolitan citizenship has its pioneers in the new sexual subjects that have moved onto the stage of history since the 1970s. Among these the 'global gay' (Altman 2001) shows the potential and the difficulties, the challenge and the opportunities. Globalization has helped create an international lesbian and gay identity which goes beyond the boundaries of the West (Altman 2001). Yet this very Western notion of what it is to be gay or lesbian is refracted through different ways of living homosexuality and gender. As Patton and Sanchez Eppler remarked:

> . . . 'being' gay, homosexual, lesbian, joto, internacional, tortillera, like that, battyman, bakla, katoi, butch, et cetera, entails answering or not answering to those terms and the desires they purport to index, in a given place, for a given duration. When a practitioner of 'homosexual acts', or a body that carries any of many queering marks moves between officially designated spaces – nation, region, metropole, neighbourhood, or even culture, gender, religion, disease – intricate realignments of identity, politics, and desire take place.
>
> (Patton and Sanchez-Eppler 2000: 3)

Globalization has produced the opportunity for recognition across distance, and for the development of elements of a common life and common cause. But it has also exposed the local peculiarities of lived experience which determine the particular identifications and distancing, the constant making and re-making of subjectivities. Similarly, whilst it is possible and necessary to recognize the common elements of homophobia, biphobia, transphobia and enforced normalization that circle the globe, it is also necessary to be sensitive to the different regimes of sexuality that govern individual ways of life. Of the nineteen countries with some recognition of same-sex relational rights or 'love rights' in 2003, all were ranked in the top twenty-four Organisation for Economic Co-operation and Development (OECD) countries for GDP per capita (Wintermute 2005: 218).

Cosmopolitanism as the ideal of establishing dialogue across chasms of difference and of establishing some sort of democracy in interpersonal as well as political life depends on breaking down the structures that separate people off and inhibit the development of a common framework of rights. Few areas have proved more controversial and contested.

Human sexual rights

Before the early 1990s, sexuality was absent from international human rights discourse (Petchesky 2000). The Universal Declaration of Human Rights, adopted by the UN General Assembly in 1948, famously declared the 'inherent dignity' and 'equal and inalienable rights' of all members of the human family. Gradually this universal subject has been seen as having different racial or ethnic origins, with different faiths or none, has different health needs, is gendered in complex ways and has different sexual preferences or orientations; but for long the UN proved reluctant to acknowledge issues of sexual diversity or transgender. The international argument for a wider agenda began to emerge with the Vienna conference on Human Rights in 1993, the UN Declaration on the Elimination of Violence against Women later that year, the world population conference in Cairo in 1994, and the women's conference in Beijing in 1995. The ground work had been going on quite clearly since the 1970s, with the various campaigns of second-wave feminism and the internationalizing of the LGBT movement. The global HIV/AIDS epidemic further helped force sexuality onto the international sexual agenda. But as Petchesky (2000) again notes, while the claim to rights can be enabling, it can as easily lead to an intensification of conflict over which rights and whose rights have priority. Conflicting rights, it has been argued, are 'the major obstacle to ensuring women's human rights in the South' (Rajan 2005: 134).

The same tension can be seen in the struggle for LGBTQ sexual rights. In his book *Desiring Arabs*, Joseph Massad (2007) is concerned with two issues he sees as fundamental to the continuing power nexus between the old imperial West and the Arab world: the distorting impact of Western interventions on the perceptions of Arab sexuality and Islam both globally and within the Islamic world itself; and the disastrous role of gay human activists – the 'gay international' – on the contemporary politics of sexuality in that world. By assuming that the Western idea of 'the gay' is a universal signifier, whose Western identity and lifestyle is applicable everywhere, the subtle and complex ways in which same-sex desire is lived in other parts of the world are ignored by these human rights advocates, and homophobic reactions are encouraged. This is compounded, Massad argues, by the alliance that has developed between human rights activists and Western governments.

It is a nice historical irony that liberal contemporary Britain, whose former empire continues to maintain the most consistently anti-homophobic attitudes across the globe (Lennox and Waites 2012), has recently positioned itself alongside the USA and other Western states as a global defender of homosexual rights especially in Africa and the Arab and broader Islamic world. Whilst the imperial West attacked Islam's alleged sexual licentiousness, the modern liberal West now attacks the alleged repression of sexual freedoms in the present Islamic world (Massad 2007). At the heart of what Altman and Symons (2016) call 'Queer Wars', the global battle over the legitimacy of LGBTQ claims to social justice, there is a fracture about the very meaning and universality of human rights.

Against such scepticism, it is important to recognize that the idea of human sexual rights has become the main vehicle for the debate on and advancement of sexual justice on a global scale. This is a relatively new development. Sexuality to a large extent was brought into human rights discourses by debates over privacy and reproduction, while the Beijing conference coalesced around questions of violence against women. Clearly there are strong links between them, especially in relation to core themes like bodily integrity or control over one's own body, personhood, equality and diversity. But reproductive rights and sexual rights can never be co-extensive, though international agencies often find it easier to deal with the former than to confront the wider questions raised by sexuality generally, and especially LGBTQ issues (see Kollman and Waites 2009). As Butler (2005) argues, issues raised globally by LGBTQ campaigners are not just particularist claims: they pose profound questions about what it means to be human in a globalized world which in many parts still seeks to deny the humanity of non-heterosexual or gender-challenging people. Sexuality is more than simply an attribute of an individual. It has come to define a relationship with the self and with others, one's very humanity. LGBTQ people *have* to raise questions about the injustices they face because if they did not do so their very humanness would continue to be questioned. Thus the central challenge of international gay and lesbian rights is to assert the reality of homosexuality, not as inner truth, not as sexual practice, 'but as one of the defining features of the social world in its very intelligibility' (Butler 2005: 64–65). To assert the value of LGBTQ identities and ways of life is to challenge existing realities and to show that there are many different ways of being sexual – and of being human.

The struggle over sexual rights has inevitable limitations (Correa et al. 2008), but it provides a necessary heuristic and mobilizing means for calling attention to injustice. Just as discrimination, prejudice, oppression and exploitation are denials of full humanity, so a positive claim for rights is an assertion of the rich diversity of human possibilities. Human sexual rights offer standards by which we can challenge both the absolutism which can find good only in traditional ways of life that have irrevocably gone, and a relativism, either descriptive or normative, that refuses to make distinctions at all. The evolution of human rights has been a process that involves a dialogue across differences, and the concept of human sexual rights that is emerging provides space and opportunity for difference to flourish within a developing discourse of our common humanity.

6

PRIVATE PLEASURES AND PUBLIC POLICIES

THE LIMITS OF SCIENCE

There are many questions we could ask about sexuality: about duty and choice, morality and immorality, goodness and evil, health and sickness, truth and falsity. Subtle, and not so subtle, debates around some or all of these dichotomies have dominated the Western discourse on sexuality for more than two thousand years, and in different languages and forms have also shaped the attitudes of many other cultures across the globe. Whatever the range of answers that may be reached, they all have the distinction of carrying a heavy weight of prescription, of telling people – often very coercively – how they must behave in order to attain the good (or moral or hygienic) life. The unifying thread of this book, however, is that the erotic has been heavily loaded with too many assumptions, that it has lumbered under a weight of expectations it cannot, and should not have to, bear. 'Sex acts', Gayle Rubin rightly said, 'are burdened with an excess of significance' (Rubin 1984: 285). We should lighten the load.

One of the major difficulties in doing this has been the privileged role claimed by the experts on sex over the past hundred years in telling us what is good or bad, appropriate or inappropriate behaviour. In his presidential address to the 1929 Congress of the World League for Sexual Reform, Magnus Hirschfeld declared that: 'A sexual ethics based on science is the only sound system of ethics' (Hirschfeld 1930: xiv). The impulse behind this statement was noble indeed. Hirschfeld, like other luminaries of this first phase of the sexological revolution, looked forward to a new enlightenment in which prejudice, religious moralism and authoritarian sexual codes would dissolve before the light of reason as provided by the new science of sex. Sexual knowledge and sexual politics marched hand in hand as the sexologists, like Hirschfeld, Havelock Ellis and Auguste Forel (joint Presidents of the World League in 1929) also became the patrons of sex reform, while sexual reformers of various hues, from feminist birth controllers to campaigners for homosexual rights, looked to the scientists for guidelines to further their activities. 'Through Science to Justice', Hirschfeld famously proclaimed as the watchword of his Scientific-Humanitarian Committee. It was the motto of the whole sex reform movement. The problem then, as now, was that the insights of this new science were not straightforward or unequivocal: to put it bluntly, sexologists disagreed with one another.

LGBTQ activists might look to Hirschfeld's theories which said that they belonged to a biologically given 'third' or 'intermediate' sex to justify their claims to social justice, but the Nazis who burned Hirschfeld's library and legacy after 1933 could equally well use more or less the same arguments to disqualify same-sexers altogether, as biological anomalies or perversions, from the new moral order – and find scientists only too willing to support them. Sexologists might point out the fact that sexuality was a rich and varied continent, but they also lent their weight to normalizing institutions, to attempts at 'cures', and to eugenic solutions to the 'problems' of overpopulation and the proliferation of the 'feeble-minded'. Havelock Ellis was not alone in being a sexual reformer, and also a supporter of the eugenic breeding of 'the best' (inevitably defined by class and racial criteria). The proliferating literature on married love from the 1920s might encourage the belief that women, too, were sexual beings deserving of satisfaction and pleasure. But these marriage experts also managed to pathologize the single woman and to sustain a burgeoning literature on the inadequacies of 'frigid' women.

The ultimate political and moral implications of sexual enlightenment were at best ambiguous and at worst dangerous as the new experts contributed a scientific justification for essentially traditional or authoritarian positions. By the 1920s, social purity organizations were looking to the writings of Ellis, Freud and others to underpin their modified but still fundamentally normalizing positions. Over the decades since, the science of sex has been drawn upon to justify a huge variety of moral positions, from passionate advocacy of sexual revolution to fervent endorsement of sexual orthodoxy. Today, even the least theoretical of moral entrepreneurs is able to call on an encyclopaedia of would-be scientific arguments to sustain her or his position, from hormonal theories, evolutionary psychology and the burgeoning evidence of DNA for explaining sexual difference and perversity and to justify the inevitability of inequality – or indeed of equality. It is particularly interesting in this regard that when the case was being made for the existence of the gay gene or gay brain by gay activists, who thought it could be used to justify their own existence, the enemies of diversity sought to use the same evidence to welcome the possibility of eliminating the gene by genetic engineering and selective breeding. Attempts to root arguments for LGBTQ rights in genetics seem to me to be both wrong-headed and dangerous because they by-pass the ethical and moral cases for equality and justice, and can lead to new forms of injustice. It is notable, for example, that a book that seeks to justify the biological causes of homosexuality concludes by condemning bisexuals for not accepting that they were truly gay (Wilson and Rahman 2005). Surely a more rational argument would be to say that the causes of any particular sexual practice are irrelevant. What matters are the ways that sexuality is lived.

This is not a polemic aimed at the rejection of any attempt at a scientific understanding of the workings of the body or the mind. As I have stressed above, we need to be alert to the biological aspects of sexuality and gender, because on and through these, cultural and social features are inscribed. I am, however, making an argument for abandoning the claim that a self-styled science of the erotic alone provides an objective guide into the truth of our bodies, and hence a code by which we should live our personal and social lives. The biological possibilities and inclinations of the body only assume meaning in historically shaped cultures. The 'science of sex' itself, like every other science, is enmeshed in the web of social relations. We should accordingly treat its more extravagant or imperialistic claims, especially when it is dealing with humans in all their contrariness, with caution and a sensitivity to their origins (see Lancaster 2003). As Steven Epstein (1996) has demonstrated in relation to the science of HIV/AIDS, the subjects of scientific investigation have their own voices, and are not prepared to simply accept what they are told as the final truth. Radical sexual activists since the 1970s have in effect created a grass-roots sexology, a counter-discourse based on experience, intimate knowledge and social interaction and struggle in which people in their thousands have voiced their own truths against the truths laid down for them. We are in the midst of a struggle over who can speak legitimately about the body, its needs and desires. Historically minded social scientists need to be sure that their voices are not drowned out in the cacophony.

Against the sexual tradition which sexology has done so much to sustain I have sought in this essay to *problematize* the idea of sexuality, to show its emergence from an intricate history, its close implication in relations of power, its deployment to sustain and normalize certain forms of erotic activity and its marginalization of others, and the crisis of meanings that has resulted from the diverse challenges which it has generated. But we are still left with a question which looms ever larger as we contemplate the domain of sexuality: what should the place of sexuality be in our individual lives in the contemporary world? This is scarcely a minor question. At its heart is the old question of ethics, of how we should live.

THE ETHICAL DILEMMA

The critique of reductionist views of sexuality which underpins this work has been very useful in casting light on hidden but controlling assumptions, and in opening up the sexual field to new questions, about history, power, meanings, diversity, choice and so on. It has, on the whole, been less successful in providing maps for navigating the highways and byways of what is still, despite all the torrents of writing about it, a partly uncharted country. The reason for this lack is quite straightforward. Sexology offered an alternative world outlook to the religious cosmology much of its initial energy was directed against. It claimed to be uncovering the truth of Nature in opposition to the truths of mere prejudice or tradition.

But if we reject the hierarchy of sexual values laid down by the science of sex, how do we distinguish the good from the bad? If, as Foucault said with reference to Sade, 'sex is without any norm or intrinsic rule that might be formulated from its own nature' (Foucault 1979: 149), how do we determine appropriate and inappropriate behaviour? If we can no longer regard sexuality as either intrinsically threatening and evil, or liberating and good, how can we escape the Scylla of moralism on the one hand and the Charybdis of anything-goes libertarianism on the other? Finally, if we can no longer accept the politics of the old 'sexual

revolutionaries' because of their reductive view of sexuality, and not believe in a transcendent 'sexual liberation',
because of the inevitable involvement of sex in the intricate
play of power, what are sexual politics for? Recent liberation movements, Foucault observed in a late interview,
'suffer from the fact that they cannot find any principle on
which to base the elaboration of the new ethics . . . [other
than] an ethics founded on so-called scientific knowledge
of what the self is, what desire is, what the unconscious is,
and so on' (Foucault 1984: 343). The trouble is that this
'scientific knowledge' is, as we know, full of divisions and
contradictions about what the self is, what desire may be,
and even whether there is such a thing as 'the unconscious'.
Yet if we reject these guidelines, is there anything left?

Foucault's own late attempt to grapple with this dilemma,
in the two volumes of his *History* published at the very end
of his life, is characteristically indirect. The two volumes
are superficially at least simple exegeses of ancient Greek
and Latin texts on how people should live (Foucault 1985,
1986). But their very indirection and lack of obvious contact with today's problems serves to clarify what is at stake.
He likens the world of the Greeks and Romans to our own
in one key respect. Like us post-moderns, they were faced
with the task of elaborating an ethic that was not founded
in religion or any other *a priori* justification, least of all
science. Like us, they were troubled with moral questions
around what we term sexuality (the nearest equivalent for
them was called *aphrodisia*). Many of the concerns have in
fact been continuous for more than 2,000 years: with the
body, the relations of men and women, of men and men.
Unlike us, however, they did not attempt a codification of

acts which made sex itself the bearer of negative values and moral anxieties, nor attempt a subordination of individuals to external rules of conduct based on such values and anxieties. They sought instead an 'aesthetics of existence', an art of life in which temperance balanced excess, self-discipline kept pleasures in order.

The ancients were preoccupied with methods of self-knowledge, with techniques of the self, rules of conduct organized around dietary matters (the individual's relation with his body), economics (the conduct of the head of the household) and the erotic (the relations of men and boys). They were, in other words, seeking modes of life which derived not from a central truth about sex, but from the set of relations in which the individual was embedded. The aim was to define the uses of pleasure in a way which neither ignored it, nor surrendered to its intoxicating force.

Foucault is not of course suggesting that this is a model for our own time. This was an ethics for 'free men', from which women, children and slaves were excluded. He rejects as a matter of principle the evocation of golden ages, and anyway the ancient world was scarcely golden. But in a typically oblique manner, what he is doing in examining a time so different from our own is to throw our own needs and aspirations into relief. What we lack, he is suggesting, is not a transcendent truth, but ways of coping with a multiplicity of truths. We need not so much a morality based on absolute values, but an ethics and politics which will enable us to cope with a variety of choices. Foucault, in taking us through the arts of existence in the ancient world, is asking us to reflect on the ways of life that could be valid for us today.

What would the basis of a modern sexual ethics be? There are hints in the distinction Foucault makes between freedom of 'sexual acts' and freedom of 'sexual choice'. He is against the first, he suggests, not least because it might involve endorsement of violent activity such as rape. It is also, of course, the mode of the sexual tradition. But he is for the second, whether it be, as he puts it 'the liberty to manifest that choice or not to manifest it' (Foucault 1982/83). The tenor of this is that the nature of the social relationships in which choice becomes meaningful is of crucial importance. We are being urged to move away from a situation where we judge the nature of the act, to one where we consider the context and the meaning of the act for the participants. I have already suggested some of the implications of this in the discussion on diversity (Chapter 4). Here I want to look at the wider implications, for it points away from an absolutist morality, based on a fundamental human nature, to a fully pluralistic ethic, based on the acceptance of diverse tastes.

Rubin argued some years ago that despite all the very real changes that have occurred: 'This culture always treats sex with suspicion. It construes and judges any sexual practice in terms of its worst possible expression. Sex is presumed guilty until proven innocent' (Rubin 1984: 278). My own position is that sex in itself is neither good nor bad, but is rather a field of possibilities and potentialities, all of which must be judged by the context in which they occur. It opens the way then, to acceptance of diversity as the *norm* of our culture and the appropriate means of thinking about sexuality.

This does not, of course, resolve all difficulties: in many ways, in fact, it compounds them. It is far easier to confront each difficult area of choice with a moral code which tells us exactly, and invariably, how we should live. In a social climate of rapid social – and moral – change, and of the emergence of new social possibilities, identities and lifestyles, it is a temptation to seek once again the security of absolute moral standards, which fixes us in a world of certainty where personal and social identities are given. Moral absolutism, as Alvin Gouldner once observed, 'serves to cut the Gordian knot of indecision', magically sweeping away doubt and anxiety and making possible the onward march of the army of the just (Gouldner 1973: 295). The approach I am advocating, in sharp distinction to the absolutist tradition, is tentative, provisional, open-ended and alive to contingency. It can be seen as partaking of some of the elements of the libertarian tradition – especially what may be called its 'sex-positive' attitudes – while at the same time it shares with the liberal tradition a recognition of the need for careful distinctions, for a grasp of meaning and context, and of the importance of the discourse of rights and choice. Where it differs from both these traditions is in its decisive recognition of the social production of sexualities, and their complex embeddedness in diverse power relations. Its aim, consequently, is to provide guidelines for decision making rather than new absolute values. It rejects the temptation of a 'radical morality'. Instead it places its emphasis on the merits of choice, and the conditions which limit choice.

TOWARDS SEXUAL DEMOCRACY

The discussion of sexual or intimate citizenship and the discourse of human sexual rights in the previous chapter pointed towards the agenda that is emerging. It implies an informalization (Wouters 2007) and democratization of sexual relationships in which the old hierarchies are fundamentally challenged, and more equal relationships are negotiated between equal moral agents. The democratization of social relationships has been a long and uneven historical process, and the term itself has only recently been fully applied to an area which seemed par excellence the domain of Nature. But it is a broader application of the term 'democracy' that is called for when we speak of the right to control our bodies, when we say 'our bodies are our own'. The claim to bodily self-determination is an old one, with roots in a number of different moral and political traditions. From liberal roots in the Puritan revolution of the seventeenth century we can trace the evolution of the idea of property in one's own person. The Marxist tradition offers a vision of society in which human needs may be satisfied harmoniously. From the biological sciences comes the understanding of the body, its capacities and limitations, establishing the boundaries of individual possibility.

All three of these recognize limits to the free exercise of bodily self-determination: through traditional, patriarchal authority, the unequal distribution of property and power, or the limits of the personality itself, with its needs for physical sustenance, emotional warmth, and above all, social involvement. From feminism has come a recognition of further limitations, the subtle and not so subtle coercions of a male-dominated society and the infiltration of inequality through all the relations of social life. A 'democratic morality', it has been suggested, would judge acts by the way partners deal with one another, the consideration they show for each other, the absence of coercion and the ability to negotiate equally and freely, their openness to one another, and the degree of pleasure and need they can satisfy (see Giddens 1992, Ch.10; Jamieson 1998, Ch.6). These are admirable goals, but their recognition can be constantly thwarted by an awareness of the constraints that limit free choice.

There are real limitations in today's world to the free play of choice. But there is another issue which looms whenever the question of choice is raised: where should choice end? Should people be free, for instance, to choose activities that may harm themselves or others, whether intentionally or not? The problem here is not so much one of physical harm – which can be measured – but of psychic or moral damage – which usually cannot. Should, say, a more just society ban pornography because of its exploitative representations of women? Should sado-masochistic sex be tolerated even between, in the famous phrase, 'consenting adults in private', when pain and violence is a frequent by-product? Should sex-workers be free to sell their bodies, and punters to buy sex, or are these transactions inevitably exploitative? 'Harm' is, of course, a notoriously difficult word to engage with. Havelock Ellis in the 1930s, in what was to become a classical liberal formulation of the issue, believed that it was such a difficult concept that condemnation or interference could only be called for in two cases: if the subjects were in danger of damaging their health, and therefore likely to call on medical or psychotherapeutic treatment; or if there was a danger of injury to the health or rights of others, in which case the law was entitled to interfere (Ellis 1946: 184). These are, on the surface at least, very sensible guidelines, but they ignore a factor that has assumed a growing importance in recent debates on sexuality, a belief that 'damage' or 'harm' can be moral as well as physical, emotional as well as psychological.

The hostility of some feminists to pornography or erotic activities that play with power disparities, such as BDSM, relies on the argument that representations of violence can cause violence or are violence and that sexual behaviour which involves power imbalances works to sustain existing power relations. The most powerful argument against this, also advanced by feminists, though of a rather different persuasion, is that attempts to suppress potentially harmful representations or fantasies do not in practice eliminate them but on the contrary reinforce their transgressive power. Jessica Benjamin argued that our culture is facing a crisis of what she describes as 'male rationality', and a resurgence of erotic fantasy. She goes on: 'A politics that denies these issues, that tries to sanitize or rationalizes the erotic, fantastic components of human life, will not defeat domination, but only vacate the field' (Benjamin 1984: 308; compare Segal 2015).

This, Benjamin believes, means the avoidance both of a simple libertarian acceptance and of moral condemnation. The primary task is to understand. And what should the basis of our understanding be? Surely it must be a recognition that the complex forces that shape our sexualities – biological potentialities, unconscious motivations and desires, emotional needs and social organization – produce many wishes and desires which often go beyond our dispassionate understanding or the canons of political correctness. Sexual excitement, Lynne Segal wrote, 'is generated by, and in the service of, a multitude of needs, not all of them "nice"' (Segal 1983: 45). This implies, rightly in my opinion, that sexuality is too difficult and elusive an idea to be tidied away into neat compartments of right or wrong. We need to be alive to its ambivalent and ambiguous qualities, and act accordingly.

Sexual 'choice', then, suggests a recognition of limits as well as possibilities, hazardous paths as much as positive goals. It must also, however, take into account another reality: the fact of conflicting choices, opposed goals. As I have already noted the debate on abortion has produced ultimately irreconcilable 'rights': those of the 'unborn child' against those of the mother who claims a right to control her own fertility. Here there are massively different conceptions in conflict: different views of what constitutes 'life', and opposing claims over the absolute autonomy of the body. But even within the broad parameters of a common social and political affiliation the 'right to choose' can have different meanings in different contexts. The claim to a right to choose abortion must also involve a right to choose *not* to have an abortion. In societies where marginalized and poor women may be encouraged (either for racist and/or population policy reasons) to limit their family size, a call for the right to abortion will appear narrowly exclusive. This has led to a crucial shift in international debates away from a campaign simply for abortion rights to a wider campaign to ensure 'reproductive rights' for women as a whole – to embrace campaigns against compulsory sterilization or compulsory abortion as well as for full access to effective birth control and the rights of women to terminate their pregnancies, if they choose (Petchesky and Judd 1998).

The context in which choice is demanded and operative is, therefore, critical. Sexual values cannot be detached from the wider social values we hold, and these themselves are increasingly diverse. We saw earlier that the world of sexuality is fragmented by a number of other relations, of race, gender and class particularly, and that subjectivities are shaped at the intersection of difference. This means that different groups will endorse different perspectives and develop often strikingly opposed priorities. The white feminist critique of the family that developed in the 1970s and 1980s appeared ethnocentric and oppressive to black women struggling to defend their families as bulwarks against the racism which may work to fragment and destroy families. Similarly, the priority given by gay and lesbian movements to 'coming out', to openly declaring your sexual preferences as a means of affirming their validity, often conflicts with the need felt by black lesbians and gay men in a racist culture to affirm their political identity with their communities of origin, whatever the family and sexual orthodoxies prevailing there (Amos and Parmar 1984; Omolade 1984). A discourse of choice must therefore be based not only on a recognition of different individual needs and goals, but of different means of living them.

There is another important factor that needs to be stressed. The priority given to diversity and choice runs the danger of appearing as a purely individual activity, with each isolated monad having to make his or her choice in the face of a multitude of options. This supermarket view of sex is in many ways complicit, as we have seen, with the vast changes that have reshaped the world since the 1980s, under the impact of globalization and neo-liberalism. The commercialization and commodification of intimate life has proceeded in parallel with greater individual freedom for many, corrupting and threatening the autonomy that it apparently offered (Hochschild 2003). Many of us may live in a world of glittering flux, where we have no choice but to choose, perhaps, but often find it impossible to make up our minds. In the hyper-market of choice, the individual is thrown back on his or her own resources, and many individuals, as we know, flail around in an apparently meaningless void.

THE HUMAN GESTURE

It is possible, however, to be more hopeful. The lessons of the history of sexuality and intimacy that I have set out in this book suggest that we are more than isolated atoms, adrift in a world of alienation. Somehow, we humans muddle through, making sense of our worlds and making decisions which are valid for us in our everyday lives. It is a sense of mutuality, an awareness of our continuing and necessary involvement with others, that ultimately provides the real guarantee of individual choice and of meaningfulness (Weeks 1995). The new patterns of intimacy that I discussed above do not presage a decline of reciprocity, but its reinvention, where individual needs and shared commitments are negotiated in a post-traditional world. More broadly, the apparent triumph of individualization in the late modern world may signal the decline of old solidarities, but it would be foolish to ignore the simultaneous rise of new possibilities. The emergence of new forms of collective and individual agency across the globe has dramatized the changes that are taking place, with often profound effects.

This is the point where the politics of sexuality and gender inevitably returns to a wider social context, and moral and political alignments. The choices we are confronted with are decided in the end not by anything intrinsic to sexuality itself but by the wider set of values and goals which we embrace. Cultural pessimists proclaim that we live in a world where common values are in sharp decline. But as Beck (1999: 13) argues, we actually live in an age *of* values, where uncertainty forces people to be creative, inventive and generative of values (see Weeks 2007). The rapid changes of the past few generations have produced, as we have seen, sharp conflicts of values, especially around sexual issues – culture wars and fundamentalisms have dramatized these but they permeate almost every aspect of everyday life. Yet in an age where pessimism – about wars, climate change, poverty, economic insecurity, ethnic clashes, racism, authoritarian nationalisms, conflicts of religion and random terror – is endemic, it is important to remember what we have gained in recent years.

The discourse of human sexual rights codifies many of the gains, and takes them on to a new plain. They signal the gap between aspiration and achievement, the chasm that sometimes seems to exist between ideal and reality. But compared to the silence around the power relationships and oppressions that enveloped sexuality and intimacy just half a century or so ago, the many clamant voices of the present signal a vital, and necessary, change. Even in the most hierarchical society men and women can develop relationships of equality and mutuality. Even in a homophobic or biphobic society men and men, women and women can find love and respect. Even in a transphobic world, trans people can live in their chosen gender, or none. Even in the most individualistic of cultures, people still manage to find sources of community and solidarity. And now there are many narratives of struggle and hope to support them, in ever more intricate global links.

Solidarity implies care and responsibility for others, a belief in the dignity of the other, a curiosity to learn about others, and a willingness to support those who seek to reduce violence and domination in private relationships as well as public institutions. It implies too a recognition of equality and interdependence, and a commitment to resolving conflict democratically, through dialogue rather than open warfare.

This is the field of the new cosmopolitanism which I sketched in the last chapter, and of a related concept, that of a critical humanism which Plummer (2003: 162, note 1; see Plummer 2015) among others have signaled: 'The humanism I would like to see developed would encourage a view of human beings as an "embedded", dialogic, contingent, embodied, universal self with a moral (and political) character'. This is humanism as a 'regulative ideal' rather than a metaphysical concept, with 'humanity' as a project of political construction – not something that has always been there (Weeks 1995: 77; Weeks 2007: 223). One of the less obvious but most vital features of globalization, and of the discourse of human sexual rights, is a growing sense of our vulnerability to others, in both their pain and their pleasures (Butler 2005: 54). It involves making the 'human gesture', affirming the human bond which links us beyond the chasms of difference.

As society becomes ever more complex it is likely that the patterns of individual sexual needs and relationships will be in ever more exotic flux. I have suggested in this book that we should be more ready than we have been to go with the flood: to fully accept the possibilities opened up by a growing social and moral pluralism, to embrace, in all their accompanying ambiguities and potential conflicts, the merits of sexual diversity and choice. The sexual tradition offered a fundamentally monolithic construct which we know as 'sexuality'. In recent years its pretensions have been punctured, its dubious origins revealed and its restrictive effects exposed. We have deconstructed the idea of sexuality. It is now time to start thinking afresh about individual needs and aspirations, and the wider social solidarities that can support them. A genuine acceptance of sexual and gender diversity seems the only appropriate starting point.

Suggestions for
Further Reading

This section on further reading can barely hint at the current richness of the literature, in breadth and depth, with a growing and challenging transnational perspective, and major contributions from the Global South. What follows is therefore highly selective, with a focus on the historical development of the core themes, and on the key issues in contemporary debates. Inevitably, there is an overlap between this note on further reading and the bibliography of the book. While the latter provides details of specific references in the text, this section is designed to allow the reader to take an argument or theme forward. As such, it will, I hope, provide many openings for a fuller exploration of human sexuality in all its richness and complexity.

GENERAL APPROACHES

The reader is entitled to know where I am coming from. The perspective outlined in this short book is elaborated in greater detail in a number of publications I have written on the history and social organization of sexuality and intimate life. These include: Jeffrey Weeks, *Coming Out. Homosexual Politics in Britain from the 19th Century to the Present*, Quartet, London (1977; 3rd edition 2016); *Sex, Politics and Society. The Regulation of Sexuality since 1800*,

Routledge, Abingdon (1981; 3rd edition 2012); *Sexuality and its Discontents. Meanings, Myths and Modern Sexualities*, Routledge & Kegan Paul, London (1985); *Against Nature: Essays on History, Sexuality and Identity*, Rivers Oram Press, London (1991); *Invented Moralities: Sexual Values in an Age of Uncertainty*, Polity Press, Cambridge (1995); *Sexual Cultures: Communities, Values and Intimacy*, edited with Janet Holland, Macmillan, Basingstoke (1996); *Making Sexual History*, Polity Press, Cambridge (2000); *Same Sex Intimacies: Families of Choice and other Life Experiments*, with Brian Heaphy and Catherine Donovan, Routledge, London (2001); *The World We Have Won: The Remaking of Erotic and Intimate Life*, Routledge, Abingdon (2007); *The Languages of Sexuality*, Routledge, Abingdon (2011); *What is Sexual History?*, Polity Press, Cambridge (2016). These all contain detailed notes and references which the interested reader can follow for further reading.

My own writings have been informed by personal and collective research but also owe immense debts to the scholarship of many others. There are a number of excellent collections which bring together the fruits of some of the best of this contemporary scholarship. The most comprehensive is the four volume collection of papers edited by Ken Plummer: *Sexualities, Vol. I, Making a Sociology of Sexualities*; *Vol. II, Some Elements for an Account of the Social Organization of Sexualities*; *Vol. III, Difference and the Diversity of Sexualities*; *Vol. IV, Sexualities and their Futures, Critical Concepts in Sociology*, Routledge, London (2002). A shorter collection, concentrating on some of the best writings on the history, sociology and politics of sexuality, is my own selection, made with colleagues: Jeffrey Weeks, Janet Holland and Matthew Waites (eds.), *Sexualities and Society: A Reader*, Polity Press, Cambridge (2003). I would also recommend the following collections, their organizing theme suggested by their titles: Richard Parker and Peter Aggleton (eds.), *Culture, Society and Sexuality: A Reader*, 2nd edition., Routledge, London (2007); Richard Parker, Marie Barbosa and Peter Aggleton, *Framing the Sexual Subject: The Politics of Gender, Sexuality and Power*, University of California Press, Berkeley, Los Angeles (2000); Peter Aggleton, and Richard Parker (eds.) *Routledge Handbook of Sexuality, Health and Rights*, Routledge, Abingdon (2010); Peter Aggleton, Paul Boyce, Henrietta L. Moore and Richard Parker (eds.) *Understanding Global Sexualities: New Frontiers*, Routledge, Abingdon, 2012; Kim M. Phillips and Barry Reay (eds.), *Sexualities in History: A Reader*, Routledge, New York (2002); Christine Williams and Arlene Stein (eds.), *Sexuality and Gender*, Blackwell, Oxford (2002); Robert Hearley and Betsy Crane (eds.), *Sexual Lives: A Reader on the Theories and Realities of Human Sexualities*, McGraw Hill, New York (2003); and Deborah Cameron and Don Kulick, *The Language of Sexuality Reader*, Routledge, Abingdon (2006). A valuable overview of the state of studies on sexuality is provided in Steven Seidman and Nancy Fischer (eds.), *Introducing the New Sexuality Studies*, 3rd edition, Routledge, Abingdon (2016).

A number of specialist journals now exist which provide ample opportunities to explore the various aspects of sexuality. Three journals in particular publish important articles relevant to the arguments in this book: *Sexualities*;

Journal of the History of Sexuality; and *Culture, Health and Sexuality*. All three have increasingly broadened their transnational coverage, and the latter is particularly rich in contributions from the Global South.

INVENTING SEXUALITIES

The shaping of gender and the 'invention' of heterosexuality and homosexuality has become a major theme in the exploration of sexuality. Recent historical scholarship is surveyed in Matt Houlbrook and H. G. Cocks (eds.), *Palgrave Advances in the Modern History of Sexuality*, Palgrave Macmillan, London (2005), and in my own *What is Sexual History?*, cited above. A helpful, if variable, survey of Western attitudes to sexuality over a long span can be found in: Philippe Aries and Andre Bejin (eds.), *Western Sexuality, Practice and Precept in Past and Present Times*, Basil Blackwell, Oxford (1985). Thomas Laqueur has traced the evolution of conceptualizations of the male and female bodies and sexualities in *Making Sex: Body and Gender from the Greeks to Freud*, Harvard University Press, Cambridge, MA (1990). A later contribution by Laqueur also provides a broad history of sexuality as well as a detailed history of its ostensible subject: *Solitary Sex: A Cultural History of Masturbation*, Zone Books, New York (2003). Randolph Trumbach has explored the 'gender revolution' of the eighteenth century in *Sex and the Gender Revolution, Volume One: Heterosexuality and the Third Gender in Enlightenment London*, University of Chicago Press, Chicago (1998). For the shift to a modern concept of sexuality see Kim M. Phillips and Barry Reay,

Sex before Sexuality: A Pre-modern History, Polity Press, Cambridge (2011); and Faramerz Dabhoiwala, *The Origins of Sex: A History of the First Sexual Revolution*, Allen Lane, London (2012). On the development of the concept of heterosexuality see Jonathan Ned Katz, *The Invention of Heterosexuality*, Dutton, New York (1995); and Louis-George Tin, *The Invention of Heterosexual Culture*, MIT Press, Boston, MA (2012).

For other general histories, each with a distinctive approach, see Angus McLaren, *Twentieth-century Sexuality: A History*, Blackwell, Oxford (1999); Anna Clark, *Desire: A History of European Sexuality*, Routledge, New York (2008); Cas Wouters, *Sex and Manners: Female Emancipation in the West, 1890–2000*, Sage, London (2004), and *Informalization: Manners and Emotions since 1890*, Sage, Los Angeles (2007); Dagmar Herzog, *Sexuality in Europe: A Twentieth-Century History*, Cambridge University Press, Cambridge (2011).

SEXOLOGY: THE SCIENCE OF SEX

The history of the study of sexuality, sexology, has rightfully become a key theme, because it illustrates that the ways in which we write about sexuality to a large extent set the parameters by which we can live it. The Viennese psychiatrist Richard von Krafft-Ebing was in a very real sense the founding father of sexology. An outstanding study of his work and influence has been written by Harry Oosterhuis: *Stepchildren of Nature: Krafft-Ebing, Psychiatry and the Making of Sexual Identity*, University of Chicago Press, Chicago (2000). For the context in which he was writing, see Roy Porter and Mikuláš Teich (eds.), *Sexual Knowledge, Sexual Science: A History of Attitudes to Sexuality*, Cambridge University Press, Cambridge (1994); Roy Porter and Leslie Hall, *The Facts of Life: The Creation of Sexual Knowledge in Britain*, Yale University Press, London (1995); two volumes edited by Lucy Bland and Laura Doan: *Sexology in Culture: Labelling Bodies and Desires*; and *Sexology Uncensored: The Documents of Sexual Science*, both Polity Press, Cambridge (1998); and Kate Fisher and Rebecca Langlands (eds.), *Sex, Knowledge, and Receptions of the Past*, Oxford University Press, Oxford (2015). For the emergence of sexual ideas in the heartland of sexual theorizing in the late nineteenth and early twentieth centuries see Robert Deam Tobin, *Peripheral Dreams: The German Discovery of Sex*, University of Pennsylvania Press, Philadelphia (2015). On the global influence of sexology, see Heike Bauer (ed.), *Sexology and Translation: Cultural and Scientific Encounters across the Modern World*, Temple University Press, Philadelphia (2015).

On the USA, which became the heartland of sexology after 1945, see Helen Lefkowitz Horowitz, *Rereading Sex: Battles over Sexual Knowledge in Nineteenth Century America*, Knopf, New York (2002); Janice M. Irvine, *Disorders of Desire: Sexuality and Gender in Modern American Sexology*, Temple University Press, Philadelphia (2005); Donna J. Drucker, *The Classification of Sex: Alfred Kinsey and the Organization of Knowledge*, University of Pittsburgh Press, Pittsburgh, PA. (2014); Lisa Downing, Iain Morland and Nikki Sullivan, *Fuckology: Critical Essays on John Money's Diagnostic Concepts*, University of Chicago Press, Chicago (2014).

BIOLOGY AND SEXUAL DIFFERENCE

Anne Fausto-Sterling, *Sexing the Body: Gender Politics and the Construction of Sexuality*, Basic Books, New York (2000) provides a stimulating overview of the relationship between biology and sexual difference. An incisive critique of the pretensions of science can be found in Roger Lancaster, *The Trouble with Nature: Sex in Science and Popular Culture*, University of California Press, Berkeley (2003). The evolution of views on the biology and psychology of sexual differences can be found in John Nicholson, *Men and Women. How Different are They*, Oxford University Press, Oxford and New York (1984); Ann Oakley, *Sex, Gender and Society* (revised edition), Gower, Aldershot (1985). Brian Sykes, *Adam's Curse*, Bantam, New York (2003), argues that men are an endangered species. Steve Jones hints at the same, though from a somewhat different perspective: *Y: The Descent of Men*, Little, Brown, London (2002). Evolutionary psychology positions are advanced in Simon Baron-Cohen, *The Essential Difference: Men, Women, and the Extreme Male Brain*, Allen Lane, London (2003); and Matt Ridley, *Nature via Nurture*, Fourth Estate, London (2003). For critiques of such positions, see Steven Rose, Leon J. Kamin and R. C. Lewontin, *Not in our Genes. Biology, Ideology and Human Nature*, Penguin Harmondsworth (1984); Julian Henriques et al., *Changing the Subject: Psychology, Social Regulation and Subjectivity*, Methuen, London and New York (1984); Hilary Rose and Steven Rose (eds.), *Alas, Poor Darwin: Arguments against Evolutionary Psychology*, Vintage Books, London (2001).

PSYCHOANALYTICAL PERSPECTIVES

For psychoanalysis, the starting point is Sigmund Freud himself, especially *Three Essays on the Theory of Sexuality*, first published in 1905 and much revised over the next 20 years. It is available in Volume 7 of *The Standard Edition of the Complete Psychological Works of Sigmund Freud* edited by James Strachey, Hogarth Press and the Institute of Psychoanalysis, London (1953). Discussions of the significance of Freud to feminist analyses of sexuality can be found in: Juliet Mitchell, *Psychoanalysis and Feminism*, Allen Lane, London (1973); Nancy Chodorow, *The Reproduction of Mothering: Psychoanalysis and the Reproduction of Gender*, University of California Press, Berkeley, CA (1978); Rosalind Coward, *Patriarchal Precedents: Sexuality and Social Relations*, Routledge & Kegan Paul, London (1983); Jacques Lacan and the Ecole Freudienne, *Feminine Sexuality*, edited by Juliet Mitchell and Jacqueline Rose, Macmillan, London (1982); Teresa de Lauretis, *Practice of Love: Lesbian Sexuality and Perverse Desire*, Indiana University Press, Bloomington (1994); and Celia Harding (ed.), *Sexuality: Psychoanalytic Perspectives*, Brunner and Routledge, Hove (2001). For debate on the relevance of psychanalytic categories for historical understanding see Sally Alexander and Barbara Taylor (eds.), *History and the Psyche: Culture, Psychoanalysis, and the Past*, Palgrave Macmillan, Basingstoke (2011). For some excellent short essays on psychoanalysis and sexuality, see Elisabeth Wright (ed.), *Feminism and Psychoanalysis: A Critical Dictionary*, Blackwell, Oxford (1992).

AFFECT AND THE EMOTIONS

Concern with the emotions in relation to sexuality is central to the subject, but in recent years it has been increasingly focused on theories of affect. Margaret Wetherell provides a clear overview of the debates in *Affect and Emotions: A New Social Science Understanding*, Sage, London (2012). There has been a revival of interest in the pioneering work of Raymond Williams on 'structures of feeling', first outlined in the 1950s: see his *Marxism and Literature*, Oxford University Press, Oxford (1977). For a broader historical approach see W. Reddy, *The Navigation of Feelings: A Framework for the History of Emotions*, Cambridge University Press, Cambridge (2001). For works on sexuality that engage with notions of affect see Eve Kosofsky Sedgwick, *Touching Feeling: Affect, Pedagogy, Performativity*, Duke University Press, Durham, NC (2003); Ann Cvetkovich, *An Archive of Feeling: Trauma, Sexuality, and Lesbian Public Culture*, Duke University Press, Durham, NC (2003); Heather Love, *Feeling Backward: Loss and the Politics of Queer History*, Harvard University Press, Cambridge, MA (2007). Gilles Deleuze and his colleague Felix Guattari developed a vitalist philosophy that sought to escape the 'oedipalization' of desire that they argue psychoanalysis produces: see Frida Beckman (ed.), *Deleuze and Sex*, Edinburgh University Press, Edinburgh (2011). Their influence can be seen in recent debates on the 'posthuman' in relation to the emotions, sexuality, gender and feminism: see Rosi Braidotti, *Transpositions: On Nomadic Ethics*, Polity Press, Cambridge (2006); and *The Posthuman*, Polity Press, Cambridge (2013).

THE SOCIOLOGY OF SEXUALITY

Recent sociological debates on sexuality can be followed in the four volumes edited by Plummer, cited above. Classic sociological contributions, especially from within the interactionist tradition, include: John H. Gagnon and William Simon, *Sexual Conduct: The Social Sources of Human Sexuality*, Hutchinson, London (1973); John H. Gagnon, *Human Sexualities*, Scott, Foresman and Co., Glenview, IL (1977); Ken Plummer, *Sexual Stigma. An Interactionist Account*, Routledge & Kegan Paul, London (1975); Ken Plummer, *Telling Sexual Stories: Power, Change and Social Worlds*, Routledge, London (1995); and William Simon, *Postmodern Sexualities*, Routledge, London (1994). For other critical sociological accounts of sexuality see Gail Hawkes, *A Sociology of Sex and Sexuality*, Open University Press, Buckingham (1996), and *Sex and Pleasure in Western Culture*, Polity Press, Cambridge (2004); Diane Richardson, *Rethinking Sexuality*, Sage, London (2000); Lisa Adkins, *Revisions: Gender and Sexuality in Late Modernity*, Open University Press, Buckingham (2002); Stevi Jackson and Sue Scott, *Theorizing Sexuality*, Open University Press/McGraw Hill, London (2010); and Momin Rahman and Stevi Jackson, *Gender and Sexuality: Sociological Approaches*, Polity Press, Cambridge (2010).

A stimulating overview of the wider theoretical debates is provided by Brian Heaphy, *Late Modernity and Social Change: Reconstructing Social and Personal Life*, Routledge, Abingdon (2007). Henrietta Moore establishes a clear agenda for transnational gender and sexuality research in *The Subject of Anthropology*, Polity Press, Cambridge (2007).

FOUCAULT AND SEXUAL THEORY

No contemporary writer on sexuality can escape the influence of Michel Foucault, even if the end result is a total rejection of his works. His views are polemically summed up in *The History of Sexuality, Vol. 1, An Introduction*, Allen Lane, London (1979). The two posthumous volumes were originally published as Michel Foucault, *Histoire de la sexualite: 2, L'Usage des plaisirs, 3, Le Souci de soi*, Editions Gallimard, Paris (1984); translated as *The History of Sexuality, Vol. 2, The Use of Pleasure*, Viking, London (1985); and *The History of Sexuality, Vol. 3, The Care of the Self*, Viking, London (1986).

Foucault's interviews often provide many clarifying insights concerning his overall project. See especially *Power/Knowledge: Selected Interviews and Other Writings 1972–1977*, edited by Colin Gordon, Harvester Press, Brighton (1980); *The Foucault Reader*, edited by Paul Rabinow, Pantheon Books, New York (1984); and J. Bernauer and D. Rasmussen (eds.), *The Final Foucault*, MIT Press, Cambridge, MA (1988). Although no substitute for reading the originals, there is a vast corpus of commentaries on Foucault. I recommend two with strongly differing approaches: Lois McNay, *Foucault: A Critical Introduction*, Polity Press, Cambridge (1994); and David M. Halperin, *Saint Foucault: Towards a Gay Hagiography*, Oxford University Press, Oxford (1995). On the historicization of sexual concepts complementary to Foucault's approach see Arnold I. Davidson, *The Emergence of Sexuality: Historical Epistemology and the Formation of Concepts*, Cambridge, MA: Harvard University Press (2001).

FEMINIST THEORIES

The feminist contribution to sexual theory and practice has been critical. Stevi Jackson and Sue Scott brought together many of the most important early contributions in their edited volume *Feminism and Sexuality: A Reader*, Edinburgh University Press, Edinburgh (1996). Two earlier and highly influential collections of articles, which were themselves interventions in the feminist debates on sexuality, contain a wide range of material on the theory, history, sociology, poetry and politics (especially feminist politics) of sex: Ann Snitow, Christine Stansell and Sharon Thompson (eds.), *Desire. The Politics of Sexuality*, Virago, London (1983), published in the USA as: *Powers of Desire: The Politics of Sexuality*, Monthly Review Press, New York (1983); and Carole S. Vance (ed.), *Pleasure and Danger. Exploring Female Sexuality*, Routledge & Kegan Paul, London and Boston (1984). A long essay in the latter by Gayle S. Rubin, 'Thinking sex: notes for a radical theory of the politics of sexuality' is particularly important, and has been widely anthologized. For her later thoughts on this essay and other aspects of her work see *Deviations: A Gayle Rubin Reader*, Duke University Press, Durham, NC (2011).

Lynne Segal has been a major documenter of and contributor to the feminist theorizing on sexuality and gender. See *Slow Motion: Changing Masculinity, Changing Men*, 3rd edition, Palgrave Macmillan, Basingstoke (2006); *Straight Sex: Rethinking the Politics of Pleasure*, Verso, London (new edition 2015); *Why Feminism? Gender, Psychology, Politics*, Polity Press, Cambridge (new edition 2015).

For her reflections on ageing, gender and sexuality see *Out of Time: The Pleasures and Perils of Ageing*, Verso, London (2013). On theories of gender see Joan W. Scott, *Gender and the Politics of History*, Columbia University Press, New York (1988) and Judith Butler and Elizabeth Weed, *The Question of Gender: J. W. Scott's Critical Feminism*, Indiana University Press, Bloomington (2011). Raewyn Connell has produced classic studies of gender, power and masculinity: *Masculinities*, 2nd edition, Polity Press, Cambridge (2005); *Gender and Power: Society, the Person and Sexual Politics*, Polity Press, Cambridge (2013); (with Rebecca Pearse) *Gender: In World Perspective*, 3rd edition, Polity Press, Cambridge (2014).

Judith Butler has been enormously influential in both feminist and queer thinking about gender and sexual 'performativity'. See her *Gender Trouble: Feminism and the Subversion of Identity*, Routledge, London (1990); *Bodies that Matter: On the Discursive Limits of Sex*, Routledge, New York (2003); and *Undoing Gender*, New York (2004).

For valuable essays from within the feminist debate on heterosexuality, see Diane Richardson (ed.), *Theorising Heterosexuality: Telling it Straight*, Open University Press, Buckingham and Philadelphia (1996); Stevi Jackson. *Heterosexuality in Question*, Sage, London (2000); Janet Holland, Caroline Ramazanoglu, Sue Sharpe and Rachel Thomson, *The Male in the Head*, The Tufnell Press, London (1998). Detailed examples of the institutionalization of heterosexuality can be found in Janet Holland and Lisa Adkins (eds.), *Sex, Sensibility and the Gendered Body*, Macmillan, Basingstoke (1996); Lisa Adkins and

Vicki Merchant (eds.), *Sexualizing the Social: Power and the Organization of Sexuality*, Macmillan, Basingstoke (1996); Lisa Adkins, *Gendered Work: Sexuality, Family and the Labour Market*, Open University Press, Buckingham (1995); Jeff Hearn, Deborah L. Sheppard, Peta Tancred-Sheriff and Gibson Burrell (eds.), *The Sexuality of Organization*, Sage, London (1989). The impact of sexual violence in sustaining male domination is explored in Joanna Bourke, *Rape: A History from 1860 to the Present*, Virago, London (2008); Janie L. Leatherman, *Sexual Violence and Armed Conflict*, Polity Press, Cambridge (2011).

INTERSECTIONALITY

The interconnections between race, class, other dimensions of disadvantage, power and sexuality have been amongst the most contested and creative aspects of recent writings. An overview of the issues as they have developed over time can be found in Jennifer C. Nash, 'Re-thinking intersectionality' *Feminist Review* 89, 1–15 (2008). Yvette Taylor, Sally Hines and Mark Casey (eds.), *Theorizing Intersectionality and Sexuality*, Palgrave Macmillan, Basingstoke (2010) is an important collection of critical essays ion the theme. Patricia Hill-Collins and Sirma Bilge offer an overview of intersectional knowledge and practice in *Intersectionality*, Polity Press, Cambridge (2016). Useful anthologies on race and sexuality include Joy James and Denean Sharpley-Whiting (eds.), *The Black Feminist Reader*, Blackwell, Oxford and Malden, MA (2000); Heidi Safia Mirza (ed.), *Black British Feminism*, Routledge, London and New York (1997); Adrian Katherine Wing (ed.),

Global Critical Race Feminism: An International Reader,
New York University Press, New York (2000). See also
Patricia Hill Collins, *Black Feminist Thought*, 2nd edi-
tion, Routledge, New York (2000); and N. Zack, *Inclusive
Feminism: A Third Wave Theory of Women's Commonality*,
Rowman and Littlefield Publishers, Lanham, MD (2005).
An overview of the theoretical and historical debates
about the intersections of race, nationalism and sexuality
can be found in Joane Nagel, *Race, Ethnicity and Sexuality:
Intimate Intersections, Forbidden Frontiers*, Oxford University Press, New York (2003). For an influential study
of the intersections of class, gender and sexuality see Bev-
erley Skeggs, *Formations of Class and Gender: Becoming
Respectable*, Sage Publications, London (1997).

SAME-SEX SEXUALITIES

A vast and ever-growing literature on the history, sociology, politics and culture of homosexuality provides major
insights into the 'invention of sexuality' in general, and
the construction of same-sex desire in particular. The
range of the debates can be seen in Peter M. Nardi and
Beth E. Schneider (eds.), *Sexual Perspectives in Lesbian
and Gay Studies: A Reader*, Routledge, London (1998);
Theo Sandfort, Judith Schuyf, Jan Willem Duyvendak and
Jeffrey Weeks (eds.), *Lesbian and Gay Studies: An Introductory, Interdisciplinary Approach*, Sage, London (2000);
and Diane Richardson and Steven Seidman (eds.), *Handbook of Lesbian and Gay Studies*, Sage, London (2002). The
'essentialist/constructionist' controversy can be traced in
Edward Stein (ed.), *Forms of Desire: Sexual Orientation*

and the Social Constructionist Controversy, Routledge, New York (1992).

Influential pioneering studies include Jonathan Ned Katz, *Gay/Lesbian Almanac*, Harper & Row, New York (1983); Jonathan Ned Katz, *Love Stories: Sex Between Men before Homosexuality*, University of Chicago Press, Chicago (2001); Lillian Faderman, *Surpassing the Love of Men. Romantic Friendship and Love between Women from the Renaissance to the Present*, Junction Books, London (1980); Kenneth Plummer (ed.), *The Making of the Modern Homosexual*, Hutchinson, London (1981), and *Modern Homosexualities, Fragments of Lesbian and Gay Experience*, Routledge, London (1992); Estelle B. Freedman et al., *The Lesbian Issue. Essays from Signs*, University of Chicago Press, Chicago (1985); Martha Vicinus (ed.), *Lesbian Subjects: A Feminist Review Reader*, Indiana University Press, Bloomington (1996); Martha Vicinus, *Intimate Friends: Women who Loved Women, 1778–1928*, Chicago University Press, Chicago (2004); Lorna Doan, *Fashioning Sapphism: The Origins of a Modern English Lesbian Culture*, Columbia University Press, New York (2001), and *Disturbing Practices: History, Sexuality and Women's Experience of Modern War*, University of Chicago Press, Chicago (2013). Concise overviews of same-sex history in the UK is provided by Matt Cook (ed.), *A Gay History of Britain: Love and Sex between Men since the Middle Ages*, Greenwood World Publishing, Oxford (2007); and Rebecca Jennings, *A Lesbian History of Britain: Love and Sex between Women since 1500*, Greenwood World Publishing, Oxford (2007). On the USA see Michael Bronski, *A Queer History of the United States*, Beacon Press, Boston (2011); Leila J. Rupp and Susan K. Freeman (eds.), *Understanding and Teaching U.S. Lesbian, Gay, Bisexual and Transgender History*, University of Wisconsin Press, Madison (2014); and Lillian Faderman, *The Gay Revolution: The Story of the Struggle*, Simon and Schuster, New York (2015).

For distinctive scholarly contributions on the evolution of same-sex desires, identities and relationships over critical periods, see John Boswell, *Social Tolerance and Homosexuality: Gay People in Western Europe from the Beginning of the Christian Era to the Fourteenth Century*, University of Chicago Press, Chicago (1980); John Boswell, *Same Sex Unions in Pre-modern Europe*, Villard Books, New York (1994); Alan Bray, *Homosexuality in Renaissance England*, Gay Men's Press, London (1982), and *The Friend*, University of Chicago Press, Chicago (2003).

For more specific studies of homosexuality in a range of cross-cultural contexts over the past century or so see: George Chauncey, *Gay New York: Gender, Urban Culture, and the Making of the Gay Male World*, Basic Books, New York (1994); Matt Cook, *London and the Culture of Homosexuality, 1885–1914*, Cambridge University Press, Cambridge (2003); Matt Houlbrook, *Queer London: Perils and Pleasures in the Sexual Metropolis*, University of Chicago Press, Chicago (2005); Gary W. Dowsett, *Practicing Desire: Homosexual Sex in the Era of AIDS*, Stanford University Press, Stanford, CA (1996); Robert Reynolds, *From Camp to Queer: Remaking the Australian Homosexual*, Melbourne University Press, Melbourne (2002), and *What happened to Gay Life?*, University of New South Wales Press, NSW (2007); Steven Seidman, *Beyond the Closet: The Transformation of Gay and Lesbian Life*, Routledge,

New York (2002); Tamsin Wilton, *Unexpected Pleasures: Leaving Heterosexuality for a Lesbian Life*, Diva Ltd, London (2003). On Africa see Marc Epprecht, *Heterosexual Africa? The History of an Idea from the Age of Exploration to the Age of AIDS*, Ohio University Press, Athens, OH (2008); Neville Hoad, *African Intimacies: Race, Homosexuality, and Globalization*, University of Minnesota Press, Minneapolis (2013); Ruth Morgan and Saskia E. Wieringer (eds.), *Tommy Boys, Lesbian Men and Ancestral Wives; Female Same-Sex Experiences in Southern Africa*, Jacana Media, Auckland Park, SA (2005).

For broader sweeps, see Rudi C. Bleys, *The Geography of Perversion: Male-to-male Sexual Behaviour outside the West and the Ethnographic Imagination, 1750–1918*, Cassell, London (1996); David M. Halperin, *One Hundred Years of Homosexuality. And Other Essays on Greek Love*, Routledge, London (1990), and *How to Do the History of Homosexuality*, University of Chicago Press, Chicago (2002); Gilbert Herdt (ed.), *Third Sex, Third Gender: Beyond Sexual Dimorphism in Culture and History*, Zone Books, New York (1994); Stephen O. Murray, *Homosexualities*, University of Chicago Press, Chicago (2000); and Jennifer Robertson (ed.), *Same-sex Cultures and Sexualities: An Anthropological Reader*, Blackwell, Oxford (2004).

Perspectives on the global emergence of LGBT movements are provided by Barry D. Adam, Jan Willem Duyvendak and Andre Krouwel (eds.), *The Global Emergence of Lesbian and Gay Politics*, Temple University Press, Philadelphia (1999); Manon Tremblay, David Paternotte, and Carol Johnson (eds.), *The Lesbian and Gay Movement and the State: Comparative Insights into A Transformed*

Relationship, Ashgate, Farnham (2011); Lisa Downing and Robert Gillett (eds.), *Queer in Europe*, Ashgate, Farnham (2011); Robert Kulpa and Joanna Mizielińska (eds.), *De-Centring Western Sexualities: Central and Eastern European Perspectives*, Ashgate, Farnham (2011); Philip M. Ayoub and David Paternotte (eds.), *LGBT Activism and the Making of Europe: A Rainbow Europe?*, Palgrave Macmillan, Basingstoke (2014); David Paternotte and Manon Tremblay, *The Ashgate Companion to Lesbian and Gay Activism*, Ashgate, Farnham (2015).

For the development of the 'queer' critique, especially of identity politics, see Steven Seidman (ed.), *Queer Theory/Sociology*, Blackwell, Oxford (1996); Anne Marie Jagose, *Queer Theory: An Introduction*, New York University Press, New York (1996); Nikki Sullivan, *A Critical Introduction to Queer Theory*, Edinburgh University Press, Edinburgh (2003); Robert J. Corber and Stephen Valocchi (eds.), *Queer Studies: An Interdisciplinary Reader*, Blackwell, Malden, MA (2003); and Iain Morland and Annabelle Willox, (eds.), *Queer Theory*, Palgrave Macmillan, Basingstoke (2004). Influential texts include Michael Warner (ed.), *Fear of a Queer Planet: Queer Politics and Social Theory*, University of Minnesota Press, Minneapolis (1993); Jonathan Dollimore, *Sexual Dissidence: Augustine to Wilde, Freud to Foucault*, Clarendon Press, Oxford (1991); and the works by Judith Butler, cited above.

FROM PERVERSITY TO DIVERSITY

Julie Peakman has written an entertaining history of early debates on perversions in *The Pleasure's All Mine: A History of Perverse Sex*, Reaktion Books, London (2013). Discussions of the meaning of 'sexual perversion' can be found in Robert J. Stoller, *Perversion: The Erotic Form of Hatred*, Quartet, London (1977); Janine Chasseguet-Smirgel, *Creativity and Perversion*, Free Association Books, London (1985); Kevin Howells (ed.), *Sexual Diversity*, Blackwell, Oxford (1984), and in Downing et al, *Fuckology* cited above.

The concept of sexual diversity opens up the discussion on sexual variations in new and often contested ways. Debates on BDSM can be traced in Bill Thompson, *Sadomasochism: Painful Perversion or Pleasurable Play?*, Cassell, London (1994); and Darren Langdridge and Meg John Barker (eds.), *Safe, Sane and Consensual: Contemporary Perspectives on Sadomasochism*, Palgrave Macmillan, Basingstoke (2007). For a critical historical perspective see Alison Moore, *Sexual Myths of Modernity: Sadism, Masochism and Historical Teleology*, Lanham, Lexington (2010).

Controversies over child abuse are discussed in Paula Reavey and Sam Warner (eds.), *New Feminist Stories of Child Sexual Abuse: Sexual Scripts and Dangerous Dialogues*, Routledge, London and New York (2003); Steven Angelides, 'Historicizing Affect, Psychoanalyzing History: Paedophilia and the Discourse of Child Sexuality', *Journal of Homosexuality* 46(1–2), 79–109 (2004); Steven Angelides, 'Feminism, Child Sexual Abuse, and the Erasure of Child Sexuality', *GLQ: A Journal of Lesbian and Gay Studies* 10(2), 141–77 (2004). An international perspective can be found in Julia O'Connell Davidson, *Children in the Global Sex Trade*, Polity Press, Cambridge (2005). Matthew Waites explores the historical controversies over minimal ages for sexual activity in *The Age of Consent: Young People, Sexuality and Citizenship*, Palgrave Macmillan, Basingstoke and New York (2008).

For bisexualities, see Marjorie Garber, *Vice Versa: Bisexuality and the Eroticism of Everyday Life*, Hamish Hamilton, London (1995); Merl Storr (ed.), *Bisexuality: A Critical Reader*, Routledge, London and New York (1999); Steven Angelides, *A History of Bisexuality*, University of Chicago Press, Chicago (2001); Clare Hemmings, *Bisexual Spaces: A Geography of Sex and Gender*, Routledge, London (2013); Surya Monro, *Bisexuality: Identities, Politics and Theories*, Palgrave Macmillan, Basingstoke (2015).

On transgender, see Marjorie Garber, *Vested Interests: Cross Dressing and Cultural Anxiety*, Routledge, New York and London (1992); Kate More and Stephen Whittle (eds.), *Reclaiming Genders: Transsexual Grammar and the Fin de Siècle*, Cassell, London (1999); Viviane K. Namaste, *Invisible Lives: The Erasure of Transsexual and Transgendered People*, Chicago University Press, Chicago and London (2000); Richard Ekins and Dave King (eds.), *Blending Genders: Social Aspects of Cross-dressing and Sex-changing*, Routledge, London and New York (1996), and *The Transgender Phenomenon*, Sage, London, Thousand Islands and New Delhi (2006); Sally Hines, *Gender Diversity, Recognition and Citizenship: Towards a Politics of Difference*, Palgrave Macmillan, Basingstoke (2013); Sally Hines and Tam Sanger (eds.), *Transgender Identities: Towards a Social Analysis of Gender Diversity*, Routledge, Abingdon; Janneke Van der Ros and Joz Motmans, 'Trans Activism and LGB Movements' (2015), in Paternotte and Tremblay, cited above, 163–77.

A queer perspective can be found in Judith/Jack Halberstam (1998) *Female Masculinity*, Duke University Press, Durham and London (1998), and *In a Queer Time and Place: Transgender Bodies, Subcultural Lives*, New York University Press, New York and London (2005). For an insight into the ambiguities of cross-dressing and 'passing' see Alison Oram, *'Her Husband was a Woman!' Women's Gender-Crossing in Modern British Popular Culture*, Routledge, London (2013). An overview of the debates can be found in Patricia Elliott, 'Engaging Trans Debates on Gender Variance: A Feminist Analysis', *Sexualities* 12(1) February, 5–32 (2009). Susan Stryker and Stephen Whittle have edited a useful collection: *The Transgender Studies Reader*, Routledge, New York and Abingdon (2006). Susan Stryker has written an important historical account: *Transgender History*, Seal Press, Berkeley, CA (2008). A collection written by young adults charts the dramatic change in attitudes to what were once regarded as perverse: David Levithan and Billy Merrell (eds.), *The Full Spectrum: A New Generation of Writing about Gay, Lesbian, Bisexual, Transgender, Questioning and Other Identities*, Random House, New York (2006).

SEXUALITY AND SPACE

The importance of the spatial organization of eroticism and sexual identities is discussed in David Bell and Gill Valentine (eds.), *Mapping Desire*, Routledge, London and New York (1995); Gill Valentine, 'Queer Bodies and the Production of Space', in Richardson and Seidman (eds.), cited above; Gordon Brent Ingram, Anne-Marie Bouthillette and Yolanda Retter (eds.), *Queers in Space: Communities, Public Spaces, Sites of Resistance*, Bay Press, Seattle (1997); William L. Leap (ed.), *Public Sex, Gay Space*, Columbia University Press, New York (1999); Phil Hubbard, *Cities and Sexualities*, Routledge, Abingdon (2011); Kath Browne, Jason Lim and Gavin Brown (eds.), *Geographies of Sexualities: Theory, Practices and Politics*, Ashgate, Farnham (2012). Applications of spatial theories in relation to sexuality can be found in the books by Matt Houlbrooke and Matt Cook cited above. See also Matt Cook and Jennifer Evans (eds.), *Queer Cities, Queer Cultures: Europe since 1945*, Bloomsbury, London (2014).

HIV/AIDS

There is now a vast literature on HIV/AIDS. For a pioneering study which captures the initial reactions in the USA, see Dennis Altman, *AIDS and the Mind of America*, New York, Doubleday (1986), published in Britain as *AIDS and the New Puritans*, Pluto, London (1986); see also Altman's *Power and Community: Organizational and Cultural Responses to AIDS*, Taylor and Francis, London and Bristol, PA (1994). He provides an autobiographical overview of the crisis and response in *The End of the Homosexual?*, University of Queensland Press, St Lucia, Queensland (2013). A pioneering examination of the historical framing of the epidemic in its early stages is provided by Elizabeth Fee and Daniel M. Fox (eds.), *AIDS: The Burdens of History*, University of California Press, Berkeley (1988) and (by the same authors) *AIDS: The Making of a Chronic Disease*, University of California Press, Berkeley

(1992). Steven Epstein produced a powerful analysis of the interface been AIDS activism and the construction of knowledge about HIV/AIDS in *Pure Science: AIDS, Activism and the Politics of Knowledge*, University of Californian Press, Berkeley, Los Angeles and London (1996). For the international dimensions of the epidemic, see Mary Haour-Knipe and Richard Rector (eds.), *Crossing Borders: Migrations, Ethnicity and AIDS*, Taylor and Francis, London and Bristol, PA (1996); and Jean-Paul Moatti, Yves Souteyrand, Annice Prieur, Theo Sandfort and Peter Aggleton (eds.), *AIDS in Europe: New Challenges for the Social Sciences*, Routledge, London and New York (2000). On the early gendering of the epidemic, see Tamsin Wilton, *En-gendering AIDS: Deconstructing Sex, Text, Epidemic*, Sage, London, Thousand Oaks, CA and New Delhi (1997). The AIDS crisis produced varying form of national activism. For the UK see: Simon Watney, *Imagine Hope: AIDS and Gay Identity*, Routledge, London and New York (2000); Virginia Berridge, *AIDS in the UK: The Making of Policy, 1981–1994*, Oxford University Press, Oxford (1994). For Canada see: Michael P. Brown, *RePlacing Citizenship: AIDS Activism and Radical Democracy*, Guilford Press, New York (1997). On Australia see Jennifer Power, *Movement, Knowledge, Emotion: Gay Activism and HIV/AIDS in Australia*, ANU Press, Canberra (2011). On the USA see: Deborah Gould, *Moving Politics: Emotions and ACT UP's Fight against AIDS*, Chicago University Press, Chicago (2009). On France see Daniel Defert, *Une Vie Politque*, Editions de Seuil, Paris (2014).

SEXUAL POLITICS AND INTIMATE CITIZENSHIP

An overview of sexual-political struggles in the first decade of the twenty-first century can be found in Sonia Correa, Rosalind Petchesky and Richard Parker, *Sexuality, Health and Human Rights* Routledge, New York and London (2008). See also Richard Parker, Rosalind Petchesky and Robert Sember (eds.), *SexPolitics: Reports from the Front Lines*, Sexuality Policy Watch, available online at www.sxpolitics.org/frontlines/home/index.php.

For valuable data on changing sexual attitudes and behaviours in two key countries, see Edward O. Laumann, Robert T. Michael, John H. Gagnon and S. Michaels, *The Social Organization of Sexuality: Sexual Practices in the United States*, University of Chicago Press, Chicago (1994); Kaye Wellings, Julia Field, Anne M. Johnson and J. Wadsworth, *Sexual Behaviour in Britain: The National Survey of Sexual Attitudes and Lifestyles*, Macmillan, London and Basingstoke (1994); Anne M. Johnson, Catherine H. Mercer, Bob Erens et al., 'Sexual Behaviour in Britain: Partnerships, Practices, and HIV Risk Behaviours', *The Lancet*, Vol. 358 (9296), 1 December 2001, pp. 1835–42. For the links between the politics of nationalism and the politics of sexuality, see Andrew Parker, Mary Russo, Doris Sommer and Patricia Yaegar (eds.), *Nationalism and Sexualities*, Routledge, New York and London (1992). Useful essays can be found in Terrell Carver and Veronique Mottier (eds.), *Politics of Sexuality: Identity, Gender, Citizenship*, Routledge, London and New York (1998). My own book, *The World We Have Won*, referenced above, explores shifting attitudes in Britain in detail.

On manifestations of the New/Moral/Christian Right from the 1980s see Anne Marie Smith, *New Right Discourses on Race and Sexuality. Britain 1968–1990*, Cambridge University Press, Cambridge (1994); Didi Herman, *The Anti Gay Agenda: Orthodox Vision and the Christian Right*, University of Chicago Press, Chicago (1997); and Amy Ansell (ed.), *Unravelling the Right: The New Conservatism in American Thought and Politics*, Westview Press, Boulder, CO (2001). The impact of the debate on pornography, amongst other things, in sexual politics can be traced in Lisa Duggan and Nan D. Hunter, *Sex Wars: Sexual Dissent and Political Culture*, Routledge, New York and London (1995); and in Bill Thompson, *Soft Core: Moral Crusades against Pornography in Britain and America*, Cassell, London (1994). On the controversies over sexual 'trafficking' in women and children see Laura Maria Agustin, *Sex at the Margin: Migration, Labour Markets and the Rescue Industry*, Zed Books, London (2007), and the O'Connell Davidson (2005) study referred to above.

Sexual or intimate citizenship has become a key theme in contemporary discussions of sexuality. The pioneering study was David Evans, *Sexual Citizenship: The Material Construction of Sexualities*, Routledge, London and New York (1985). For subsequent critical interventions see David Bell and Jon Binnie, *The Sexual Citizen: Queer Politics and Beyond*, Polity Press, Cambridge (2000); Shane Phelan, *Sexual Strangers: Gays, Lesbians, and Dilemmas of Citizenship*, Temple University Press, Philadelphia (2001); Ken Plummer, *Inventing Intimate Citizenship*, University of Washington Press, Seattle (2003); Francesca Stella, Yvette Taylor, Tracey Reynolds and Antoine Rogers, *Sexuality, Citizenship and Belonging: Trans-National and Intersectional Perspectives*, Routledge, Abingdon (2016). My own contribution to the debate can be found in 'The Sexual Citizen', *Theory, Culture and Society* 15(3–4), 35–52 (1998).

Changes in patterns of intimacy are crucial to understanding contemporary patterns of sexuality. See especially Anthony Giddens, *The Transformation of Intimacy: Sexuality, Love and Eroticism in Modern Societies*, Polity Press, Cambridge (1992); Lynn Jamieson, *Intimacy: Personal Relationships in Modern Societies*, Polity Press, Cambridge (1998); Alan Frank, Patricia T. Clough and Steven Seidman (eds.), *Intimacies: A New World of Relational Life*, Routledge, Abingdon (2013); Sasha Roseneil, Mariya Stoilova, Isabel Crowhurst, Tone Hellesund and Ana Cristina Santos, 'Living Apart Together in Contemporary Europe: Accounts of Togetherness and Apartness', *Sociology* 48(6), 1075–91 (2015); Jacqui Gabb and Janet Fink, *Couple Relationships in the 21st Century*, Palgrave Macmillan, Basingstoke (2015).

Same-sex marriage is an obvious focus for debates about the meanings of intimacy, and it became the subject of heated controversy in the 2000s. See Kelly Kollman, *The Same-Sex Unions Revolution in Western Democracies: International Norms and Domestic Policy Change*, Manchester University Press, Manchester (2013); and David Paternotte, 'Global Times, Global Debates? Same-Sex Marriage Worldwide', *Social Politics* 22(4), 653–74 (2015). Although there was a common policy objective, each national case was subtly different. On Scandinavia see: Jens Rydström, *Odd Couples: A History of Gay Marriage in Scandinavia*, Aksant, Amsterdam (2011). For France: Eric Fassin, 'Same Sex, Different Politics: "Gay Marriage" Debates in France and the United States', *Public Culture* 13(2), 215–32 (2001); C. Johnston, 'The PACS and (Post)Queer Citizenship in Contemporary Republican France', *Sexualities* 11(6), December, 688–705 (2008). On Britain: Nicola Barker and Daniel Monk (eds.), *From Civil Partnership to Same-Sex Marriage: Interdisciplinary Reflections*, Routledge, Abingdon (2015). On the Netherlands: K. Waaldijk, 'Small Change: How the Road to Same-Sex Marriage Got Paved in the Netherlands', in Robert Wintermute and M. Andenaes, *Legal Recognition of Same-Sex Partnerships: A Study of National, European and International Law*, Hart Publishing, Oxford, 437–64 (2001). On southern Europe: Ana Cristina Santos, *Social Movements and Sexual Citizenship in Southern Europe*, Palgrave Macmillan, Basingstoke (2013). On the USA: George Chauncey, *Why Marriage: The History Shaping Today's Debate over Gay Equality*, Basic Books, New York (2004); M. J. Klarman, *From the Closet to the Altar: Courts, Backlash and the Struggle for Same-sex Marriage*, Oxford University Press, Oxford (2013); A. L. Brandzel, 'Queering Citizenship? Same-sex Marriage and the State', *GLQ: A Journal of Lesbian and Gay Studies* 11(2), 171–204 (2005); P. Kandaswamy, 'State Austerity and the Racial Politics of Same-Sex Marriage in the United States', *Sexualities* 11(6), 706–25 (2008).

On same-sex parenting see: Karen Griffin and Linda Mulholland (eds.), *Lesbian Mothers in Europe*, Cassell,

London (1997); Ellen Lewin, *Lesbian Mothers: Accounts of Gender in American Culture*, Cornell University Press, Ithaca (1993); Judith Stacey, *Unhitched: Love, Marriage, and Family Values from West Hollywood to Western China*, New York University Press, New York (2011); Daniel Winunwe Rivers, *Radical Relations: Lesbian Mothers, Gay Fathers, and their Children in the United States since World War II*, University of North Carolina Press, Chapel Hill, NC (2013). On 'friends as family' see Kath Weston, *Families We Choose: Lesbians, Gays, Kinship*, Columbia University Press, New York (1991); Jeffrey Weeks, Brian Heaphy and Catherine Donovan, *Same Sex Intimacies: Families of Choice and other Life Experiments*, Routledge, London (2001). For an important analysis of same-sex relationships in the last century see Matt Cook, *Queer Domesticities: Homosexuality and Home Life in Twentieth Century London*, Palgrave Macmillan, Basingstoke (2014).

SEXUALITY AND GLOBALIZATION

The globalized context of contemporary intimacies and sexualities is discussed in Dennis Altman, *Global Sex*, University of Chicago Press, Chicago (2001). There are a range of studies and examples in Aggleton et al., *Understanding Global Sexualities* referenced fully above. Ken Plummer has provided a stimulating, comprehensive and sophisticated analysis in *Cosmopolitan Sexualities: Hope and the Humanist Imagination*, Polity Press, Cambridge (2015). Peter L. Stearns offers an overview of *Sexuality in World History*, Routledge, Abingdon (2009). For discussion of the impact of global perspectives on writing sexual see Margot Canaday, 'Thinking Sex in the Transnational Turn', *American Historical Review* 114(5), 1250–1 (2009), and other contributions to the same journal; Elizabeth A. Povinelli and George Chauncey, 'Thinking Sexuality Transnationally', *GLQ: A Journal of Lesbian and Gay Studies* 5(4), 439–50 (1999).

On the globalization of gay identities see Cindy Patton and Benigno Sanchez-Eppler (eds.), *Queer Diasporas*, Duke University Press, Durham, NC and London (2000); Arnaldo Cruz-Malavé and Martin F. Manalansan IV (eds.), *Queer Globalizations: Citizenship and the Afterlife of Colonialism*, New York University Press, New York (2002); Evelyn Blackwood and Saskia E. Wieringa (eds.), *Female Desires: Same-sex Relations and Transgender Practices across Cultures*, Columbia University Press, New York (1999); Leila J. Rupp, *Sapphistries: A Global History of Love between Women*, New York University Press, New York (2009). Dennis Altman and Jonathan Symons examine some of the resulting *Queer Wars*, Polity Press, Cambridge (2016).

Critical analyses of sexual globalization can be found in Rosemary Hennessy, *Profit and Pleasure: Sexual Identities in Late Capitalism*, Routledge, New York (2000); Jon Binnie, *The Globalization of Sexuality*, Sage, London (2004); Elizabeth Bernstein and Laurie Schaffner (eds.), *Regulating Sex: The Politics of Intimacy and Identity*, Routledge, New York and London (2005).

For analyses of different cultures and nations see: Saskia Wieringa and Horacio Sívori (eds.), *The Sexual History of the Global South in Africa, Asia and Latin America*, Zed Books, London (2013); Joseph A. Massad, *Desiring Arabs*,

Chicago University Press, Chicago (2007); S. N. Nyeck and Marc Epprecht (eds.), *Sexual Diversity in Africa: Politics, Theory and Citizenship*, McGill-Queens University Press, Montreal (2013); Sylvia Tamale, *African Sexualities: A Reader*, Pambauka Press, Cape Town (2011); Susan L. Mann, *Gender and Sexuality in Modern China*, Cambridge University Press, Cambridge (2011); Richard G. Parker, *Bodies, Pleasures and Passions: Sexual Culture in Contemporary Brazil*, Beacon Press, Boston (1991), and *Beneath the Equator: Cultures of Desire, Male Homosexuality and Emerging Gay Communities in Brazil*, Routledge, London (1999); Corinne Lennox and Matthew Waites (eds.), *Human Rights, Sexual Orientation and Gender Identity in the Commonwealth*, Institute of Commonwealth Studies and Human Rights Consortium, London (2012). For the political deployment of homophobia in various nations and cultures see Meredith L. Weiss and Michael J. Bosia (eds.), *Global Homophobia: States, Movements, and the Politics of Oppression*, University of Illinois Press, Urbana (2013).

HUMAN SEXUAL RIGHTS

The emergence of new discourses on human sexual rights has been one of the most important shifts since the end of the last century. For a short but powerful discussion of the evolution of the concept of human rights see Lynn Hunt, *Inventing Human Rights: A History*, W.H. Norton and Co, New York and London (2007). On the meanings of humanity see Joanna Bourke, *What it Means to be Human: Reflections from 1791 to the Present*, Virago, London

(2011). For a stimulating and powerful discussion of 'critical humanism' see Ken Plummer, *Cosmopolitan Sexualities*, fully referenced above. For the evolution of specific ideas of human sexual rights see Nicholas Bamforth (ed.), *Sex Rights*, Oxford Amnesty Lectures, Oxford University Press, Oxford and New York (2005); Rosalind Petchesky and Karen Judd, *Negotiating Reproductive Rights: Women's Perspectives across Countries and Cultures*, Zed Books, London (1998); and Rosalind Petchesky, 'Sexual Rights: Inventing a Concept, Mapping an International Practice', in Parker et al. (2000); Correa et al., *Sexuality, Health and Human Rights* (2008), fully referenced above. The development of LGBT human rights are discussed in detail in Kelly Kollman and Matthew Waites (eds.), 'The Global Politics of LGBT Human Rights', Special Issue of *Contemporary Politics* 15(1), (2009).

BIBLIOGRAPHY

Adam, Barry D. (1978) *The Survival of Domination: Inferiorization and Everyday Life*, Elsevier, New York.

Adam, Barry D. (1995) *The Rise of a Lesbian and Gay Movement*, Twayne, New York.

Adam, Barry D., Jan Willem Duyvendak and Andre Krouwel (eds.) (1999) *The Global Emergence of Gay and Lesbian Politics: National Imprints of a Worldwide Movement*, Temple University Press, Philadelphia.

Adkins, Lisa (1995) *Gendered Work: Sexuality, Family and the Labour Market*, Open University Press, Buckingham.

Adkins, Lisa (2002) *Revisions: Gender and Sexuality in Late Modernity*, Open University Press, Buckingham.

Aggleton, Peter and Richard Parker (eds.) (2010) *Routledge Handbook of Sexuality, Health and Rights*, Routledge, Abingdon.

Aggleton, Peter, Paul Boyce, Henrietta L. Moore and Richard Parker (eds.) (2012) *Understanding Global Sexualities: New Frontiers*, Routledge, Abingdon.

Alexander, Sally and Barbara Taylor (eds.) (2011) *History and the Psyche: Culture, Psychoanalysis, and the Past*, Palgrave Macmillan, Basingstoke.

Altman, Dennis (1982) *The Homosexualization of America, The Americanization of the Homosexual*, St Martin's Press, New York.

Altman, Dennis (1994) *Power and Community: Organizational and Cultural Responses to AIDS*, Taylor and Francis, London.

Altman, Dennis (2001) *Global Sex*, University of Chicago Press, Chicago.

Altman, Dennis (2013) *The End of the Homosexual?*, University of Queensland Press, St Lucia, Queensland.

Altman, Dennis and Jonathan Symons (2016) *Queer Wars*, Polity Press, Cambridge.

American Psychiatric Association (2013) *Diagnostic and Statistical Manual of Mental Disorders*, 5th edition (DSM-5), American Psychiatric Association, Washington, DC.

Amos, Valerie and Pratibha Parmar (1984) 'Challenging imperial feminism', *Feminist Review* 17, 3–19.

Angelides, Steven (2001) *A History of Bisexuality*, University of Chicago Press, Chicago.

Angelides, Steven (2004a) 'Historicizing affect, psychoanalizing history: Paedophilia and the discourse of child sexuality', *Journal of Homosexuality* 46(1–2), 79–109.

Angelides, Steven (2004b) 'Feminism, child sexual abuse, and the erasure of child sexuality', *GLQ: A Journal of Lesbian and Gay Studies* 10(2), 141–77.

Anthias, Floya and Nira Yuval Davis (1983) 'Contextualizing feminism – gender, ethnic and class divisions', *Feminist Review* 15, Winter, 62–75.

Anthias, Floya and Nira Yuval Davis (1993) *Racialized Boundaries: Race, Nation, Gender, Colour and Class and the anti-Racist Struggle*, Routledge, London.

Archer, John and Barbara Lloyd (1982) *Sex and Gender*, Penguin, Harmondsworth.

Archer, John and Barbara Lloyd (2002) *Sex and Gender*, 2nd edition, Cambridge University Press, Cambridge.

Asexuality Archive.com (2012) *Asexuality: A Brief Introduction*, Asexuality Archive.com.

Attwood, Feona (ed.) (2009) *Mainstreaming Sex: The Sexualization of Western Culture*, I. B. Tauris, London.

Baird, Vanessa (2007) *The No-Nonsense Guide to Sexual Diversity*, New edition, New Internationalist Publications, Oxford.

Bamforth, Nicholas (ed.) (2005) *Sex Rights*, Oxford Amnesty Lectures, Oxford University Press, Oxford.

Barker, Meg John and Darren Langdridge (eds.) (2010) *Understanding Nonmonogamies*, Routledge, New York.

Barker, Nicola and Daniel Monk (eds.) (2015) *From Civil Partnership to Same-Sex Marriage: Interdisciplinary Reflections*, Routledge, Abingdon.

Bauman, Zygmunt (2003) *Liquid Love: On the Frailty of Human Bonds*, Polity Press, Cambridge.

Bauman, Zygmunt (2005) *Liquid Life*, Polity Press, Cambridge.

Bayer, Ronald (1981) *Homosexuality and American Psychiatry. The Politics of Diagnosis*, Basic Books, New York.

BBC (2015) 'Teenage pregnancy rate continue to fall', at http://www.bbc.co.uk/news/health-34050975, 25 April 2015, accessed 9 June 2016.

Beccalossi, Chiara (2012) *Female Sexual Inversion: Same-Sex Desire in Italian and British Sexology, c. 1870–1920*, Palgrave Macmillan, Basingstoke.

Beck, Ulrich (1999) *Risk Society: Towards a New Modernity*, Sage, London.

Beck, Ulrich (2002) 'The cosmopolitan society and its enemies', *Theory, Culture and Society* 19(1–2), 17–44.

Beck, Ulrich and Elisabeth Beck-Gernsheim (1995) *The Normal Chaos of Love*, Polity Press, Cambridge.

Beck, Ulrich and Elisabeth Beck-Gernsheim (2002) *Individualization: Institutionalized Individualism and its Social and Political Consequences*, Sage, London.

Beckman, Frida (2011) *Deleuze and Sex*, Edinburgh University Press, Edinburgh.

Bell, Alan P., Martin S. Weinberg and Sue Keifer Hammersmith (1981) *Sexual Preference: Its Development in Men and Women*, Indiana University Press, Bloomington.

Bell, David and Gill Valentine (eds.) (1995) *Mapping Desire*, Routledge, London.

Bell, Mark (1998) 'Sexual orientation and anti-discrimination policy: The European Community', in Terrell Carver and Veronique Mottier (eds.), *Politics of Sexuality: Identity, Gender, Citizenship*, Routledge, London, 58–67.

Benedict, Ruth (1980, first published 1935) *Patterns of Culture*, Routledge and Kegan Paul, London.

Benjamin, Jessica (1984) 'Master and slave: The fantasy of erotic domination', in Ann Snitow, Christine Stansell and Sharon Thompson (eds.), *Desire: The Politics of Sexuality*, Virago, London, 292–311.

Bernstein, Elizabeth and Laurie Schaffner (eds.) (2005) *Regulating Sex: The Politics of Intimacy and Identity*, Routledge, New York.

Bhatt, Chetan (1997) *Liberation and Purity: Race. New Religious Movements and the Ethics of Postmodernity*, UCL Press, London.

Binnie, Jon (2004) *The Globalization of Sexuality*, Sage, London.

Boswell, John (1994) *Same Sex Unions in Pre-modern Europe*, Villard Books, New York.

Bouhdiba, Abdelwahab (1985) *Sexuality in Islam*, translated by Alan Sheridan, Routledge and Kegan Paul, London.

Brandzel, A. L. (2005) 'Queering citizenship? Same-sex marriage and the state', *GLQ: A Journal of Lesbian and Gay Studies* 11(2), 171–204.

Bray, Alan (1982) *Homosexuality in Renaissance England*, Gay Men's Press, London.

Bristow, Joseph (2011) *Sexuality*, Routledge, New York and London.

Brooks-Gordon, B., L. Gelsthorpe, M. Johnson and A. Bainham (eds.) (2004) *Sexuality Repositioned: Diversity and the Law*, Hart Publishing, Oxford.

Broque, Christophe (2015) 'AIDS activism from north to global', in Paternotte and Tremblay (eds.), 59–72.

Brown, Gavin (2015) 'Queer movement', in Paternotte and Tremblay (eds.), 73–86.

Brown, Wendy (2006) *Regulating Aversion: Tolerance in the Age of Identity and Empire*, Princeton University Press, Princeton, NJ.

Brown, Wendy and Rainer Forst (2014) *The Power of Tolerance: A Debate*, edited by Luca di Blasi and Christoph F. E. Holzhey, Columbia University Press, New York.

Bryant, Karl and Salvador Vidal-Ortiz (eds.) (2008) 'Introduction to retheorizing homophobia', *Sexualities* 11(4), August, 387–96.

Bullough, Vern L. (1976) *Sex, Society and History*, Science History Publications, New York. The particular essay, 'Sex in history: A virgin field', was first published in 1972.

Butler, Judith (1990) *Gender Trouble: Feminism and the Subversion of Identity*, Routledge, New York.

Butler, Judith (1993) *Bodies that Matter: On the Discursive Limits of Sex*, Routledge, New York.

Butler, Judith (2005) 'On being besides oneself: On the limits of sexual autonomy', in Bamforth (ed.), 48–78.

Califia, Pat (1979) 'Unraveling the sexual fringe. A secret side of lesbian sexuality', *The Advocate* 27, December, 19–21.

Califia, Patrick (2014) *Sex Changes: Transgender Politics*, Cleiss Press, Berkeley, CA.

Canaday, Margot (2009) *The Straight State: Sexuality and Citizenship in Twentieth Sexuality America*, Princeton University Press, Princeton, NJ.

Carnes, Patrick (2001) *Out of the Shadows: Understanding Sexual Addiction*, Hazeldon Publishing, Centre City, MN.

Carrigan, Mark, Kristina Gupta and Todd G. Morrison (eds.) (2014) *Asexuality and Sexual Normativity: An Anthology*, Routledge, Abingdon.

Cartledge, Sue and Joanna Ryan (eds.) (1983) *Sex and Love: New Thoughts on Old Contradictions*, The Women's Press, London.

Cerankowski, June Karli and Megan Milks (eds.) (2014) *Asexualities: Feminist and Queer Perspectives*, Routledge, New York.

Chasseguet-Smirgel, Janine (1985) *Creativity and Perversion*, Free Association Books, London.

Chauncey, George (2004) *Why Marriage? The History Shaping Today's Debate over Gay Equality*, Basic Books, New York.

Cherfas, Jeremy and John Gribbin (1984) *The Redundant Male*, The Bodley Head, London.

Chodorow, Nancy (1978) *The Reproduction of Mothering: Psychoanalysis and the Reproduction of Gender*, University of California Press, Berkeley, CA.

Chodorow, Nancy (1980) 'Gender, relation and difference in psychoanalytic perspective', in Hester Eisenstein and Alice Jardine (eds.), *The Future of Difference*, G. K. Hall, Boston, MA, 3–19.

Connell, Raewyn (2005) *Masculinities*, 2nd edition, Polity Press, Cambridge.

Connell, Raewyn (2009) *Gender*, 2nd edition, Polity Press, Cambridge.

Connell, Raewyn (2013) *Gender and Power: Society, the Person and Sexual Politics*, Polity Press, Cambridge.

Cook, Matt (2003) *London and the Culture of Homosexuality, 1885–1914*, Cambridge University Press, Cambridge.

Cook, Matt (2014) *Queer Domesticities: Homosexuality and Home Life in Twentieth Century London*, Palgrave Macmillan, Basingstoke.

Correa, Sonia, Rosalind Petchesky and Richard Parker (2008) *Sexuality, Health and Human Rights*, Routledge, New York.

Coveney, Lal, Margaret Jackson, Sheila Jeffreys, Leslie Kaye, and Pat Mahony (1984) *The Sexuality Papers. Male Sexuality and the Social Control of Women*, Hutchinson, London.

Coward, Rosalind (1983) *Patriarchal Precedents: Sexuality and Social Relations*, Routledge and Kegan Paul, London.

Coward, Rosalind (1984) *Female Desire: Women's Sexuality Today*, Paladin, London.

Davidson, Arnold I. (2001) *The Emergence of Sexuality: Historical Epistemology and the Formation of Concepts*, Harvard University Press, Cambridge, MA.

Davis, Murray S. (1983) *Smut: Erotic Reality/Obscene Ideology*, University of Chicago Press, Chicago.

Dawkins, Richard (1978) *The Selfish Gene*, Granada, St Albans.

D'Emilio, John (1983) *Sexual Politics, Sexual Communities: The Making of a Homosexual Minority in the United States 1940–1970*, University of Chicago Press, Chicago.

Dollimore, Jonathan (1991) *Sexual Dissidence: Augustine to Wilde, Freud to Foucault*, Clarendon Press, Oxford.

Downing, Lisa, Iain Morland and Nikki Sullivan (2014) *Fuckology: Critical Essays on John Money's Diagnostic Concepts*, University of Chicago Press, Chicago.

Duggan, Lisa (2003) *The Twilight of Equality? Neoliberalism, Cultural Politics, and the Attack on Democracy*, Beacon Press, Boston, MA.

Duggan, Lisa and Nan D. Hunter (1995) *Sex Wars: Sexual Dissent and Political Culture*, Routledge, New York.

Dyer, Richard (1985) 'Male sexuality in the media', in Andy Metcalf and Martin Humphries (eds.), *The Sexuality of Men*, Pluto Press, London, 28–43.

Edholm, F. (1982) 'The unnatural family', in Elizabeth Whitelegg et al. (eds.), *The Changing Experience of Women*, Martin Robertson, Oxford, 166–177.

Egan, R. Danielle and Gail Hawkes (2010) *Theorizing the Sexual Child in Modernity*, Palgrave Macmillan, New York and London.

Ekins, Richard and Dave King (2006) *The Transgender Phenomenon*, Sage, London.

El Feki, Shereen (2013) *Sex and the Citadel: Intimate Life in a Changing Arab World*, Chatto and Windus, London.

Elliott, Anthony and Charles Lemert (2006) *The New Individualism: The Emotional Costs of Globalization*, Routledge, London.

Elliott, Patricia (2009) 'Engaging trans debates on gender variance: A feminist analysis', *Sexualities* 12(1), February, 5–32.

Ellis, Havelock (1946; first published 1933) *The Psychology of Sex*, William Heinemann, London.

Engels, Friedrich (1972) *The Origin of the Family, Private Property and the State*, Lawrence & Wishart, London.

Epstein, Steven (1996) *Impure Science: AIDS, Activism and the Politics of Knowledge*, University of California Press, Berkeley, CA.

Evans, David (1985) *Sexual Citizenship: The Material Construction of Sexualities*, Routledge, London.

Eysenck, H. J. and G. D. Wilson (1979) *The Psychology of Sex*, Dent, London.

Faderman, Lillian (1981) *Surpassing the Love of Men*, Junction Books, London.

Faderman, Lillian (2015) *The Gay Revolution: The Story of the Struggle*, Simon and Schuster, New York.

Fausto-Sterling, Anne (2000) *Sexing the Body: Gender Politics and the Construction of Sexuality*, Basic Books, New York.

Flandrin, Jean-Louis (1985) 'Sex in married life in the early Middle Ages: The Church's teaching and behavioural reality', in Philippe Aries and Andre Bejin (eds.), *Western Sexuality: Practice and Precept in Past and Present Times*, Blackwell, Oxford, 114–29.

Ford, C. S. and F. A. Beach (1965; first published 1952) *Patterns of Sexual Behavior*, Methuen, London.

Forst, Rainer (2013) *Toleration in Conflict: Past and Present*, Cambridge University Press, Cambridge.

Foucault, Michel (1979) *The History of Sexuality, Vol. 1. An Introduction*, translated by Robert Hurley, Allen Lane, London.

Foucault, Michel (1980a) *Power/Knowledge*, edited by Colin Gordon, Harvester Press, Brighton.

Foucault, Michel (1980b) *Herculine Barbin, Being the Recently Discovered Memoirs of a Nineteenth-Century French Hermaphrodite*, Pantheon Books, New York.

Foucault, Michel (1982/83) 'Sexual choice, sexual acts', *Salmagundi* 12, 58–59.

Foucault, Michel (1984) 'On the genealogy of ethics: An overview of work in progress', in Paul Rabinow (ed.), *The Foucault Reader*, Pantheon Books, New York, 340–372.

Foucault, Michel (1985) *The History of Sexuality, Vol. 2, The Use of Pleasure*, Viking, London.

Foucault, Michel (1986) *The History of Sexuality, Vol. 3, The Care of the Self*, Viking, London.

Freeman, Derek (1983) *Margaret Mead and Samoa: The Making and Unmaking of an Anthropological Myth*, Harvard University Press, Cambridge, MA.

Freud, Ernst (ed.) (1961) *Letters of Sigmund Freud 1873–1939*, Hogarth Press, London.

Freud, Sigmund (1905) *Three Essays on the Theory of Sexuality* in Freud 1953–74, Vol. 7.

Freud, Sigmund (1910) *Leonardo da Vinci and a Memory of his Childhood*, in Freud 1953–74, Vol. 11.

Freud, Sigmund (1916–17) *Introductory Lectures on Psychoanalysis*, in Freud 1953–74, Vol. 16.

Freud, Sigmund (1920) *The Psychogenesis of Homosexuality in a Woman*, in Freud 1953–74, Vol. 18.

Freud, Sigmund (1921) *Group Psychology and the Analysis of the Ego*, in Freud 1953–74, Vol. 18.

Freud, Sigmund (1930) *Civilisation and its Discontents*, in Freud 1953–74, Vol. 21.

Freud, Sigmund (1953–74) *The Standard Edition of the Complete Psychological Works of Sigmund Freud*, edited by James Strachey, Hogarth Press and The Institute of Psychoanalysis, London.

Gagnon, John H. (1977) *Human Sexualities*, Scott, Foresman and Co., Glenview, Illinois.

Gagnon, John. H. and William Simon (1973) *Sexual Conduct: The Social Sources of Human Sexuality*, Hutchinson, London.

Garber, Marjorie (1992) *Vested Interests: Cross Dressing and Cultural Anxiety*, Routledge, New York and London.

Garber, Marjorie (1995) *Vice Versa: Bisexuality and the Eroticism of Everyday Life*, Routledge, New York.

Giddens, Anthony (1992) *The Transformation of Intimacy: Sexuality, Love and Eroticism in Modern Societies*, Polity Press, Cambridge.

Gilder, George F. (1973) *Sexual Suicide*, Quadrangle, New York.

Gilroy, Paul (2004) *After Empire: Melancholia or Convivial Culture*, Routledge, Abingdon.

Gittins, Diana (1982) *Fair Sex: Family Size and Structure 1900–1939*, Hutchinson, London.

Gouldner, Alvin (1973) *For Sociology*, Allen Lane, London.

Halberstam, Judith/Jack (1998) *Female Masculinity*, Duke University Press, Durham.

Halberstam, Judith/Jack (2005) *In a Queer Time and Place: Transgender Bodies, Subcultural Lives*, New York University Press, New York.

Halperin, David M. (1990) *One Hundred Years of Homosexuality. And Other Essays on Greek Love*, Routledge, London.

Halperin, David M. (2002) *How to Do the History of Homosexuality*, University of Chicago Press, Chicago.

Hamer, Dean, S. Hu, Vicki L. Magnusen, N. Hu, and Angela M. Pattatuci (1993) 'A linkage between DNA markers on the X chromosome and male sexual orientation', *Science* 261, 421–27.

Haour-Knipe, Mary and Richard Rector (eds.) (1996) *Crossing Borders: Migrations, Ethnicity and AIDS*, Taylor and Francis, London.

Haritaworn, Jinthana (2012) *The Biopolitics of Mixing: Thai Multiculturalities and Haunted Ascendencies*, Ashgate, Farnham.

Hawkes, Gail (2004) *Sex and Pleasure in Western Culture*, Polity Press, Cambridge.

Heaphy, Brian (2007) *Late Modernity and Social Change: Reconstructing Social and Personal Life*, Routledge, Abingdon.

Heaphy, Brian, Carol Smart and Anna Einarsdottir (2012) *Same Sex Marriages: New Generations, New Relationships*, Palgrave Macmillan, Basingstoke.

Hearn, Jeff, Deborah L. Sheppard, Peta Tancred-Sheriff and Gibson Burrell (eds.) (1989) *The Sexuality of Organization*, Sage, London.

Heath, Stephen (1982) *The Sexual Fix*, Macmillan, London.

Hennessy, Rosemary (2000) *Profit and Pleasure: Sexual Identities in Late Capitalism*, Routledge, New York.

Herdt, Gilbert (1994) *Third Sex, Third Gender: Beyond Sexual Dimorphism in Culture and History*, Zone Books, New York.

Herdt, Gilbert (ed.) (2009) *Moral Panics, Sex Panics: Fear and the Fight over Sexual Rights*, New York University Press, New York.

Herman, Didi (1997) *The Anti Gay Agenda: Orthodox Vision and the Christian Right*, University of Chicago Press, Chicago.

Herzog, Dagmar (2011) *Sexuality in Europe: A Twentieth-Century History*, Cambridge University Press, Cambridge.

Hill-Collins, Patricia and Sirma Bilge (2016) *Intersectionality*, Polity Press, Cambridge.

Hines, Sally (2013) *Gender Diversity, Recognition and Citizenship: Towards a Politics of Difference*, Palgrave Macmillan, Basingstoke.

Hines, Sally and Tam Sanger (eds.) (2012) *Transgender Identities: Towards a Social Analysis of Gender Diversity*, Routledge, Abingdon.

Hirschfeld, Magnus (1930) 'Presidential address: The development and scope of sexology', in Norman Haire (ed.), *World League for Sexual Reform: Proceedings of the Third Congress*, Kegan Paul, London, xii–xv.

Hochschild, A. R. (2003) *The Managed Heart: Commercialization of Human Feeling* (20th anniversary edition), University of California Press, Berkeley.

Holland, Janet, Caroline Ramazanoglu, Sue Sharpe and Rachel Thomson (1998) *The Male in the Head*, The Tufnell Press, London.

Hunt, Lynn (2007) *Inventing Human Rights: A History*, W. H. Norton and Co, New York.

Hunt, Stephen (2015) 'Faith and religion', in Paternotte and Tremblay (eds.), 243–58.

Ignatieff, Michael (1984) *The Needs of Strangers*, Chatto and Windus, London.

Jackson, Stevi (2009) *Heterosexuality in Question*, Sage, London.

Jackson, Stevi and Sue Scott (2010) *Theorizing Sexuality*, Open University Press and McGraw Hill, London.

Jagose, Anne Marie (1996) *Queer Theory: An Introduction*, New York University Press, New York.

Jamieson, Lynn (1998) *Intimacy: Personal Relationships in Modern Societies*, Polity Press, Cambridge.

Johnson, Anne M., Catherine H. Mercer, Bob Erens, Andrew J. Copas, Sally McManus, Kaye Wellings, et al. (2001) 'Sexual behaviour in Britain: Partnerships, practices, and HIV risk behaviours', *The Lancet* 358(9296), 1835–42.

Johnson, Mark (1997) *Beauty and Power: Transgendering and Cultural Transformation in the Southern Philippines*, Berg, Oxford.

Johnston, Cristina (2008) 'The PACS and (post-) queer citizenship in contemporary Republican France', *Sexualities* 11(6), December, 688–705.

Jones, Ernest (1955) *The Life and Work of Sigmund Freud*, Vol. 2, Basic Books, New York.

Jones, Steve (2002) *Y: The Descent of Men*, Little-Brown, London.

Jones, Steve (2009) *Darwin's Island: The Galapagos in the Garden of England*, Little-Brown, London.

Kafer, Alison (2013) *Feminist, Queer, Crip*, Indiana University Press, Bloomington, Indiana.

Kandaswamy, Priya (2008) 'State austerity and the racial politics of same-sex marriage in the US', *Sexualities* 11(6), December, 706–25.

Katz, Jonathan Ned (1995) *The Invention of Heterosexuality*, NAL and Dutton, New York.

Kinsey, Alfred C., Wardell B. Pomeroy and Clyde E. Martin (1948) *Sexual Behavior in the Human Male*, W. B. Saunders, Philadelphia.

Kinsey, Alfred C., Wardell P. Pomeroy, Clyde E. Martin and Paul H. Gebhard (1953) *Sexual Behavior in the Human Female*, W. B. Saunders Company, Philadelphia.

Klesse, Christian (2006) 'Heterornormativity, Non-monogamy and the marriage debate in the bisexual movement', *Lesbian and Gay Psychology Review* 7(2), 162–73.

Klesse, Christian (2007) *The Spectre of Promiscuity: Gay Male and Bisexual Non-monogamies and Polyamories*, Ashgate, Aldershot.

Kollman, Kelly (2007) 'Same-sex unions: The globalization of an idea', *International Studies Quarterly* 51(2), 329–57.

Kollman, Kelly (2013) *The Same-sex Union Revolution in Western Democracies: International Norms and Domestic Policy Change*, Manchester University Press, Manchester.

Kollman, Kelly (2015) 'Same-sex partnership and marriage: The success and costs of transnational activism', in Paternotte and Tremblay (eds.), 307–21.

Kollman, Kelly and Matthew Waites (eds.) (2009) 'The global politics of LGBT human rights', Special Issue of *Contemporary Politics* 15(1), March.

Krafft-Ebing, Richard von (1931) *Psychopathia Sexualis. A Medico-Forensic Study, with especial attention to the Antipathic Sexual Instinct*, Physicians and Surgeon's Book Company, Brooklyn, NY.

Kulick, Don (1998) *Travesti: Sex, Gender and Culture Among Brazilian Transgendered Prostitutes*, University of Chicago Press, Chicago.

Kulick, Don and Jens Rydström (2015) *Loneliness and its Opposite: Sex, Disability, and the Ethics of Engagement*, Duke University Press, Durham, NC.

Lancaster, Roger (2003) *The Trouble with Nature: Sex in Science and Popular Culture*, University of California Press, Berkeley, CA.

Langdridge, Darren and Meg John Barker (eds.) (2007) *Safe, Sane and Consensual: Contemporary Perspectives on Sadomasochism*, Palgrave Macmillan, Basingstoke.

Laplanche, J. and J. B. Pontalis (1980) *The Language of Psychoanalysis*, The Hogarth Press and the Institute of Psychoanalysis, London.

Laqueur, Thomas (1990) *Making Sex: Body and Gender from the Greeks to Freud*, Harvard University Press, Cambridge MA.

Laumann, Edward O., Robert T. Michael, John H. Gagnon and S. Michaels (1994) *The Social Organization of Sexuality: Sexual Practices in the United States*, University of Chicago Press, Chicago.

Lauretis, Teresa de (1994) *Practice of Love: Lesbian Sexuality and Perverse Desire*, Indiana University Press, Bloomington.

Lennox, Corinne and Matthew Waites (eds.) (2012) *Human Rights, Sexual Orientation and Gender Identity in the Commonwealth*, Institute of Commonwealth Studies and Human Rights Consortium, London.

LeVay, Simon (1991) 'A difference in hypothalamic structure between heterosexual and homosexual men', *Science* 253, 1034–37.

Linden, Robin Ruth, Darlene R. Pagano, Diana E. H. Russell, and Susan Leigh Star (eds.) (1982) *Against Sadomasochism: A Radical Feminist Analysis*, Frog in the Web, East Palo Alto, CA.

Loe, Meika (2004) *The Rise of Viagra: How the Little Blue Pill Changed Sex in America*, New York University Press, New York.

Loseke, Donileen R., Nancy Scheper Hughes, John Devine, John Gagnon, Colin Samson, Benjamin Shephard, et al. (2003)

'Forum: The Catholic Church, paedophiles and child sex abuse', *Sexualities* 6(1), 6–64.

Love, Heather (2007) *Feeling Backward: Loss and the Politics of Queer History*, Harvard University Press, Cambridge, MA.

Lowe, Donald M. (1982) *History of Bourgeois Perception*, Chicago University Press, Chicago.

Mahdavi, Pardis (2009) *Passionate Uprisings: Iran's Sexual Revolution*, Stanford University Press, Stanford, CA.

Malinowski, Bronislaw (1929) *The Sexual Life of Savages*, Routledge and Kegan Paul, London.

Malinowski, Bronislaw (1963) *Sex, Culture and Myth*, Rupert Hart-Davis, London.

Marwick, Arthur (1998) *The Sixties: Cultural Revolution in Britain, France, Italy and the United States, c. 1958-c.1974*, Oxford University Press, Oxford.

Massad, Joseph A. (2007) *Desiring Arabs*, Chicago University Press, Chicago.

Masters, William H. and Virginia E. Johnson (1966) *Human Sexual Response*, Little, Brown, Boston.

McIntosh, Mary (1968) 'The homosexual role', *Social Problems* 16(2), 182–92.

McLaren, Angus (1978) *Birth Control in Nineteenth Century England*, Croom Helm, London.

McLaren, Angus (1984) *Reproductive Rituals*, Methuen, London.

Mead, Margaret (1948) *Sex and Temperament in Three Primitive Societies*, Routledge and Kegan Paul, London.

Mead, Margaret (1949) *Male and Female. A Study of the Sexes in a Changing World*, Victor Gollancz, London.

Mead, Margaret (1977; first published 1928) *Coming of Age in Samoa. A Study of Adolescence and Sex in Primitive Societies*, Penguin, Harmondsworth.

Mesli, Rostom and Gayle Rubin (2015) 'SM politics, SM communities in the United States', in Paternotte and Tremblay (eds.), 291–306.

Micklethwaite, John and Adrian Wooldridge (2009) *God is Back: How the Global Rise of Faith is Changing the World*, Allen Lane, London.

Mitchell, Juliet (1974) *Psychoanalysis and Feminism*, Allen Lane, London.

Moatti, Jean-Paul, Yves Souteyrand, Annice Prieur, Theo Sandfort and Peter Aggleton (eds.) (2000) *AIDS in Europe: New Challenges for the Social Sciences*, Routledge, London.

Moberly, Elizabeth R. (1983) *Psychoanalysis: The Early Development of Gender-identity*, Routledge and Kegan Paul, London.

Money, John (1980) *Love and Love Sickness*, Johns Hopkins University Press, Baltimore and London.

Monro, Surya (2015) *Bisexuality: Identities, Politics and Theories*, Palgrave Macmillan, Basingstoke.

Moore, Henrietta L. (2011) *Still Life: Hopes, Desires and Satisfactions*, Polity Press, Cambridge.

Moore, Susan (2010) *Sexual Myths of Modesty: Sadism, Masochism and Historical Teleology*, Lanham, Lexington.

More, Kate and Stephen Whittle (eds.) (1999) *Reclaiming Genders: Transsexual Grammar at the fin de siecle*, Cassell, London.

Morgan, D. (1999) 'What does a transsexual want? The encounter between psychoanalysis and transsexualism', in More and Whittle (eds.), 219–39.

Nagel, Joane (2003) *Race, Ethnicity and Sexuality: Intimate Intersections, Forbidden Frontiers*, Oxford University Press, New York.

Namaste, Viviane K. (2000) *Invisible Lives: The Erasure of Transsexual and Transgendered People*, Chicago University Press, Chicago and London.

Nash, Jennifer C. (2008) 'Re-thinking intersectionality', *Feminist Review* 89, 1–15.

Neale, Palena R. (1998) 'Sexuality and the international conference on population and development. The Catholic Church in international politics', in Terrell Carver and Veronique Mottier (eds.), *Politics of Sexuality: Identity, Gender, Citizenship*, Routledge, London, 147–57.

Nicholson, John (1984) *Men and Women: How Different Are They?* Oxford University Press, Oxford.

Nicol, Nancy and Miriam Smith (2008) 'Legal struggles and political resistance: Same-sex marriage in Canada and the USA', *Sexualities* 11(6), December, 667–87.

Nussbaum, Martha (1999) *Sex and Social Justice*, Oxford University Press, New York and Oxford.

O'Carroll, Tom (1980) *Paedophilia. The Radical Case*, Peter Owen, London.

O'Connell Davidson, Julia (1998) *Prostitution, Power and Freedom*, Polity Press, Cambridge.

O'Connell Davidson, Julia (2005) *Children in the Global Sex Trade*, Polity Press, Cambridge.

O'Connell Davidson, Julia and J. Sanchez Taylor (2005) 'Travel and taboo: Heterosexual sex tourism to the Caribbean', in Bernstein and Schaffler (eds.), 83–100.

Omolade, Barbara (1984) 'Hearts of darkness', in Ann Snitow, Christine Stansell and Sharon Thompson (eds.), *Desire: The Politics of Sexuality*, Virago, London, 361–77.

Oosterhuis, Harry (2000) *Stepchildren of Nature: Krafft-Ebing, Psychiatry and the Making of Sexual Identity*, University of Chicago Press, Chicago.

Padgug, Robert A. (1979) 'Sexual matters: On conceptualizing sexuality in history', *Radical History Review* 20, Spring/Summer (special issue on 'Sexuality in History'), 3–23.

Parker, Richard (1991) *Bodies, Pleasures and Passions: Sexual Culture in Contemporary Brazil*, Beacon Press, Boston.

Parker, Richard (1999) *Beneath the Equator: Cultures of Desire, Male Homosexuality and Emerging Gay Communities in Brazil*, Routledge, London.

Parker, Richard, Marie Barbosa and Peter Aggleton (2000) *Framing the Sexual Subject: The Politics of Gender, Sexuality and Power*, University of California Press, Berkeley, CA.

Paternotte, David and Hakan Seckinelgin (2015) ' "Lesbian and gay rights are human rights": Multiple globalizations and LGBTI activism', in Paternotte and Tremblay (eds.), 209–42

Paternotte, David and Manon Tremblay (2015) *The Ashgate Companion to Lesbian and Gay Activism*, Ashgate, Farnham.

Patton, Cindy and Benigno Sanchez-Eppler (eds.) (2000) *Queer Diasporas*, Duke University Press, Durham, NC.

Petchesky, Rosalind (2000) 'Sexual rights: Inventing a concept, mapping an international practice', in Parker, Barbosa and Aggleton (eds.), 81–103.

Petchesky, Rosalind (2003) 'Negotiating reproductive rights', in Weeks, Holland and Waites (eds.), 227–40.

Petchesky, Rosalind and Karen Judd (1998) *Negotiating Reproductive Rights: Women's Perspectives across Countries and Cultures*, Zed Books, London.

Phillips, Kim M. and Barry Reay (eds.) (2002) *Sexualities in History: A Reader*, Routledge, New York.

Playdon, Z-J. (2004) 'Intersecting oppressions: Ending discrimination against lesbians, gay men and trans people in the UK', in Brooks-Gordon, Gelsthorpe, Johnson, and Bainham (eds.), 131–54.

Plummer, Ken (1975) *Sexual Stigma: An Interactionist Account*, Routledge and Kegan Paul, London.

Plummer, Ken (ed.) (1980) *The Making of the Modern Homosexual*, Hutchinson, London.

Plummer, Ken (1981) 'The paedophile's progress', in Brian Taylor (ed.), *Perspectives on Paedophilia*, Batsford, London, 113–32.

Plummer, Ken (1984) 'Sexual diversity: A sociological perspective', in K. Howells (ed.), *Sexual Diversity*, Blackwell, Oxford, 219–53.

Plummer, Ken (1995) *Telling Sexual Stories: Power, Change and Social Worlds*, Routledge, London.

Plummer, Ken (2002) 'The square of intimate citizenship', *Citizenship Studies* 5(3), 237–53.

Plummer, Ken (2003) *Intimate Citizenship: Private Decisions and Public Dialogues*, University of Washington Press, Seattle.

Plummer, Ken (2010) 'Generational sexualities, subterranean traditions, and the hauntings of the sexual world: Some preliminary research', *Social Interaction* 33(2), 163–91.

Plummer, Ken (2015) *Cosmopolitan Sexualities: Hope and the Humanist Imagination*, Polity Press, Cambridge.

Pomeroy, Wardell, B. (1972) *Dr Kinsey and the Institute for Sex Research*, Harper and Row, New York.

Prosser, J. (1999) 'Exceptional locations: Transsexual travelogues', in More and Little (eds.), 83–114.

Puar, Jasbir (2007) *Terrorist Assemblages: Homonationalism in Queer Times*, Duke University Press, Durham, NC.

Rajan, R. S. (2005) 'Women's human rights in the Third World', in Bamforth (ed.), 119–36.

Rattray Taylor, Gordon (1953) *Sex in History*, Thames and Hudson, London.

Raymond, Janice (1979) *The Transsexual Empire*, Boston: Beacon.

Reay, Barry, Nina Attwood and Claire Gooder (2015) *Sex Addiction: A Critical History*, Polity Press, Cambridge.

Reavey, Paula and Sam Warner (eds.) (2003) *New Feminist Stories of Child Sexual Abuse: Sexual Scripts and Dangerous Dialogues*, Routledge, London.

Renvoize, Jean (1982) *Incest: A Family History*, Routledge and Kegan Paul, London.

Reynolds, Robert (2002) *From Camp to Queer: Remaking the Australian Homosexual*, Melbourne University Press, Melbourne.

Rich, Adrienne (1984) 'Compulsory heterosexuality and lesbian existence', in Ann Snitow, Christine Stansell and Sharon Thompson (eds.), *Desire: The Politics of Sexuality*, Virago, London, 212–41.

Richardson, Diane (ed.) (1996) *Theorising Heterosexuality: Telling it Straight*, Open University Press, Buckingham.

Richardson, Diane (2000) *Rethinking Sexuality*, Sage, London.

Richardson, Diane (2004) 'Locating sexualities: From here to normality', *Sexualities* 7(4), 391–411.

Richardson, Diane (2015) 'Neoliberalism, citizenship and activism', in Paternotte and Tremblay (eds.), 259–71.

Richardson, Diane and Steven Seidman (2002) *Handbook of Lesbian and Gay Studies*, Sage, London.

Rivers, Daniel Winunwe (2013) *Radical Relations: Lesbian Mothers, Gay Fathers, and their Children in the United States since World War II*, University of North Carolina Press, Chapel Hill, NC.

Robinson, Shirleene (ed.) (2008) *Homophobia: An Australian History*, The Federation Press, Annandale, NSW.

Rose, Hilary (1996) 'Gay brains, gay genes and feminist science theory', in Jeffrey Weeks and Janet Holland (eds.), *Sexual Cultures: Communities, Values and Intimacy*, Macmillan, Basingstoke, 53–72.

Rose, Hilary and Steven Rose (eds.) (2001) *Alas, Poor Darwin: Arguments against Evolutionary Psychology*, Vintage Books, London.

Rose, Jacqueline (1986) *Sexuality in the Field of Vision*, Verso, London.

Rose, Steven, Leon J. Kamin and R. C. Lewontin (1984) *Not in our Genes. Biology, Ideology and Human Nature*, Penguin, Harmondsworth.

Ross, Ellen and Rayna Rapp (1984) 'Sex and society: A research note from social history and anthropology', in Ann Snitow, Christine Stansell and Sharon Thompson (eds.), *Desire: The Politics of Sexuality*, Virago, London (USA edition published in 1983 as

Powers of Desire: The Politics of Sexuality, Monthly Review Press, New York).

Rubin, Gayle (1974) 'The traffic in women: Notes on the "political economy" of sex', in Reiner R. Rapp (ed.), *Towards an Anthropology of Women*, Monthly Review Press, New York, 157–210.

Rubin, Gayle (1984) 'Thinking sex: Notes for a radical theory of the politics of sexuality', in Carole S. Vance (ed.), *Pleasure and Danger: Exploring Female Sexuality*, Routledge and Kegan Paul, Boston, 267–319.

Rubin, H. S. (1999) 'Trans studies: Between a metaphysics of presence and absence', in More and Whittle (eds.), 174–92.

Ruthven, Malise (2004) *Fundamentalism: The Search for Meaning*, Oxford University Press, Oxford.

Sahlins, Marshall (1976) *The Use and Abuse of Biology: An Anthropological Critique of Sociobiology*, Tavistock, London.

Samois (ed.) (1982) *Coming to Power: Writings and Graphics on Lesbian S/M*, Samois, Berkeley, CA.

Schur, Edwin (1980) *The Politics of Deviance: Stigma Contests and the Uses of Power*, Prentice-Hall, Englewood Cliffs, NJ.

Scruton, Roger (1983) 'The case against feminism', *The Observer*, 22 May.

Scruton, Roger (1986) *Sexual Desire: A Philosophical Investigation*, Weidenfeld and Nicolson, London.

Seabrook, Jeremy (2001) *Travels in the Skin Trade: Tourism and the Sex Industry*, Pluto Press, London.

Sedgwick, Eve Kosofsky (2003) *Touching Feeling: Affect, Pedagogy, Performativity*, Duke University Press, Durham, NC.

Segal, Lynne (1983) 'Sensual uncertainty, or why the clitoris is not enough', in Sue Cartledge and Joanna Ryan (eds.), *Sex and Love: New Thoughts on Old Contradictions*, The Women's Press, London, 30–47.

Segal, Lynne (1998) 'Only the literal: The contradictions of anti-pornography feminism', *Sexualities* 1(1), 43–62.

Segal, Lynne (1999) *Why Feminism?*, Polity Press, Cambridge.

Segal, Lynne (2015) *Straight Sex: Rethinking the Politics of Pleasure*, Verso, London.

Seidman, Steven (2014) *The Social Construction of Sexuality*, 3rd edition, W.W. Norton and Company, New York.

Sexualities (2006) 'Viagra culture', special issue edited by A. Potts and L. Tiefer, *Sexualities* 9(3), July.

Sexualities (2008) 'Regulating sexuality: Contemporary perspectives on lesbian and gay relationship recognition', special issue edited by Elizabeth Peel and Rosie Harding, *Sexualities* 11(6), December.

Shakespeare, Tom, Kath Gillespie-Sells and Dominic Davies (eds.) (1996) *The Sexual Politics of Disability*, Cassell, London.

Shipley, Heather (ed.) (2014) *Globalized Religion and Sexual Identity: Context, Contestations, Voices*, Brill Academic Press, Leiden, NL.

Silva, Elizabeth and Carol Smart (eds.) (1999) *The 'New' Family?* Sage, London, Thousand Oaks.

Simon, William (1996) *Postmodern Sexualities*, Routledge, London.

Simon, William (2003) 'The postmodernization of sex', in Weeks, Holland and Waites (eds.), 22–32.

Singer, Irving (1973) *The Goals of Human Sexuality*, Wildwood House, London.

Skeggs, Bev (1997) *Formations of Class and Gender: Becoming Respectable*, Sage, London.

Smart, Carol (2007) *Personal Life: New Directions in Sociological Thinking*, Polity Press, Cambridge.

Smart, Carol (2008) ' "Can I be bridesmaid?" Combining the personal and political in same-sex weddings', *Sexualities* 11(6), December, 761–76.

Snitow, Ann, Christine Stansell and Sharon Thompson (eds.) (1983) *Desire: The Politics of Sexuality*, Virago, London.

Socarides, Charles W. (1978) *Homosexuality*, Jason Aranson, New York.

Sontag, Susan (1983) *Illness as Metaphor*, Penguin, Harmondsworth.

Sontag, Susan (1989) *AIDS and its Metaphors*, Allen Lane, London.

Stein, Edward (ed.) (1992) *Forms of Desire: Sexual Orientation and the Social Construction Controversy*, Routledge, New York and London.

Stoler, Ann Laura (1995) *Race and the Education of Desire: Foucault's History of Sexuality and the Colonial Order of Things*, Duke University Press, Durham, NC.

Stoller, Robert J. (1977) *Perversion: The Erotic Form of Hatred*, Quartet, London.

Stone, Lawrence (1977) *The Family, Sex and Marriage in England 1500–1800*, Weidenfeld and Nicolson, London.

Storr, Merl (2003) 'Postmodern bisexuality', in Weeks, Holland and Waites (eds.), 153–61.

Stryker, Susan (2008) *Transgender History*, Seal Press, Berkeley

Symons, Donald (1979) *The Evolution of Human Sexuality*, Oxford University Press, Oxford.

Taylor, Brian (1981) 'Introduction', in Brian Taylor (ed.), *Perspectives on Paedophilia*, Batsford, London, vii–xxii.

Taylor, Yvette (2016) *Making Space for Queer-Identifying Religious Youth*, Palgrave Macmillan, Basingstoke.

Taylor, Yvette, Sally Hines and Mark Casey (eds.) (2010) *Theorizing Intersectionality and Sexuality*, Palgrave Macmillan, Basingstoke.

Taylor, Yvette, and Ria Snowden (eds.) (2014) *Queering Religion, Religious Queers*, Routledge, New York and London.

Therborn, Göran (2004) *Between Sex and Power*, Routledge, London.

Thompson, Bill (1994) *Sadomasochism: Painful Perversion or Pleasurable Play?*, Cassell, London.

Thornhill, Randy and Craig Palmer (2000) *A Natural History of Rape: Biological Bases of Sexual Coercion*, MIT Press, Cambridge, MA.

Threlfal, M. (ed.) (1996) *Mapping the Women's Movement*, Verso, London.

Tiefer, Leonore (2006) 'The Viagra phenomenon', *Sexualities* 9(3), July, 273–94.

Trumbach, Randolph (1998) *Sex and the Gender Revolution. Volume 1, Heterosexuality and the Third Gender in Enlightenment London*, University of Chicago Press, Chicago.

Van der Ros, Janneke and Joz Motmans (2015) 'Trans activism and LGB movements', in Paternotte and Tremblay (eds.), 163–77.

Vance, Carole S. (1984) Pleasure and danger: Towards a politics of sexuality', in Carole S. Vance (ed.), *Pleasure and Danger: Exploring Female Sexuality*, Routledge and Kegan Paul, Boston, 1–27.

Veyne, Paul (1985) 'Homosexuality in ancient Rome', in Philippe Aries and Andre Bejin (eds.), *Western Sexuality: Practice and Precept in Past and Present Times*, Blackwell, Oxford, 26–35.

Waites, Matthew (2005) *The Age of Consent: Young People, Sexuality and Citizenship*, Palgrave Macmillan, Basingstoke.

Walters, Suzanna Danuta (2014) *The Tolerance Trap: How God, Genes and Good Intentions are Sabotaging Gay Equality*, New York University Press, New York.

Warner, Michael (ed.) (1993) *Fear of a Queer Planet: Queer Politics and Social Theory*, University of Minnesota Press, Minneapolis.

Warner, Michael (1999) *The Trouble with Normal: Sex, Politics and the Ethics of Queer Life*, The Free Press, New York.

Weeks, Jeffrey (1985) *Sexuality and its Discontents: Meanings, Myths and Modern Sexualities*, Routledge and Kegan Paul, London.

Weeks, Jeffrey (1995) *Invented Moralities: Sexual Values in an Age of Uncertainty*, Polity Press, Cambridge.

Weeks, Jeffrey (1998) 'The sexual citizen', *Theory, Culture and Society* 15(3–4), 35–52.

Weeks, Jeffrey (2000) *Making Sexual History*, Polity Press, Cambridge. Weeks,

Weeks, Jeffrey (2007) *The World We Have Won: The Remaking of Erotic and Intimate Life*, Routledge, Abingdon.

Weeks, Jeffrey (2011) *The Languages of Sexuality*, Routledge, Abingdon.

Weeks, Jeffrey (2012; 1st published 1981) *Sex, Politics and Society: The Regulation of Sexuality since 1800*, 3rd edition, Routledge, Abingdon.

Weeks, Jeffrey (2015) 'Liberalism by stealth? The civil partnership act and the new equalities agenda in perspective', in Barker and Monk (eds.), 29–44.

Weeks, Jeffrey (2016) *What Is Sexual History?* Polity Press, Cambridge.

Weeks, Jeffrey (2016; 1st published 1977) *Coming Out: The Emergence of LGBT Identities in Britain from the Nineteenth Century to the Present*, Quartet, London.

Weeks, Jeffrey, Brian Heaphy and Catherine Donovan (2001) *Same Sex Intimacies: Families of Choice and other Life Experiments*, Routledge, London.

Weeks, Jeffrey, Janet Holland and Matthew Waites (eds.) (2003) *Sexualities and Society: A Reader*, Polity Press, Cambridge.

Weinberg, George (1972) *Society and the Healthy Homosexual*, St Martin's Press, New York.

Weinberg, Thomas and G. W. Levi Kamel (eds.) (1983) *S and M: Studies in Sado Masochism*, Prometheus Books, Buffalo, NY.

Weinstein, Fred and Gerald M. Platt (1969) *The Wish to be Free: Psyche and Value Change*, University of California Press, Berkeley, CA.

Weiss, Meredith L. and Michael J. Bosia (eds.) (2013) *Global Homophobia: States, Movements, and the Politics of Oppression*, University of Illinois Press, Urbana.

Wellings, Kaye, Julia Field, Anne M. Johnson and Jane Wadsworth (1994) *Sexual Behaviour in Britain: The National Survey of Sexual Attitudes and Lifestyles*, Macmillan, London.

Weston, Kath (1991) *Families We Choose: Lesbians, Gays, Kinship*, Columbia University Press, New York.

Wetherell, Margaret (2012) *Affect and Emotions: A New Social Science Understanding*, Sage, London.

Williams, Raymond (1977) *Marxism and Literature*, Oxford University Press, Oxford.

Wilson, E. O. (1975) *Sociobiology: The New Synthesis*, Harvard University Press, Cambridge, MA.

Wilson, E. O. (1978) *On Human Nature*, Harvard University Press, Cambridge, MA.

Wilson, Glenn and Qazi Rahman (2005) *Born Gay: The Psychobiology of Sex Orientation*, Peter Owen, London.

Wintermute, Robert (2005) 'From "sex rights" to "love rights": Partnership rights as human rights', in Bamforth (ed.), 186–224.

Wintermute, Robert and Mads Andenaes (eds.) (2001) *Legal Recognition of Same-Sex Partnerships*, Hart Publishing, Oxford.

Witz, Anne, Susan Halford and Mike Savage (1996) 'Organized bodies: Gender, sexuality, and embodiment', in Lisa Adkins and Vicki Merchant (eds.), *Sexualizing the Social: Power and the Organization of Sexuality*, Macmillan, Basingstoke, 173–90.

Wolmark, Jenny (ed.) (1999) *Cybersexualities: A Reader in Feminist Theory, Cyborgs and Cyberspace*, Edinburgh University Press, Edinburgh.

Wouters, Cas (2007) *Informalization: Manners and Emotions since 1890*, Sage, Los Angeles.

INDEX